PRAISE FOR

Putting the Rabbit in the Hat

'A hugely readable memoir from a giant of stage and screen'
Mark Kermode

'A life well lived and a story well told. From first page to last, Brian Cox the great actor is Brian Cox the great storyteller, and nobody is spared his sharp eye and his caustic wit, himself and some big Hollywood names included'
Alastair Campbell

'Simply a delight, so much so that it's tempting to consume it in one sitting . . . mesmerizing'
Peter Biskind

'Clever, perceptive . . . brilliant'
The Times

'It's a book full of wonderful stories and huge insight into the whole business of acting and the workings of the human soul . . . absolute heaven'
Sunday Times

'Blisteringly brilliant'
Daily Telegraph

'One of the best showbiz memoirs ever written'
Mail on Sunday

'The sort of riveting, candid read you might expect from the illustrious *Succession* actor'
Independent

'Amusi
Guardian

'An insightful look into his extraordinary life and career – which sees no signs of slowing down'   *Radio Times*

'Wildly enjoyable'   *Evening Standard*

'I've never read a book that conveys the joy, grace and pain of the journey of being an actor and a human more honestly and with such straightforward blistering charm'   Kate Beckinsale

'It is much more than a rabbit Mr Cox pulls out of his hat. In this candid vision of his life, it is revealed how it is he is able so convincingly, authentically and uniquely to play such an abundance of characters. All of them different, all of them real, all of them him'   Hampton Fancher

'Brian Cox is not only one of the greatest actors of his generation, he is a gentleman among men. Kind, wise, funny and intense in the best ways possible, Brian is also a wonderful tale teller as this book proves'   Ryan Murphy

'Wonderfully honest, touching and funny'   Gemma Jones

'This book is like listening to him talk, switching from anecdote to diatribe to honest self-reflection and back to his original story before he interrupted himself. The effect is of undiminished curiosity and passion for life and work. All his observations are laced with his characteristic generosity, self-deprecation and cut-the-crap wisdom'   Harriet Walter

'A tale like no other, it's a seminal autobiography'   *Edinburgh Evening News*

'Cox's book is digressive and gossipy, as all celebrity biographies should be. It's also very funny, and as salty as you would expect from the man who has conclusively proved that there are at least 50 different ways of saying f*** off'   *Irish Independent*

'The iconic Scottish actor traces his life story from his childhood in Dundee to his extraordinary career on both screen and stage'
Scots Magazine

'Cox writes beautifully . . . *Putting the Rabbit in the Hat* is a rare and brilliant thing: an honest, genuinely funny and moving memoir from a star who has a real story to tell'   *Sunday Business Post*

'His writing is as compelling as any of his memorable performances'   *The Lady*

'A splendid memoir [and] a deeply intelligent exploration of his chosen profession, its joyous rewards and its mind-scratching demands . . . Throughout, his honesty is disarming'   Tortoise

Born in Dundee, Scotland, in 1946, Brian Cox has enjoyed a formidably prolific career in theatre, film and television. He has worked extensively with the Royal Shakespeare Company, where he gained recognition for his portrayal of Titus Andronicus, as he did several years later when he played the part of King Lear at the National Theatre. Cox was the first Hannibal Lecter in *Manhunter*. He is also famous for his roles in, amongst others, *Succession*, *Sharpe*, *Rob Roy*, *Braveheart*, *The Boxer*, *Rushmore*, *L.I.E*, *Super Troopers*, *Troy*, *The Bourne Identity*, *The Bourne Supremacy*, *X2: X-Men United*, *Red* and *Churchill*.

Putting the
Rabbit in the Hat

BRIAN COX

MY AUTOBIOGRAPHY

QUERCUS

First published in Great Britain in 2021 by Quercus Editions Ltd

This paperback published in 2022 by

QUERCUS

Quercus Editions Ltd
Carmelite House
50 Victoria Embankment
London EC4Y 0DZ

An Hachette UK company

A CIP catalogue record for this book is available
from the British Library

PB ISBN 978 1 52941 652 7
Ebook ISBN 978 1 52941 650 3

PICTURE CREDITS

First plate section: p. 3 (bottom) used by kind permission of DC Thomson & Co Ltd;
p. 4 (bottom right) © BBC; p.5 (bottom) used by kind permission of DC Thomson & Co Ltd;
p. 6 (top) © Sophie Baker / ArenaPAL; p. 7 (top) © Nobby Clark / ArenaPAL,
(bottom) © Donald Cooper / Photostage; p. 8 (top) © BBC.
Second plate section: p. 1 (top) © Frazer Ashford / ArenaPAL, (bottom) © STV;
p. 2 (top left) © Alamy, (top right) © Richard Mildenhall / ArenaPAL;
p. 3 (top) © Donald Cooper / Photostage; p. 4 (top left) © Donald Cooper / Photostage,
(top right) © Geraint Lewis / ArenaPAL, (bottom left) © Neil Libbert; p. 5 (bottom) © Sean Hudson;
p. 6 (top left and right) © Alamy, (bottom right) © John McConville;
p. 7 (top) © Cate Gillon, (bottom left) © Elke Rosthal;
p. 8 (top) © Graeme Hunter/Salon Pictures, (bottom) photographs courtesy of Home Box Office, Inc.

10 9 8 7 6 5 4 3 2 1

Typeset by CC Book Production
Printed and bound in Great Britain by Clays Ltd, Elcograf S.p.A.

To my Ma and Dad,
and to the other three great influences in my life:
Fulton Mackay, Michael Elliott and Lindsay Anderson.
And, of course, to the family Circus Coximus.

FOREWORD

The first time I saw Brian Cox on stage was in 1985 when, in a mere three months, he stormed New York in two roles that could have not been more antithetical: first, on Broadway opposite Glenda Jackson, as a dashing doctor in Eugene O'Neill's five-hour Freudian epic *Strange Interlude* of 1928, and then at Joseph Papp's Public Theater downtown as a savage detective in Northern Ireland in *Rat in the Scull*, a fierce contemporary drama by Ron Hutchinson. Rarely has an actor so little known in America unfurled his dazzling range in such prominent venues in so compact a time before New York's tough audiences. This coup soon led to a rapid expansion of his career from the British stage to theatre, film and television productions all over the world. The pace, quality and fearless variety of his work has never let up since.

I would not meet Brian until more than three decades later, when we gathered at Silvercup Studios in Queens for the table read of the pilot of the HBO dramatic series *Succession* in November 2016. As I discovered in the long days on set to come, he is both a dedicated artist with a relentless curiosity and boundless work ethic, and the natural leader of a company of actors, most of them considerably younger, whom he cheers on at every turn. Plus he is witty and devilish company; he takes his work seriously but never himself. I can't believe that, as a producer of *Succession*, I have had the good fortune to be in his presence for nearly five years.

There have been so many dividends and delights in being Brian's colleague that I would have to write a book of my own to catalogue them. So I must focus on one day that stands out as a landmark in my lifetime of watching actors at work, whether on stage, on screen, or on set. The *Succession* gang was aboard a yacht in Croatia in the spring of 2019, preparing for the final shot of the final episode of our second season. Brian's character, the tyrannical family patriarch Logan Roy, is seated in his boat's gilded salon watching the live cable-news broadcast of a New York press conference in which his once favoured son Kendall, played by Jeremy Strong, accuses him of enabling unspeakable crimes in the family firm.

We shot the scene first thing on a sunny morning. The television screen Brian was watching was blank, since the press conference itself would not be shot until the following week in New York. So Kendall's diatribe was not acted by Jeremy but instead read by a young female production assistant crouched a few feet away from where Brian was seated. I was also a few feet away from Brian. His performance could not have been more different from those I'd seen him give on stage. He had no dialogue. His assignment was simply to listen. Not that there was anything simple about the delicate interplay of emotions the camera captured in close-up.

In this memoir, Brian quotes our *Succession* collaborator, the writer Tony Roche, as telling him, 'You do stillness like nobody I know . . . One just has to give you stage directions and then film.' Tony of course is engaging in artistic license. But not by much. Here's the stage direction for Logan, as written by the show's creator, Jesse

Armstrong, on the final page of the script: 'Slowly across his face there cracks just the hint of, not quite a smile, but a smile-smirk of appreciation. His son is a killer after all.' Brian conveyed all that from the very first take. Mesmerized viewers have been analysing it and talking about it ever since.

The story of how Brian attained such mastery is told in full in *Putting the Rabbit in the Hat*. The tale kicks off with custodial jobs at a theatre in Dundee, Scotland, where he grew up in Dickensian circumstances. The youngest of five, with a beloved father who died when he was eight and a mother who spent the rest of her life battling mental illness, he left school at fifteen. He survived repeated tragedies thereafter, from near-poverty after his father's death to a devastating fire that incinerated the playhouse of his tutelage. Yet somehow he found his way to London, where he studied acting at the renowned LAMDA. Soon he was revelling in the new 'social mobility' of the 1960s, personified in the theatre by working-class iconoclasts in acting (Albert Finney) and playwriting (John Osborne) who showed him a path to a career.

How Brian ended up collaborating with so eclectic a cast of characters over the ensuing half-century is deliciously told in these pages and illuminated with his spicy cameos of the whole sprawling ensemble. What other actor has intersected with Steven Seagal and Tom Stoppard, Spike Lee and Vanessa Redgrave, Ralph Richardson and Mel Gibson, Nicol Williamson and Woody Allen? Played Hannibal Lecktor as well as Harold Hill in *The Music Man* and King Lear? Had an instant wedding in Las Vegas, directed *The Crucible* at the Moscow Art Theatre, served as the rector of the University of Dundee, taken up tango dancing and been felt up by Princess Margaret? It's all here, along with the marriages, love affairs and children, the struggles with afflictions of the mind and body, and his impolitic takes on Margaret Thatcher, Michael Caine, Quentin Tarantino and Lee Strasberg (among others). Also present is an overarching humanity that drives him to find the good in (most of) those whose work or behaviour he finds appalling.

At one point in this riveting, candid and touching memoir Brian writes, with characteristic generosity, of Morgan Freeman, that Freeman was 'the Morgan Freeman you would hope to meet'. Brian Cox is the Brian Cox you would hope to meet, as you are about to discover for yourself.

Frank Rich
August 2021

PROLOGUE

In 1996, I found myself seated next to the actor Nigel Hawthorne on a plane, and we got talking about our respective work.

'I once did a film with Sylvester Stallone,' he moaned at one point, apropos of exactly what, I don't remember.

'Oh, that's nothing,' I told him, playing my ace. 'I can beat that. I've just done a film with Steven Seagal.'

'Oh,' said Hawthorne. 'Really? What was that like? Do tell.'

'Well . . .'

Steven Seagal, I told Nigel, is as ludicrous in real life as he appears on screen. He radiates a studied serenity, as though he's on a higher plane to the rest of us, and while he's certainly on a *different* plane, no doubt about that, it's probably not a higher one. Seagal suffers from that Donald Trump syndrome of thinking himself far more capable and talented than he actually is, seemingly oblivious to the fact that an army of people are helping to prop up his delusion.

Seagal would never do off-lines for others. Off-lines are when you do a scene and the camera's on your character, while the other actor stands there to provide you with your feeds. It's a bit boring for the one off-camera but most actors, the ones who aren't Steven Seagal, will do it because it's part of the job. But on *The Glimmer Man*, the director, a lovely man called John Gray, took me to one side and said, 'The continuity person will be doing your off-lines, I'm afraid. Steven won't do them. Steven doesn't *do* off-lines.'

'That's a relief,' I said, 'it would only be a distraction.'

One particular day when Seagal was showing a girl around the set he stopped by where I sat with the script in my hand. 'You see,' he purred serenely at the girl, 'this is how a great actor works.'

'No, Steven,' I sighed. 'I'm just learning my lines, that's all.'

The next thing I knew, he materialized, mysteriously keen as mustard to do his off-lines for me. *But Steven doesn't do off-lines*, I thought. Confused, I glanced across to see John Gray shrugging, and I wondered if Steven's attendance had anything to do with the girl he'd been escorting around the set. Could it be a coincidence that she stood not far away?

Action. We began the scene, but the problem was that Steven didn't know his lines. He kept fluffing them. 'Steven, it's very nice of you to do this,' I said at last, 'but it's really not necessary. Why don't you go back to your trailer?'

Thankfully, Seagal agreed that his absence would make our hearts grow fonder, and there were audible sighs of relief as he left us to it.

And that was what I told Nigel Hawthorne about my experience of working with Steven Seagal.

'Well, I can't do that sort of thing any more,' he shuddered, 'I can't play that kind of action movie type part.'

'I don't feel that way,' I told him. 'To me, the nature of the actor's life is that we do the job, we do the best we can and move on.' I added that I'd just read a book by Michael Powell, *A Life in Movies: An Autobiography*, about how he and Emeric Pressburger became the pre-eminent film-makers of their generation. In the book, Powell says something along the lines of, 'In movies, there are no big parts or small parts. There are only long parts and short parts.' He means that no matter what the part, it can be as big or as small, as slight or as impactful as the film or actor allows.

It was a piece of wisdom that had stuck with me, and as someone who had decided their future lay as a supporting actor, it lit the way for me from that moment on. It freed me, in fact. It removed ego from the equation and allowed me to disregard the size of the role, the star wattage of my co-performers, even, to a certain extent, the quality of the film I was in, and concentrate solely on what I was able to contribute to my character and what my character could contribute to the film. Actor, character, text. That's all it is.

No doubt my words fell on deaf ears, because even though Hawthorne had put *Demolition Man* behind him and gone on to make *The Madness of King George* as well as a brace of well-received Shakespeare adaptations, he was still fixated on that Stallone experience. That, too, is a characteristic familiar to the actor, that feeling of deep-seated insecurity. All actors suffer from it. We're all desperately insecure.

All of us, that is, except Steven Seagal.

CHAPTER 1

Saturday, 1st June 1946, about 1.45 in the afternoon

Throughout my childhood I'd hear it from my poor old ma. How my beginning was almost her end.

You see, it was with considerable reluctance that I came into this vale of tears. There was no abseiling down Fallopio and into the light for me. I was going in the other direction, my wee hands clasping at the funiculus umbilicalis, wrapping the cord around my neck, while to make matters even more perilous and potentially fatal for at least one of the participants, my legs had joined the party too.

What's that now? Something cold and metallic on my backside. These forceps are tugging me, dragging me, pulling me down, until out I come, arse first through a sea of red – farting and shitting my way into the world . . .

'Molly has had a baby boy, a wee Gemini!'

The cry was rallied throughout the nearest and dearest, including my Aunt Susie, who trilled, 'I gotta a horse,' as was her habit. And if that looks like a typo, I can assure you, it's not. 'I gotta a horse,' was the catchphrase of Ras Prince Monolulu, a West Indian tipster who at the time was famous for espousing his spurious equine knowledge at racecourses up and down the country. (Monolulu, incidentally, died in 1965, when he was visited in hospital by legendary bon viveur Jeffrey Bernard. Bernard had brought with him a box of Black Magic and Monolulu choked to death on a strawberry cream.)

Susie was my dad's sister, a larger-than-life personality. Her husband, the wee and wily bonnet-clad Geordie McWha (and it's true, he was called McWha – I believe his Irish ancestors must have had an unpronounceable name and ended up with McWha) was her polar opposite, although he did once pour a bucket of water over Winston Churchill when Churchill was running for re-election as Dundee's MP – a contest Churchill went on to lose, possibly as a result of the soaking. 'He had it coming,' Geordie would tell you if you asked him why he did it. Perhaps Aunt Susie had a bet on the election's outcome, for both she and Geordie were inveterate punters, and Susie, whose own birthday was also 1st June, had decided my arrival was, 'An omen, a blessing. A wee Gemini, just like me.'

'Well . . . not quite like you, Susie,' retorted Chic, my dad – Chic being short for Charles, especially in that part of the world.

'Bugger off. Y'ken what I mean. I gotta a horse.'

She meant for that Wednesday's Derby, of course. The horse? A grey. A rank outsider with the odds to match. She picked it for the name: Airborne. Gemini being an air sign.

So, bets were laid. And Airborne did indeed win the 1946 Derby at fifty to one. But as small transient fortunes were made, the celebrations of my extended relations overshadowed the physical hell of my mother. Since the birth of my elder brother Charlie, she had suffered four or five miscarriages before I came along. Scarred inside and out, mentally and physically, she suffered alone in her hospital bed, and although nobody knew it at the time, she would never be the same again.

Nevertheless, she rallied enough to instruct my da to register the birth. After some discussion around the issue of naming, my dad reluctantly agreed to my mother's preferred suggestion and set off to the register office, not at all convinced by my intended name but with a task to complete nonetheless.

The story was told to me later by my gambling-mad Auntie Susie – how my dad found himself at the desk of an affable and, as it would turn out, somewhat presumptuous registrar.

'And what would the wee man's name be?' asked the registrar.

'Colin,' replied my father, with ebbing confidence.

'Colin?' responded the registrar, pulling a face. 'Really?'

'Aye . . .' was my father's shaky response.

Still the same face. 'Are you convinced?'

'Aye . . .' my dad replied, not at all convincingly.

'Och, I dinnae like that name,' countered the registrar, shaking his head. 'The laddie will get all that police emergency nonsense. "Calling all cars." Colin all cars. Get it? Have you no got a better name than that?'

'Not really,' was my father's sheepish reply.

'Well, to be frank, I've always had a hankering for the name Brian.'

'Och, that's better, that's much better. Oh, yeah. That's a relief. Brian it is, then.'

The registrar made a note. 'Now what about a middle name?'

'A middle name?' My dad's confidence had well and truly evaporated by now. 'I really don't know . . .'

'Oh, he should have a middle name. He should certainly have a middle name,' insisted the registrar, now firmly in his stride. 'What about Donald? Very popular. David? Douglas? Dominic? I know. I know. *Denis*.'

Who knows why the registrar should have been so obsessed with the letter D. Either way, my dad, now on the edge of hysteria, agreed. 'Yes indeed, let it be Denis. Let it be Denis.'

Thus I was registered Brian Denis Cox.

Later, my dad confided to my aunt. 'Susie, I couldn't wait to get out of that bloody registrar's office. It was like being cross-examined by the Gestapo.'

Nothing is recorded as to my mother's reaction to the name change. I suspect given how ill she was that all questions and decisions were subsumed in a morphine haze.

Meantime, I had joined 'Clan Cox': generation after generation of dislocated Mick-Macks besieged by the forces of tribalism and the Catholic faith. Acceptance without question, that was us. I call it 'conditioned ignorance'.

Not that I knew any different back then, of course. My world was my father, Chic, my mother, Mary Ann (also known as Molly) née McCann (and affiliated with the Clan McCann), and my siblings in descending age order: Bette, May, Irene and Charlie. Together we lived at our house at 19 Brown Constable Street in Dundee.

I call it our house, as in our 'hoose', which is a very Scottish expression. You talk about your 'hoose', but your 'hoose' could just be two rooms, and that's precisely what we had at Brown Constable Street. My elder sisters would end up moving out and going to live with their respective husbands, but for a while there were all seven of us in that two-bedroom flat. Bette, May and Irene all shared the bed settee in one room (and in order to sleep, May would sing to her sisters at Bette's insistence); my father and mother in the small bedroom, and my brother Charlie and me in the bed-alcove in the living room. I slept with wet cloths on my feet as a result of terrible ankle problems I suffered during childhood. Just growing pains, I think, since they didn't last long, but in the meantime, the cloths did a grand job of soothing me to sleep.

Our kitchen was a tiny scullery off to one side where the cooking was done. My ma had a terrifying accident in there once when, while remonstrating with Charlie, she knocked a pan of hot chip fat all over her arm and collapsed. I remember afterwards, we were all playing with this meringue that she had on her arm – this huge white meringue it was.

From our house you could see the Tay, the longest river in Scotland. I'd marvel at its silvery swell spread out before me, dominating the city, every time I left the house on my way to school or off to play games of 'lone wolf' with my pals. That river acted both as barrier and portal. On the one hand it reminded me of the city's roots in the whaling industry via the famous Tay whale, a humpback which found itself lost and stranded in the estuary. The whale was slaughtered and dissected, its blubber oil contributing to the town's huge jute industry by being used in processing and extending the jute yarn. Then of course there was the famous Tay Railway Bridge, which literally fell down with a great loss of life during a storm in December 1879.

And on the other hand?

On the other hand, I'd look at that river and think, *I'm gonna cross that bugger one day, find out what's on the other side.* From about the age of four I'd think that. Every time I left the house.

I see myself now as an infant determinist. Later on in life I'd have a mentor who told me, 'It'll be the long haul for you, Brian,' a condition I accepted, unconditionally. And I see now how Dundee's whaling history acts as a metaphor for that state of being. The long haul meant keeping astride the lost whale through sea and estuary, wave after wave after wave. The infant determinist would be tossed and thrown in his pursuit. I would challenge oceans in pursuit of 'the reason why' – *why be an actor?* – and on occasion I would get severely drenched.

CHAPTER 2

In 2013, I was part of a documentary, *Secrets from the Workhouse*, in which I joined the writer Barbara Taylor Bradford, Felicity Kendal and Charlie Chaplin's great-granddaughter, Kiera Chaplin, on a journey to investigate our respective ancestors' links with the poorhouse, as it was rightly known in Scotland, *not* the workhouse as it was known to the south (of England), where there was no 'work', only flagrant misery.

Look at the documentary now and you'll see me getting cross. Not quite the works – Logan Roy in full flight – but still, I probably shouldn't have got as worked up as I did, or at least kept it for behind closed doors. By Christ, though, it was a downright unjust system, and I was angry on behalf of all those like my great-grandfather on my mother's side, Patrick McCann.

Patrick had been injured working on the Forth and Clyde Canal in Glasgow and also suffered from bronchitis. At the age of thirty-nine – having lost five of his eight children and his own wife who'd died at the age of thirty-six – Patrick took his youngest son, Sam, and threw himself on the mercy of the poorhouse. There he should have found sanctuary.

Fourteen times – *fourteen* times – he attempted, primarily, to have his youngest son taken into care, which through his persistence, eventually happened. But as to himself, the poorhouse labelled him a malingerer and turfed him out as one of the undeserving poor. In 1908, Patrick was briefly united with his three sons, and a new two-year-old granddaughter who was my mother, Molly. This was in Dundee and Patrick would have loved to stay there with his family, but as he was registered in Glasgow he had to return there. Three unhappy years later he was declared insane at Gartcosh asylum, where he wandered the wards believing he was a fourteen-year-old boy from Derry. He died later that year, taking the stigma of being a 'malingerer' to his grave.

So, yes, my blood boiled at the sheer injustice of it all. From an injury sustained by building the city's transport links to a lonely, wretched death in an insane asylum, shunned by a system that should have supported him. That was my great-grandfather's life. 'Malingerer', in-fuckin'-deed.

As you might imagine, the tales of my great-grandparents, grandparents, aunts and uncles are legion, and we could fill another book with a dizzying array of Bernards and Annes and Hughs and Kathys and Jeans. We could talk of Uncle Tom, who had been in the First World War as a stretcher bearer. Tom married a young French woman called Zelie Valembois, had two sons, Andrew and Harry, and the family settled in Béthune, in the suburb of Labeuvrière, France. There, thanks to his medical experience, Tom found work as a masseur for the local football team. In May 1940, Germany advanced into France, trapping Allied troops on the beaches of Dunkirk. By sheer mischance, my uncle's team were playing an away game somewhere on the coast of Normandy, cutting him off from his family. Informed that the only way out of his dilemma was to join the evacuating Allied troops, he ended up getting on one of the last boats out of Dunkirk, and was thus separated from his family for the whole war.

Back in Béthune, my Aunt Zelie and her two children found themselves in the clutches of an occupying force. The Germans saw a photograph of my uncle in his British army uniform and interned my cousin Andrew, being the eldest, in a labour camp in Silesia, where he ended up serving time with P.G. Wodehouse. His brother Harry would join him a year later. In time Andrew would write a book about their experiences.

Uncle Tom lived with us back in Scotland for a while, as did Aunt Zelie, who looked after me when I was a wee boy. She used to sing 'J'attendrai' by a French singer called Dalida to me, an influence I remember as being distinctly not-Scottish, something different, something kind of special.

But like I say, these tales could fill another book. For the time being we'll be content to keep the focus on my mum and dad, beginning with my maternal grandfather, James McCann, who was one of the unfortunate Patrick's children.

James was a tram driver, a drill sergeant in the Black Watch militia, an alcoholic and a rather abusive man by all accounts. Not to excuse his abusive behaviour, merely to put it into context, but he was a veteran of the First World War, having been invalided out with frozen feet. My mother used to say that he had a look in his eyes as though he'd seen the dark side of the moon. No doubt he had.

James McCann died in 1927.

On the other side of my own particular gene pool was my paternal grandfather, name of Hugh Cox. Hugh was married to Elizabeth, who between the years of 1877 and 1904 gave birth to thirteen children, one of that baker's dozen being my pa, Chic.

Hugh Cox died in 1927.

So, in other words, both of my grandfathers died the same year, and it was their passing that was indirectly responsible for bringing my parents together. In those days you had to serve an appropriate mourning period of three months, during which time you wore a black armband and weren't supposed to socialize. To get around that and go dancing, for example, you'd have to slip out of town, where you could remove your armband.

Chic and Molly, then, both of whom having lost their dads and wanting to cut loose, happened to go to the same dancehall in Montrose at the same time. My mother saw my dad sitting alone and, my God, the sheer brass of it, asked him to dance.

And that was it. He was twenty-three. She was twenty-one.

We Scots are a peripatetic, nomadic lot – I'm like that now, shuttling between London and New York – and so it was that just after they met, my mum left for Canada to take up a life in service. My dad was okay about it. Pretty sanguine, you might say. *'Ah well, you've got to go, you know. It was an arrangement,'* and off she went.

The thing was, she didn't get on all that well out there. Plus, she had my dad waiting for her back in Dundee, so she returned home after about a year, reconnected with him and they got married.

She shouldn't have done that. She regretted having done it. If I could choose one word to describe my ma, it's 'thwarted'. She would always talk about how she should have stayed in Canada, and she maybe felt that things would have been different – as in *better* – for her if she had, because after all, coming back to Scotland meant re-entering a society which was essentially quite feudal, where everybody was supposed to know their place, where women in particular were expected to knuckle down, bear children, and tough shit if you don't like it. In Canada she'd been in service and I've no doubt that it was bloody hard, but it was a job with pay and fixed hours and the occasional day off. It was arduous and restrictive, but I dare say not as arduous, nor as restrictive and imprisoning as life as a spinner in the jute mills, followed by three daughters, a son and then me, not to mention the four or five miscarriages in between.

Money, at least, was not a problem. Not at first anyway. Not then. See, there was a twenty-two-year gap between my dad and his sister, my Aunt Anne, which explains why she was more like a surrogate mother than big sister to him, and also why she used her war widow's pension to help set him up in business when her husband, Joe, was killed in the Great War.

It was Anne's hope that my pa and his family would escape the cycle of poverty that had afflicted both the Cox and the McCann clans since time immemorial. (In common with Joe Biden's ancestors, my Irish Cox forefathers were victims of the 1840s Irish famine. Joe's forebears escaped to the US, mine to Dundee.)

The money from my Auntie Anne was used to open a grocer's shop in the small working-class ghetto of Charles Street in the Wellgate area of Dundee.

At first my dad wasn't keen, and in fact it was my mum who ran the shop while he played out the final few bars of his pre-married life. Along came us children, though, and Ma was needed at home to look after the kids and stare out of the windows wondering how life in Canada might have been, so Da took over the running over the shop.

It's odd that he should ever have been wary of assuming life as a grocer, because he soon realized that running a local shop was something of a calling, and he quickly came to see himself as a community service first, shopkeeper second, filling days that were very hard and very long with acts of kindness and civic duty, lending a hand to the old and infirm, lending money to those that needed it. Fortunately, the war years brought him some prosperity. As a grocer he was an excused occupation, and thus in a position to make a bit of money. Being a true socialist in the best sense of the word, he paid his good fortune forward.

The first time I remember trying to visit the shop, I was just three. He used to return at lunchtime for his 'denner' and forty winks. 'Take me back with you, Da,' I asked him on one particular occasion.

'Oh no, son, best you stay here,' he told me kindly but firmly.

Not even me crying my eyes out would persuade him, and so he left without me. I waited for my ma's back to be turned and decided to follow him.

Outside our front door I promptly got horribly lost. In fact, I was only two streets away, but that might as well have been the other side of the world as far as three-year-old Brian was concerned. Unsurprisingly, being so far away from home for the first time, and having lost sight of my father and with not the foggiest idea how to get back, I shat myself. I don't mean metaphorically, either. I literally shat myself.

Eventually, almost the entire afternoon later, I was picked up by two policemen who took me to Bell Street police station in the centre of town. There was an old lady there who was the station housekeeper – bet they don't have one of those any more – and she cleaned me up before they returned me to my frantic parents.

So my *actual* first visit to the shop happened later, and what I remember about the shop was that it was sawdusty and seemed to sell everything. That everything on sale was fresh. These days you'd walk into a shop like that and think you'd chanced upon a quaint little delicatessen, but back then it was a case of needs must: everything was fresh because we had no refrigeration.

What else? Oh yes, he had a ham machine. He got very excited about his new ham machine. He could operate that ham machine with the same expertise and dexterity that he used to prepare butter pats with two wooden paddles or cut cheese with wire or look at a stream of figures and add them up very, very quickly (a skill that was denied to me, sadly). I remember thinking that my dad seemed to possess all these skills, these secret shopkeeper skills that I never even knew he had. They just made him even greater in my eyes. My king and my hero.

Mostly I remember him with the customers. That generosity, already legendary, at work. How people would arrive with a sad face and leave with a smiley one. How to them he was hero and confessor of their day-to-day struggle against the poverty of the Great Depression. How he treated everyone the same, and how to him they were all his brother.

'Are you all right, brother?'

'How are you today, brother?'

It wasn't just financial help he provided, either. It wouldn't be at all uncommon for him to close the shop at ten o'clock and go straight to help an old couple decorate their home. This after a day during which he'd got up at five or six to fetch the milk and do the cheese and ham rolls and then open up.

For my mother, however, his generosity and care were a source of constant frustration. After the war, and by the time I came on the scene, we had a little bit of money behind us. We were what you'd call lower middle class, and she thought his working-class customers were taking advantage of him, seeing him as a soft touch.

'Remember, Brian,' she would say to me tartly, 'charity begins at home.'

He didn't see it that way, of course. I think of him now as being very much a medium for other people's joy and happiness, though sadly not his own. I was told about a big party they held in 1936 for the Coronation, and guess who organized that? And as for Hogmanay . . . He loved Hogmanay. He loved to put on a party.

There is one particular Hogmanay that stands out. I was three years old again, and my family were eagerly awaiting the coming year. Guests – otherwise known as 'first footers' – would begin to arrive at our house as soon as church bells announced the arrival of the new year, and my ma and da, both adept at creating the perfect ambience for a New Year's 'do', stood like greyhounds in the slips. Our troubles were some years in the future. Life was good then and it was especially good at Hogmanay.

How important is Hogmanay to Scots? Very, very important is the answer. It's Christmas and Thanksgiving and a Scottish Cup win all rolled into one and we celebrate accordingly. My family were Mick-Macks, a mix of Irish and Scottish who, although they liked to party and had innately sociable bones, were by no means what you'd call 'party animals'. Even they were drunk for a week at Hogmanay. It's tradition, you see. The same tradition which says that the first footer who brings luck to the house should be blue-eyed and dark-haired, and that they should enter bearing a lump of coal to signify the bringing of a year's good fortune to the home.

Meanwhile, my sister May was ready to sing her heart out at a moment's notice while Bette and Irene were primed to do my mother's bidding in preparation of the festivities, busily laying out knives, forks, plates, various cordials and alcohol of numerous varieties – all in hopeful contribution to a successful evening's spree.

Me, I'd be resigned to missing out on the majority of the festivities, knowing that early in the evening I would be consigned to bed in my folks' bedroom – the living room, where Charlie and I slept, having been requisitioned for the do. At some point, at around say, 1 a.m., I'd be woken by my da, and invited to join the throng. He'd carry me into the chamber of drunken revellers, a room filled with intoxicated joy and happiness.

On this particular occasion, my dad stood me on the coal bunker, which was situated in the window recess of our living room and equipped with heavy curtains to keep out the winter's excesses. This, it turned out, was to be my first stage. Mine was a family of performers at heart. Whether it was May with her singing or my other sisters staging the show of Hogmanay, my father the master of ceremonies in his shop, my mother the tragic figure haunting the scullery kitchen. Of course, I had to make my own debut.

I don't remember how it was planned, or even if it was. Just that I had seen – and loved – *The Jolson Story* at the cinema, and so it seemed only natural that when the curtains drew open, I should kneel and launch into a medley of his songs, accompanied by a complete set of physical actions, but minus blackface.

It was the effect, the electric effect it had on the room, that stayed with me. It was how my actions seemed somehow to unify the gathering. It was the attention, the acceptance, the sense of purpose. Of course, there was an element of vanity, of 'showing off', but it was more about that effect, about being some kind of transmitter and creating a shared experience that brought the room together.

I could not have articulated it at the time, naturally, but even at that young age I was given an insight into the power of performance, and in that very moment the path of my life was confirmed. My *purpose* was confirmed, and it would fill my wee spirit for days. The young Brian did not need to know the nature of the purpose. It's not like I knew *I want to act*. Just that I had that feeling of purpose. And with that feeling came freedom.

Nestled within my safe familial bubble, I was allowed to develop my nascent performing tendencies, which even extended to the games I would play. The rain kept us indoors a lot, so me and my pals would build a bomber in my big front room, recreating raids on the enemy. It was all performance. And yet, because my life was settled and comfortable, I never really saw it as a means of escape, because I had nothing to escape from.

Not then, anyway. Oh, but one day, my mother ran away and I didn't know why. I just came home and she wasn't there, and my dad was having to deal with the fallout and not doing a very good job of it. Befuddled, almost, by my mother's lack of fulfilment.

It turned out that she had gone to Blackpool. My dad went after her by way of my sister May in Chester, only that didn't work out so he placed me in Prestatyn holiday camp, and then went on to negotiate with my ma for her return. All told she was gone about a month.

There were also, I think, religious differences between the two of them, my father being a confirmed agnostic in the face of my mother's even more fervent Catholicism. Or was that just the pretext for any number of other issues? Either way, I remember seeing them fighting. I was woken up one night by the noise of them arguing. I remember vividly seeing my father with a scratch down his face where my mother had lashed out at him.

Looking back now, I can see that there was a disconnect between the two of them. An essential lack of understanding. She, in her own way, was doing bird when she wanted to fly like one. She was looking for a creative outlet and was jealous that Pa had found one in performing acts of kindness for other people.

But still, no life is without its share of affliction and overall ours wasn't at all bad. My Auntie Anne's wish had been granted; we had indeed escaped the mouse-wheel of poverty that had gripped our clans since the middle of the previous century. My dad was as generous with his family as he was with his customers. My sisters, Bette and May, both benefited from grand weddings; we took family holidays to Butlin's and even to Lourdes. Often, on a Sunday, my mother and I would load up on Patterson's crisps and Robb's lemonade and take half- or whole-day bus trips on a Dickson's or Watson's tour bus. They left from just outside the city library on Albert Square and would negotiate the narrow, winding Scottish Highland roads to such places as Pitlochry, Blair Atholl and Killiekrankie.

These days out, as well as creating a close bond between me and my mother, instilled in me a love of travel, that nomadic urge I'm talking about that is common to Celts – and particularly we Scots – and that has never truly left me.

All in all, life was good. And it stayed good, right up until the age of eight, when my world fell in.

CHAPTER 3

It was a Friday afternoon, and I arrived home from school to find Mrs Robbie, who always wore Edwardian black and suffered from goitre, standing on the landing outside the door to our flat. Mrs Robbie lived next door, so her being on the landing was the first thing to strike me as odd.

It's funny, because as an adult you know – you know that a certain expression augurs bad tidings, or that a phone ringing in the middle of the night is never good news, or that a stammering, shell-shocked neighbour spells trouble. But as a kid you've got animal instinct, and it was that very instinct which told me something was wrong as Mrs Robbie struggled to find the words – struggled because it wasn't her place to tell me what lay in wait over the threshold of our flat.

'Oh, Brian,' she was saying, with one hand at her swollen throat. 'Brian, Brian. Poor Brian. I'm so, so sorry, Brian.'

Sorry for what? I wondered, as I walked into our flat, which was even busier than usual, bustling with sad-faced folk who all seemed to be hovering around a table laden with food. Among them was my mother, sitting in an armchair. And it was as though my gaze travelled on rails towards her. She'd been weeping but then, as my arrival prompted a respectful hush to fall across those assembled, she looked up at me, and she told me, 'Your da's gone, Brian. He passed away this afternoon at two o'clock.'

I knew he'd been ill, of course. I knew he'd been ill because he was always hunting out the Andrews Liver Salts for what he said was indigestion, and I knew that he'd been sufficiently ill to require a hospital stay. My mother and I had paid him a visit.

But I didn't know he'd been *that* ill – not ill enough to die one Friday afternoon while I was struggling with arithmetic at school. I later discovered that he'd only been diagnosed with pancreatic cancer three weeks previously, but at that stage I didn't even know that much. Just that one minute he'd been hunting out the Liver Salts and having to go for an inconvenient hospital stay. The next my ma was weeping, and all our lives had changed.

I was sent to my cousin Rose, who put me in front of the TV, an invention that was still new and very much a rarity back then. I stayed in front of that television for a long time. To this very day, television is still a great comfort to me. I wonder if there is a link?

My father's funeral was amazing, so they said. Packed to the rafters with over 200 mourners, and not just family and friends, but his customers – those many, many beneficiaries of his generosity.

But I missed all that. I was in front of the TV.

I know why they did it. They did it for my own good, in the name of protecting me. But my reaction to that emotional bulwark was to create a fantasy in which I went to fetch a shirt from a back room, there to be confronted by the sight of my father lying in state.

It wasn't true. There was indeed a wake, as is Irish tradition, but I didn't see it. My chancing upon it was complete fabrication on my part, a story made up in order to connect in some way with this bizarre event that I was not allowed to take part in, not even being allowed to attend the funeral.

Hardly surprising, then, that for years afterwards – right up until my late twenties – I had a recurring dream of searching for my father, only to see him in the distance but never being able to reach him, his dream-state form remaining forever out of my reach.

I tell a story about how I attended the funeral of an uncle with my son, Alan, who was twelve years old at the time. When my uncle's coffin was lowered carefully into the ground, Alan broke from the mourners, ran to the edge of the grave and solemnly watched as the cemetery workers began filling the hole. After a while he returned to me with a look on his face that took me a moment or so to decipher.

It was closure. It was journey's end seen and understood.

I envied Alan that. I envied him because I never got there with my father, never would and never will.

My father's death affected us all in different ways. People would say, 'Aw, it must have hit wee Brian hard, being so young,' but in actual fact, I think my elder brother, Charlie, at sixteen, suffered the most. While writing this book, I spoke to May, who told me a story about Charlie at the funeral. How people were laughing at fond remembrances of my father, but Charlie was crying. How he tried to disguise his tears by peeling an orange. Concentrating too hard on peeling the orange. Pouring himself into the task. Using the orange to avoid having to confront his own feelings of utter and outright desolation, shoving the fruit into his mouth as though to keep his motor functions occupied and thus prevent the tears.

I don't remember much of Charlie after Pa's death. Despite the fact that he could have been excused on compassionate grounds, he ran off to do his national service, and that took him out of the picture for a while.

As for my other siblings, Bette and May had got married, left home and had families of their own. My other sister, Irene, was unmarried, still at home, and was expected to take care of me as our mother grieved. Irene's own dreams of travelling abroad had to take a back seat for a while.

And Ma? My already frail mother? My thwarted mother who had always chafed at the bonds of her life of maternal servitude, scarred mentally and no doubt physically by five births and an equal number of miscarriages? As for her?

Where do I start?

Well, a many-sided dice was my mother. One of those sides was funny and eccentric and sweet in a beguiling, unworldly sort of way. You and I will be talking more about my great friend and mentor Fulton Mackay in due course, but when my mum first met him in the early 1970s, she curtsied.

I was taken aback. 'Ma, what are you . . . did you just curtsy?'

She said, 'I never. I never did, Brian.'

I said, 'Ma, you did, you went . . . you bobbed . . . you curtsied. What's all that about?'

She said, 'Oh I don't know, it's just . . . we used to do that in the old days.'

In Canada, she'd meant. And you'd have thought Canada might have been a little less *Downton Abbey*, you know? A wee bit more relaxed and not quite so hierarchical. But no. Everybody – even in Canada – likes that form of servility, and for those of my mother's generation, and particularly of her standing, deference was baked into their DNA.

'Please don't do that again, Ma,' I asked her, feeling a bit bemused by the whole thing if I'm honest. I wasn't used to that side of her; I knew her as queen of her own domain, an environment in which she'd sooner die than yield to another. But that was one of her many contradictions. Like on the one hand I remember the great excitement when, during the years of prosperity, she got a fur coat, while on the other hand one of my abiding memories of her is wearing a worn-out red dressing gown night and day, a garment that seemed to symbolize her fragility and ill health.

She never was one to go overboard. That was another thing about my mother. When I married my first wife, Caroline, she wrote to my mother-in-law, a letter that included the memorable passage, 'Brian's not awfully bright, but he's got a good heart.' Praise indeed.

Her greatest praise was that something was 'quite nice'. You have to read that in a Dundonian accent: 'Oh it's *quite nice.*' That was praise indeed from my ma, and it carried her through the early years of my career. One time not long after I'd left drama school, she said to me, 'Brian, listen, I've got a petition up.'

And I said, 'What's this petition, Ma?'

She said, 'It's a book saying that I think we should see you more on television. I'm getting the neighbours to sign it, and I'm going to send it to the BBC.'

And I had to say, 'Ma, it doesn't work like that. You can't just tell the BBC to put me on TV and they'll do it.'

Thankfully she dropped her petition idea.

Another time, Caroline and I were living in a wonderful place called Vincent Square, just overlooking the Westminster School playing fields, and my mum came to visit. I'd been doing a bit of TV and working late, and I was hung-over for some reason, but I staggered home to the flat only to find my ma sitting at the kitchen table, smoking a Player's, as was her habit.

'Oh, Ma . . .'

I'll be honest, I'd forgotten she was due to arrive that day.

'Oh hi, Brian,' she said, and if she minded my forgetfulness, she didn't show it.

'So, how are you?'

'Oh. I'm fine.'

I said, 'How was the journey?'

'Oh, it was quite nice. It was quite nice.'

I said, 'It was your first time in an airplane, wasn't it?'

'Oh yes, it was, it was. And you know, Brian, I never knew – I never knew the sky was in bits.'

'In bits?'

She said, 'Well, when you see it from the ground, it looks like it's all in one piece. But when you're up in the plane and you look out, there's a bit here, there's a bit over there and there's a bit up there. It's all in bits.'

And I went, 'Yeah, Ma, that's cloud, you know. Clouds – they're not necessarily at the same level.'

We ended up having an existential conversation about the sky: me in a slightly altered state; her, pondering with the ubiquitous Player's, and both of us wondering whether the sky is a single, intricately embroidered sheet or a glorious gaseous patchwork.

But that was her. Very sweet. Very endearing. Almost eccentric in her way.

But then, on the other hand, came an incident in 1971. Caroline was pregnant with twins. She'd put her acting career on hold as a result. I'd been doing Alan Bennett's *Getting On* at Brighton when I got the call, and it was Caroline, who I should point out has a dark, almost gallows sense of humour.

'I've got good news and bad news,' she told me. 'The good news is that we had twins.'

'What's the bad news?' I asked.

'The bad news is that they didn't make it.'

See what I mean?

Which is not to say that it was anything but a matter of profound sadness to her. I came home one day to find her going through all the drawers. 'What are you doing?'

'Oh, nothing . . . nothing . . . I just thought . . .'

'What?'

'Oh, I don't know . . . it's stupid . . . I thought they might be here.'

'Who?'

'Um . . . the twins.'

Ach. Dark times. Dark times, indeed.

And I remember telling my mum about what we were going through, trying to explain Caroline's suffering. But she just looked at me coldly, with a somewhat bemused expression on her face. 'Ah, Brian,' she said to me, as though I had much to learn about the world, 'we've all dropped bairns.'

That was her phrase. *We've all dropped bairns.* It was said in such a matter-of-fact way that it absolutely floored me, and it took me a moment or so to realize that she wasn't being insensitive, or at least not deliberately, maliciously so; she was just being a product of her environment. A woman who had lived through and survived – and so very nearly succumbed to –periods of almost intolerable hardship.

You might argue that she was deliberately denying my wife the empathy that she had been denied during her own periods of loss?

What goes around comes around. That kind of thing. I don't think so. Or again, if so, then not callously so. It was more the expectation and ethos of one generation – a generation that had been deprived of empathy – rubbing up against the next.

And you know something? There's no real response to it. In a situation like that you can't tell your ma she's got it wrong. You have to show a bit of understanding. You have to try and be in her shoes. You have to see it as just another aspect of her character.

In the wake of my father's death, those various sides of my mother folded in on themselves. What she felt, I can't even begin to imagine, but I assume that guilt and regret figured in the mix. Much later my brother-in-law – Bill Chidlow, May's husband – told me that my mum had visited my dad in hospital. 'Your mother came to see your dad and I remember him looking at her with such contempt,' and what was really going on there, I don't know, or even if my brother-in-law misinterpreted what he saw, but what I took from it was how terribly tragic that even at the end they couldn't work it out. They couldn't cross the chasm of their differences to manage a last rapprochement. My parents were people of imagination. This was their sin: imagination. But they weren't allowed to give it rein.

My mother was destroyed. Like cracks in a vase, her life up to Pa's death had weakened her, and now the vessel smashed.

Even so, she might have coped. *Might have.* If not for one thing.

All of a sudden we were dirt poor.

What had happened was that Pa had invested a lot of money – and for the time it really was a lot, like £28,000 – which he sank into a building project. That was the trouble with him. He wasn't built for capitalism. This was a man who would give the shirt off his back for someone in need, and when you look at it like that, the idea of him profiting from a canny business deal seems a fanciful notion at best. No doubt my mum understood that. Perhaps deep down she feared what eventually happened: that his business partners would take advantage of him, it would all go bad and he would lose the money. And that he would die and leave us with barely a penny to our name.

And that made my mother terribly frail. So frail, both mentally and physically, that she was unable to work, which meant that the money dried up, and there was the odd occasion when we'd be waiting for her widow's pension to arrive on Friday with the cupboards bare on Thursday night, when I'd have to go across to the chip shop and beg batter bits from the back of the chip pan off them. They were very sweet about it, actually, and it wasn't as though it happened often. But still.

Deep she went. Deep into a hole of ill health and mental fragility. Over the years, and at various times, I would see her in the black depths of despair, watching helplessly as she lost her fervent Catholic faith. Watching as she became hostage to her own mental health.

On one occasion, I returned home to find her with her head in the oven.

'What are you doing, Ma?'

That child's instinct again. That sixth sense. *Something is wrong.*

Oh, but, 'I'm just cleaning the oven, Brian,' she told me hurriedly. 'And it is a hell of a duty.'

And it took a good few years for the penny to drop. How it formed a pattern. That suicide attempt. The breakdowns she had. The electroshock therapy and hospitalizations. Me, picking up the pieces of my ma. Knowing what had caused the already fragile vessel to smash but not really knowing what to do with the shards.

The way things fell was that around the new year of 1956 she was admitted to hospital, so for over a year, until Irene emigrated to Canada in the Spring of 1957, it was just me and Irene in the house. After Irene left (or should that be 'escaped'?) for Canada, I stayed with Bette, her husband Dave and their two young boys, all of us in a two-bedroom flat, sharing an outside toilet with three other families. I was ten then, and apart from spending a brief time with May at her home in Warrington in the summer of 1957, I stayed with Bette until Ma was discharged at the beginning of 1958. I was back living with my mum in a new flat again – this one on the west side of Dundee – intermittently from 1958 until 1961.

The upshot of all of this was that I became a peripatetic child. A peripatetic child of a peripatetic family spawned by a peripatetic nation.

My sisters of course were preoccupied with lives of their own, and as a result, it's fair to say, did not give me the gold-standard *in loco parentis* care. In interviews these days I often recount that my sisters looked *out* for me rather than *after* me, and that's all very well to say wearing my goggles of adult retrospection, but at the time? Put it this way, it was during the first year after my dad's death that I wrote a note to my sister: *'Dear Irene, you've never looked after me, you don't look after me probably. I'm not going any more messages for you.'*

('Messages', I should point out, is what we called 'errands' back then, and I'm fairly certain I meant to say 'properly' and not 'probably'. Otherwise? You get the gist. It was ironic that after that year of looking after me, Irene should bugger off to Canada. I'm sure it wasn't my note that sent her in search of a new life overseas, just as I'm sure that she didn't choose Canada because of its associations with Ma's broken dreams. But that doesn't stop it being ironic.)

In one sense, self-sufficiency was a gift my sisters gave to me. It meant that from then on my journey through life was largely unaccompanied by feelings of homesickness, loneliness and/or fear; that I had mettle at my core. And yet on the other hand they say that strong, stable relationships, especially parental ones, help the child form better and stronger connections in later life. Certainly, I can look at my own parenting and see that principle – or lack of it – in action, because let's be honest here, I have, in my time, been a fairly crappy father.

My first son, Alan, was born in 1970, when I was still married to Caroline. At the time, I was in rehearsal for *A Midsummer Night's Dream* at the University Theatre in Manchester, the forerunner to the Royal Exchange. The cast was sharing a house in Manchester. I was on the first floor, and Zoë Wanamaker, who was playing Hermia – her first job, I think – had the downstairs room, a few feet away from the only phone in the house. Which meant that apart from playing Hermia, Zoë was also cast in the role of house messenger.

At 5 a.m. on 6th August, I was awoken by a rapping on the door. *Bang, bang, bang.*

'It's happening,' called Zoë from the landing outside, her voice pillowy with sleep.

Bustling past Zoë – 'Thank you, thank you, thank you' – I hurtled downstairs in my PJs, grabbed the dangling receiver. 'Hullo?'

It was my mother-in-law. Once upon a time I'd been driving her someplace, said something that displeased her, and she'd slapped me. I had to pull over. 'Look, I'm not your son, you can't punch me like that,' for which she rewarded me with a look as if to say, *suck it up, sunshine.*

Now she was as matter-of-fact as ever. 'Caroline's on the way now, she's going to the hospital.'

'Okay, fine. Thank you. I'll be there.'

Back up the stairs I ran, got dressed (couldn't find my underpants, had to go commando), rushed to the station, got the train from Manchester to London, hot-footed it to St George's Hospital on Hyde Park Corner and . . . missed the birth by ten minutes.

Alan had slight jaundice when he was born, but he was fine and soon developed into a very, very sweet boy with a really lovely nature. And yet missing his birth by ten minutes somehow set the template for my role as a father. The following year was when we lost the twins, which was hard for Caroline, and I'm ashamed to say, I wasn't much help. Too young, too focused on my career and not quite mature enough. I became mature as a result. Well, I got on the road to maturity, shall we say, because I still don't know if I'm mature or not, but there you go, the esteemed jury remains out on that one.

My daughter, Margaret, arrived in the September of 1977. She was born using the Leboyer method, which advocates the use of low light and silence during the process – as described in *Birth Without Violence* by the French obstetrician Frédéric Leboyer. Not until the mucus had been cleared from her throat did Margaret utter a sound.

The age gap between Margaret and Alan hasn't stopped them being close, although – a bit like a married couple – they sometimes get on each other's nerves. Because I'd left school at fifteen, I didn't know what to do about the whole political thing of whether to send them to private schools or not. Caroline took the reins on that, I'm glad to say. I was busy ploughing other furrows at the time, so I wasn't being particularly domestic (translation: I was busy being a crap dad), and so I agreed – being in no position not to, frankly – that the kids should have the best possible opportunities. I would have preferred Alan to go through the university system, but he really wanted to be an actor and like me went to the London Academy of Music and Dramatic Art. Margaret, on the other hand, is the first person in my family to go to university.

With my second wife – and my soulmate – Nicole, I have two more kids: Orson, who was born in 2002, and Torin, born in 2004. We were in Morocco with Alan when I announced that Nicole was pregnant with Orson. 'So, Alan,' I said to him, feeling a little nervous, as only a father can be when breaking such news to his son. 'I have to tell you that Nicole is pregnant.'

'Oh,' he said. 'Well. Then I shall have to think about that.'

'Okay,' I said.

So he went out into the desert for a walk. I stood in the hotel room looking at him wandering on the outskirts of the desert, thinking, *I wonder what's going through his head?* Until in the end, he returned. 'Didn't you think to take precautions?' he asked, rather impertinently.

'No,' I said, 'it was meant.' At that he pulled a face, so I added, 'You know, I wouldn't mind grandchildren, so I've decided to make my own.'

He looked at me. *Typical.*

Anyway, that was that. Orson was born by Caesarean section. He was supposed to be a home birth, but following in his father's footsteps decided to make an about-turn and locked his head under his mother's ribs.

His full name is Orson Jonathan Cyrus Cox. Orson was originally intended to be Spencer, but when he was born, his arms were so stiff we named him Orson like the stuffed bear. Cyrus (pronounced 'Sirrus') goes to his mother's Iranian roots. We added Jonathan because it means 'gift of God'.

After that, Nicole really wanted a natural birth with Torin but his labour was going on for some time, and there were blood pressure problems so another Caesarean became inevitable. Torin is an ancient Celtic name that Nicole discovered. It goes back to the Viking invasions (Thor –Tor-in). As for his middle names, Kamran nods to Nicole's Iranian roots and Charles is after my father.

These days, the four of us live in New York, where I've been based pretty much full-time since 2008 when I came to Broadway with the West End transfer of Tom Stoppard's *Rock 'n' Roll*, directed by Trevor Nunn.

And, my God, the kids are so hormonal. I mean, among all the wet towels and the collections of fungus-infested mugs left to fester in bedrooms, we sometimes forget that teenage boys are such slaves to their hormones. How as a result they need to sleep long hours – hours that are not always convenient for the rest of polite, civilized society. How that means you're always having to wake them up. 'Torin, it's five past eight . . .'

'Torin, ten past eight!'

'Torin, a quarter past!!'

'*Torin!!!*'

And I hate all that. 'I wasn't designed to be your wake-up call,' I'll say, day in, day out, like a stuck record. I hate having to drag them off their videogames and failing miserably. I hate the fact that while I had a hand in creating them, I seem to have absolutely nothing in common with them.

Which is all a long and roundabout way of saying that while I consider my children to be wonderful miracles – and I really do, I'm not just saying it for the cameras – I have little affinity with the process of fathering them. Thank God, they have a wonderful mother who bears the brunt and, more often than not, has to fulfil both roles.

One of my very favourite lines is from the play *Alpha Beta* by Ted Whitehead, all about a working-class couple's marriage breakdown. The husband has finally persuaded the wife that they should part, and she says, 'But the children. Who'll take care of the children?'

To which he replies, 'Professionals.'

I love that line. It makes me roar with laughter every time. I love it because it says all that needs to be said about parenting. It says, *We need training.*

And my own parental deficiency – and you must understand that I take no pleasure in admitting this – stems from that. A lack of training. My examples were either not good enough or too good. Because I was so young when my father died, he was never anything other than a mythic creature to me. Death conferred on him a sainthood. Compared to him I am and always will be clumsy and dithering and indecisive, and to me the inevitability of that and the futility of trying to live up to his example is an ever-present thing. It's an impossible ideal that haunts me every day.

It is said that Joan Crawford, having been abandoned by two fathers in short order, spent her life in search of paternal figures to replace them. A succession of lovers, husbands, directors and producers might fit the bill for a while, but Joan would grow suspicious when they didn't reject her and would strike a pre-emptive blow, ending the relationship. Bette Davis, on the other hand, when her father left, said that she 'became my own father and everyone else's'.

My own reaction was less clear-cut than either. Certainly, I went on to find mentors, perhaps the equivalent of Crawford's father figures. But the flip side was Bette's fierce sense of self-reliance. And on top of that, something else: an absence.

It's funny. In the early years of our marriage, Caroline and I would hold amazing New Year's Eve parties, where the guest list was incredible: John Osborne, Lindsay Anderson, Alan Bates, Albert Finney. And at the last minute, literally just before we threw open the doors, I'd say, 'I think we need some more napkins,' and disappear before the guests turned up, purely because I wouldn't want to be there when the first person arrived.

And that's my flaw. One of them, anyway. It's this propensity for absence, this need to disappear. I have a photograph of Pa and me together. I'm about three or four, and he's sitting on my tricycle, fitting a buttonhole to my lapel at the same time, and there's such love and care and devotion in the act. It shines through the ancient photograph. It reaches through the years. I love that photograph and it means the world to me. Diamonds form in my eyes every time I look at it. But it also reminds me of my own fatherly shortcomings. My own inability to be truly present.

Meanwhile, when Ma came out of hospital, she cut a severely reduced figure, gone from being the once-proud matriarch to a shadow of that – thin and pinched and frail. An old phobia re-emerged – coal – which was particular inconvenient since the coalman lived in the tenement above ours. If only she'd developed an aversion to camels, or something else rarely seen in Scotland. But, oh no, it had to be coal.

My instructions were that under no circumstances should I pass the neighbour's coal lorry parked outside the entrance to our close, which meant taking a long, circuitous route home through the back-yards of Lyon Street, all the time knowing that Ma would be keeping watch from the bedroom window. One time I decided to risk it and snuck in through the front door.

'*Brian!*'

She'd been lying in wait and pounced on me, dragging me to the bathroom where I was forced to scrub down in case I'd inadvertently brought coal dust into the flat. Not only that, but she would also always take advantage of the situation to check my head for nits with a steel comb.

In addition, her knitting became erratic. Once upon a time she'd been a consummate knitter, but after hospital she'd lost some crucial aspect of her skill with the needles. The things she made me became increasingly idiosyncratic. I'd get hats aimed at people with shrunken heads, sweaters clearly designed to fit two or three fully grown adults at once. Long into my time at drama school I'd dread the sight of the brown-paper packages that arrived from her, wondering what homemade horrors lurked within.

Thankfully, things would eventually calm down with my ma, and from being mentally unable to work, she rallied and got a job as a chalet maid at Butlin's, as well as rediscovering her faith.

I, however, had changed. I had become much more the person I am today. Self-sufficient and self-reliant. Toughened-up and nomadic. I suppose you'd have to say that it was a good foundation for life as an actor. But having lived through every grisly moment of it, it's not the training I'd recommend.

CHAPTER 4

My primary school was Our Lady of Victories at St Mary's, Forebank. One of my first memories there was of a playground fight. If you can call it that. A bunch of pupils were goading me into beating up another kid who was a bit backward. A poor, bullied kid. And as the bullies gathered and stood, baying for blood, I saw a terrible, hunted look in the lad's eyes and knew there was no way I could go through with it. At the same time, I knew the terrible price I would pay for *not* going through with it.

And so, instead of either beating the kid up or backing out and offering myself as human chum for the bullies, I turned it into a gag. I began a scrap with an imaginary opponent. At first my fight with fresh air took the assembly by surprise, but then the laughter started, proper hysterical laughter, increasing as I threw myself with even greater vigour onto the ground and into the performance. Because that's what it was – a performance. It was me locating that urge inside and using it once more, only this time as a form of protection.

Thus I learned one of the first important lessons of being an actor: you've got to be able to think on your feet, turn on a dime. It also corresponds with an idea very close to my heart, which is that the best actors are child actors. Children have such a sense of being and of being in the moment. There is no past, or present, only the now. A child doesn't research, doesn't adhere to some bogus process, doesn't look for his or her motivation, isn't bound by personal history. A child doesn't do 'method'.

He or she just *is*.

There's no better example of this than in December 2010, when I visited my friends John and Clara Archer at their home in Drymen, Scotland. We'd just had breakfast with their toddler, Theo, and since it had already been remarked upon that Theo showed a surprising aptitude and skill for language, well beyond his years, I decided to try a little experiment – teaching him Hamlet's 'to be, or not to be' soliloquy.

It was Christmas, Theo was distracted by a toy on a shelf and, perhaps even more to the point, was just two-and-a-half years old – not an age noted for its desire to learn Shakespeare. Even so, he did a grand job of maintaining focus.

It was quite incredible. You can actually see this online. It's worth looking up. And what you'll see is a surprising and comical moment when, with Theo's response to 'to be or not to be, that is the question', he breaks with convention and says, 'Yeah.'

I repeat the phrase, and he then replies, 'Yeah, it is.'

At one point, entirely of his own volition, he responds physically to the phrase 'the slings and arrows of outrageous fortune'. Earlier in the experiment he had mimicked a movement I made, but this 'slings and arrows' gesture is entirely of his own making. He also picks up the word 'suffer' and says it so strongly, with full emphasis on the two syllables, 'suf-fer', that it hits the listener with a sense of sadness.

How does a two-year-old have such an instinct that he can pick this up? Where does it come from? I'll tell you. It comes from where I drew the inspiration to convert my audience in the school playground from bloodthirsty to beguiled. It comes from the gut.

Sure enough, school, while being pretty horrendous in most ways, saw me begin to develop what you might call the gift of the gab. I gained a reputation as someone who liked to be in the limelight, and it was no doubt for that reason that Mr Robertson, the headmaster, singled me out one day.

'Cox!'

'Sir.'

'Right, Cox, I want you to go to Larg's . . .'

Larg's was a big shop selling gramophones, records and such. 'I need a stylus for my Philips radiogram. I need you to go and pick it up today.'

Only too happy to miss a chunk of school, I spent hours wandering around, got the stylus, came back and gave it to him. And he never noticed that I'd missed most of my day at school.

And after that? Well, as you can imagine, the floodgates well and truly opened. Any messages that needed doing, I was your man, and about three times a week I'd be doing the messages for Mr Robertson or any other teacher who needed anything from town, and each time I went in, I'd spend all of five minutes doing the message and the rest of the time – *hours* – just wandering around, a wee boy in a Dundonian daydream, thinking about all those saps at school, stuck in classrooms studying for their eleven-plus exam while I was plunking off and munching sweets.

There was a flaw in my plan, of course. The flaw in my plan was the fact that I did no studying for the eleven-plus, and as a result failed with flying colours. Had I passed I would have gone to an academy, gained experience of humanities and my horizons would no doubt have been broadened at a more formative age.

But that's not what happened. Instead I found myself with my fellow deadbeats at a secondary modern, St Michaels, fed into a sausage-meat system geared towards churning out skilled workers. The work bit I was fine with. I have no problem with work, either as an abstract concept or in practice. It was the skill I lacked. Our first task in woodwork was to make a model boat, which should have been a simple enough job. The trouble being that my boat looked like the *Pequod* after the fight with the whale. Other kids took their boats home to show their parents, but I didn't have a dad, and my mother wouldn't have been interested in any boat I'd made, especially not a ravaged, pathetic approximation of one, so it was all kind of pointless.

Thank God for two teachers: George Hackett, an art teacher, who saw something in me, and Bill Dewar, who introduced me to the stage. Thanks to Bill I did a sort of performance at school. It was a thing about a trial. I can't remember the title, but I do remember a few lines from it. '*And the end of all the fuss, was nothing less than us, an upright and official British jury. So, raise your voices, bang the drum with a hey nonny-no, and a rum-tum-tum . . .*'

I played a police sergeant. I was a sergeant in a play about a trial with a hey nonny-no. And the only thing that frustrated me was that there wasn't nearly enough of it. We just did that one performance. One.

But of course I was at the wrong school, and there were to be no more stage appearances for me – not for a while, anyway.

Outside of school I did the normal things. I hung about with a group of lads, the Lyon Street Gang. Our favourite game was lone wolf, where one of us would go off and we had to track them and find them. I loved lone wolf and got so good at it that on one occasion I found a perfect hiding place and was still there at 1 a.m. – at which point it dawned on me that everybody had probably gone home, and that maybe I should follow suit. Still, I won. I mean, not that we had such a thing as the Lyon Street Gang Lone Wolf Champion, but if we did then the title would have been mine, and I dare say I'd hold it to this day.

It was also a great time for music. My sisters played records all the time and it rubbed off. In fact, they say I learned to read through looking at album sleeves. That's how I'd know it was Frank Sinatra singing 'Fools Rush In', or Vaughn Monroe crooning 'Where the Wild Things Go'. I remember my pal David Strachan introducing me to this American singer, Buddy Holly, and being completely smitten.

I was also into books. Well, at first I was into comics. Besides the jute mills, Dundee was also famous for DC Thomson, publishers of the *Beano* and the *Dandy*, and I was an avid and very loyal reader of the *Dandy* on a Tuesday and the *Beano* on a Thursday, as well another comic, which also came on a Thursday, *Film Fun*, which I loved.

Eventually I graduated to DC Comics and *Superman*. I loved *Batman*, too. In fact, my early love for Batman is the reason why I've no truck with Christopher Nolan's *Batman* films. The whole dark and brooding thing? That's just not Batman to me. Batman was witty and funny. The adventures were thrilling and a little bit surreal, not all angsty and dark the way Nolan has them. That's his interpretation, fair enough, but I don't think they need depth forced on them. It's all there anyway; it's allegory.

The other thing I liked was the Classics Illustrated comics, which were classic stories told in a comic-book style. *Moby-Dick*, *Hamlet*, *Macbeth*, *The Three Musketeers*, *The Last of the Mohicans*, *David*

Copperfield, A Tale of Two Cities . . . Oh my God, I used to love them. About fifteen years ago, I was staying at the Covent Garden Hotel and I discovered eBay. I'm not sure why it took me staying at the Covent Garden Hotel to discover eBay, but there you go. I went mad. I raided almost the entire collection of Classics Illustrated, over 150 of them. I've even got a copy from 1946, the year I was born.

Which reminds me. In 1997, I made *The Boxer*, Jim Sheridan's film set in Northern Ireland and starring Daniel Day-Lewis in the lead. I played the father of his beloved, who was played by Emily Watson.

Back then, Daniel was full method, of course. I remember Emily arriving on set and he greeted her in character, complete with his Northern Irish accent, which took her by surprise, to say the least.

'What do I do?' she asked me from the side of her mouth.

'Oh, just talk to him normally,' I advised. 'Just use your normal voice, he'll be fine.'

Another time, Jim and I were in the director's caravan watching Dan go through his paces outside. Skipping. Shadow-boxing. The works. Ye gods, it was exhausting just watching him.

'You know, Brian,' mused Jim, 'I'm just not sure that boxing works as a metaphor for this film.'

We watched Dan a bit longer. He'd slapped a rolled towel over his shoulders and was popping some jabs.

'I'll tell you what, Jim,' I said, 'I think it might be a bit late for that.'

This could well be the reason after all that extracurricular, exhausting character creation, he found himself worn out. He threw in the towel, decided *No more* and announced he was taking early retirement. Perhaps he realized how silly it all was. Nonetheless, he's a superb actor, and he was brilliant in *The Boxer*. And if I wasn't wholly enamoured of *There Will Be Blood*, either by the film or his performance, I did think he was brilliant in *Lincoln*. Watch how he listens. He is truly one of the great listeners.

Anyway, during the making of *The Boxer*, Dan announced that when the film wrapped he was going to give up acting and become a cobbler. Actually, I think it was a shoe designer, but collectively we in the cast and crew decided it was a cobbler. I, in particular, cherished the notion that Dan might become a cobbler simply because the image that came to mind was from the Classics Illustrated edition of *A Tale of Two Cities* in which Dr Manette is pictured at a cobbler's last, cobbling away with this hammer held high – cobbling as a means of distraction. That, to me, was Dan. Dan in a nutshell. And after that, he was always Dr Manette to me, even when he didn't give it all up to be a cobbler.

Meanwhile, back in my childhood, and I graduated to books. It took me a while, actually; I didn't really have the patience for books when I was a lad, but I got the bug, thankfully, and I got into Hardy, read most of those and have reread them since. *The Mayor of Casterbridge* is one of the great, great books of the English language. I was also tremendously influenced by Herman Melville's *Moby-Dick*, which would come in handy later, and of course the work of my fellow countryman Robert Louis Stevenson, who for me is one of the great, great writers.

Later on I was in Stevenson's *The Master of Ballantrae* on the television. It's a fantastic story that always feels a bit overlooked in favour of the likes of *Kidnapped* and *Treasure Island*. Both brilliant works, but I think *The Master of Ballantrae* and *Dr Jekyll and Mr Hyde* represent the core of Stevenson's literary obsession. The eternal struggle between devil and angel. So much to do with Celtic archetypes.

Later on, I got into other Scottish authors, in particular Alexander

Trocchi. Trocchi's *Young Adam* is about Joe, who works on a barge on the Forth and Clyde Canal, where my great-grandfather Patrick McCann once worked. Joe and his co-worker find the body of a woman in the water, but as the book goes on we learn of Joe's connection with the dead woman and his part in her death.

I love the notion of *Young Adam*. I love its themes of connection and disconnection. The fact that Joe's not connected to the girl and then realises that he is, and that – spoiler ahead – he's responsible for her death. Then there's – another spoiler coming up – his fascination with watching somebody else being tried for her murder. It asks how you deal with problems you don't feel connected to, and although it came out around the time when existentialism was a really big thing –Jean-Paul Sartre, Albert Camus – it's not languid and French. It locates those same themes in a completely different geographical context and it's very, very Scottish.

In about 1969, I worked on a script for a film adaptation with a guy called Roger Williams, who's sadly no longer with us. Roger and I went on a tour of what was left of the Forth and Clyde Canal, and after that we got to work on the script. I remember typing it up. I'm not a typist. Proper search-and-bash merchant, I am. But as I was typing I got this strange sensation. It was the weirdest thing ever. I looked up, and I saw myself sitting on top of the door watching myself typing.

I thought, *That's weird*, and then went back to typing. But it was a real, proper existential moment, completely in keeping with the work we were doing. I was thinking, *Is this real, or is this pretending*? And that of course is where the whole discipline of acting is open to question, because what is real and what is pretend? When do we pretend and when are we real? When are we true and when are we not necessarily being false, but not quite being true? I find that fascinating from my work point of view.

(The film never got made, by the way. There is an adaptation from 2003 starring Ewan McGregor, which I'm sure is very good, but I haven't seen it – I think perhaps because it just feels too personal.)

All of which means that I can feel my way back along a guide rope from the likes of Alexander Trocchi and *Young Adam* to the comics and Classics Illustrated I used to read as a kid. And, while we are at it, from pretty much any point in my life right now back to the movies I used to watch.

Because I loved movies. I mean, while I might have loved music, comics and books, my love for the cinema was on an entirely different level. So much so, it deserves its own chapter.

CHAPTER 5

The first movie I ever saw was a Dean Martin and Jerry Lewis film, and I became a big fan as a result. The only thing I have in common with the French is that they and I are both huge Jerry Lewis fans.

After that, I went to the cinema regularly, obsessively, religiously. Those days I used to plunk off school? If the timing was right, then I went to the cinema. Weekends? Cinema. Trips out with my sisters or my ma? 'Where do you want to go, Brian? The picture house again, is it?'

Aye. There were twenty-one cinemas in Dundee and I was a regular at every single one, especially the Green's Playhouse, the Broadway and the Royal. I loved double features, the ones that started at 6 p.m. and went through until 11 p.m. I could see as many as eight movies in a week that way. You'd see the new releases, like Alan Ladd and Edward G. Robinson in *Hell on Frisco Bay*, alongside the films that had already been out a while. I remember seeing *Wuthering Heights* with Larry Olivier and Merle Oberon. The Agatha Christie thriller *And Then There Were None* directed by René Clair. I liked them all, old and new. Considering I was just a wee boy, my tastes were pretty sophisticated.

I went to see *Giant* starring James Dean, Elizabeth Taylor and

Rock Hudson at the Green's Playhouse. This was during one of my illicit excursions from school, and I loved it so much that when it finished, I stayed on in the cinema to see it again because you could do that kind of thing in those days, if you knew what you were doing, and I certainly did, being a seasoned campaigner.

The trouble was that while *Giant* is a brilliant film, it's well over three hours, and I'd already seen it once, so what did I do?

I nodded off.

I awoke with a start to find that the film had finished and the cinema was dark and cold. I had no watch, but I could tell that it was late – very late. You could just sense it. There was that 'very late' feel to the place, as if all human life had withdrawn, leaving the clammy dark to take its place. I groped my way out of the auditorium and set eyes on a clock. It was four in the morning.

I crapped myself. Only metaphorically this time, being that much older.

At least I had the wherewithal to unlock, escape the cinema and flee into the street, where I looked fearfully this way and that, gulping hard. Talk about frying pans and fires. Sure, the cinema was spooky, but Dundee's darkened, tramlined streets at night were, if anything, even more foreboding.

Next thing you know I was panic-running – running, running – when suddenly I came upon a police box, one of the old Tardis types, at Nethergate, which was at the bottom of Reform Street. I'd just reached it and was about to run past when from within came a deep voice.

'And where are you going at this time in the morning, young man?'

No sign of anyone. Just the Tardis.

'I'm late.' I told the Tardis.

'What do you mean, you're late?' Still no sign of the copper inside. He'd no doubt decided this was an issue best resolved from the comfort of the police box interior. You could hardly blame him – it was bloody cold.

I said, 'Well, I should be home, but I was at the pictures and I fell asleep.'

The Tardis said, 'Are you by any chance Brian Cox?'

'Yes,' I squeaked.

'And is your sister Irene Cox?'

'Yes.'

He said, 'Aye, well, she's looking for you. She's crazy-mad. She's beside herself. You'd better get home.'

Off I went home, only to discover that my sister Irene was indeed frantic with worry, crazy-mad and beside herself. That was a lively homecoming, I can tell you.

But that was me and the cinema. I was obsessed. I mean, seeing James Dean, for example, in *East of Eden*. There's a moment when he's talking to Julie Harris as he's on a swing, a child's swing in the garden. He's having problems with his father, who he can never please enough, and he's estranged from his mother who's now running a whorehouse, and he's all pent up and angry, when suddenly he swings and deliberately hits his head on the tree above.

I later discovered that this moment wasn't in the script, the head-hitting bit. He just did it, and Elia Kazan, the director, let it go in. And while that knowledge lends the moment an extra power, I was still totally blown away at the time. I just thought, *Wow, what was that? Where does that come from?* That pain.

Same with Brando in *On the Waterfront* – Brando's trying to talk to Eva Marie Saint about her hair 'like a hunk of rope' and he does this thing with her glove. He tries it on. And even at that young age, I was blown away by that gesture – by the texture and the detail in the performance.

I preferred American movies. These days I like British films, especially the Ealing comedies, but back then the likes of *Doctor in the House*, Dirk Bogarde and Kenneth More were a little middle class for my tastes. They were too far away from my own experience to resonate; not far enough to give me the same exotic thrill I got from *A Place in the Sun* or *A Streetcar Named Desire*. Even *The Bridge on the River Kwai* was a bit on the formal side for me. This was a problem, because even at that young age I was eyeing up a future as one of those guys on the screen although I hadn't foggiest idea how to go about it. How does a wee kid from Dundee get to be in films (films being the only outlet I was aware of back then – theatre not even on the horizon)?

But then one afternoon I went to the Plaza Cinema in Hilltown to see *Saturday Night and Sunday Morning*, and it changed me. And I mean really, radically changed me at a cellular level. Because I looked at Albert Finney, who was working-class English, in a film that wasn't all about the lives of posh folk in drawing rooms, or struggling nobly in far-off places, or having faintly amusing high-jinks on hospital wards; it was all about working-class people – people like us.

To me, this was proper eye-opening stuff. This was a transformative moment. I thought, *My God, that could be me. If that guy up there can do it, I can do it, too.*

I ended up working with Albert in 1973, when we were in David Storey's play *Cromwell* together. The late Pete Postlethwaite was in it, too, and so was Alun Armstrong. Albert was playing an Irishman, and he wasn't very good, unfortunately, but that didn't stop me being utterly overawed by him. I remember it was a very 'corpsey' cast, and there was a scene where a family is carting away the dead body of a soldier in a coffin ready for burial, but they're met by Cromwellian soldiers on the way. One night there was something about the corpse – a Royal Court dummy that had been in many productions and was now confined to this coffin – which for some reason struck us as funny, and Pete, Alun and I got a fit of the giggles while Albert was trying to do his scene.

Just as the scene went to black and we were out of sight of the audience, Albert broke character, grabbed me and snarled, 'You're not that fooking good, you know.'

God, it scared the shit out of me, but he was so right. We weren't so good that we could afford to be distracted like that. Besides, he wasn't so cross that we didn't eventually become quite friendly, and he never stopped being an important figure for me. I remember something he said once – he said, 'There I was having sex on a beach in Hawaii, thinking, no other Finney has ever done this. I'm having sex on a beach in Hawaii on behalf of all other Finneys.' And I understand completely what that meant. Not the sex on a beach in Hawaii – I've never had the pleasure – but the sense of breaking out, of escaping that great Damoclean sword of wretched poverty. Escaping a system that is designed to thwart you and keep you down and make sure you know your place.

These days, I'd never go back to live in Dundee but I've maintained my links with the city because it reminds me of the gift I've been given, because my upbringing is so much a part of me it's written through me like words through a stick of rock; it informs my overall vision of being bona fide, of being legitimate, of trying to do what does me good, even when it's been enormously difficult. And that means all kinds of things. It means my career, my marriages, my children. It also means the spiritual pursuits I've embarked on over the years. All of which have been about doing me good. It's not a selfish thing, it's just, *How do I get better? How do I improve?* And that's my MO.

Anyway, we're getting ahead of ourselves. The point is that for me, as a lad, Albert was the standard bearer. He was the vanguard. And of course Albert was followed by Richard Harris in *This Sporting Life*, Tom Courtenay in *The Loneliness of the Long Distance Runner*, Alan Bates in *A Kind of Loving*. All just regular blokes-down-the-pub doing regular bloke-down-the-pub stuff, except up there on the big screen, in the place normally reserved for Montgomery Clift and Rock Hudson, who just by virtue of being there were shining a torch onto the path ahead for me. Even, a little later, Peter O'Toole in *Lawrence of Arabia*, was very much part of that generation. Though the film was ostensibly cut from the same cloth as *Bridge on the River Kwai* – same director, David Lean, for a start – Peter, again, was different. He was one of us. I got to work with him later, too, on *Troy*, but I'll save that for a later chapter.

And I still love films above all else, even the theatre. Especially the old ones. I mean, I love long-form drama, of course; I love what television does. The way it develops something over a period of time, how it's not about the powerful opening and the dramatic close, it's all about the middle. But by the same token, I'm not sure if you can beat the classic movies, I'm really not. The Covid thing was a great period for me, watching stuff, going back to the wellspring. Turner Classic Movies. The Criterion Channel. I found myself appreciating the styles as they've developed from the thirties onwards. The incredible speed at which actors used to perform, for example. They had that wonderful sense of momentum, so if you see a film like Howard Hawks's *His Girl Friday* with Rosalind Russell as Hildy and Cary Grant as Walter Burns, it's played at a phenomenal rate, and it's just fantastic. It's so snappy. I find that watching them teaches me so much, because the thing about my job is that you never stop learning. You never stop learning how to take a moment, how to circumvent it, how to knock it forward, how to not dwell, how to understand the verb but keep it moving and not get trapped into it.

I'm still a good audience member, despite having been an actor for sixty years. I give myself over to the experience of it, because I don't ever want to lose that love I have for it.

I'm not very good at watching myself, funnily enough. My wife makes me do it and I'm not bad, but it's the *doing* that is the thing I like, not the seeing.

I think I'm always more keen to see other people's work anyway. I'm particularly interested in the young director, the guy or girl doing their first movie. Recently, I watched a film called *Smithereens* which was Susan Seidelman's first movie – the one she made before *Desperately Seeking Susan* – and it's an extraordinary piece of work. It's about a punk girl who's travelling across the States trying to hook up with like-minded outsiders, and though it's a film I would never normally watch in a million years, I thought I'd give it a go, and was completely entranced by it.

So I love seeing that kind of great work, that flowering of talent. I'm not the biggest fan of *The Crown*, but you do see some really special acting in it. I'm thinking of Tobias Menzies playing the Duke of

Edinburgh. There were a couple of episodes where the Duke's world is shaky, to say the least, and Tobias just understood something about that inner torment and how to channel it.

And that's what actors do. We touch on the inner life of people, what they are, where their disappointments are, where their love is, where their desire is, what they're seeking, and we become conduits for it. I appreciated that from an early age – right from seeing James Dean bash his head and Marlon Brando do that business with the glove – and I still appreciate it now.

My mother was very keen on the cinema, of course. Apparently she went all the time when she was pregnant with me, and in fact my sister Irene used to say it was why I got into acting – because I'd been absorbing it in the womb.

As I grew up, our shared love of the cinema was something that bonded me and Ma. Spencer Tracy was her favourite actor, and he's mine, too. As far as my mum was concerned, it didn't hurt that Tracy was Catholic. For me, he's just the greatest film actor ever. He's part of my life's blood. And to pick a favourite film of his is a near-impossible task because they're all brilliant. I mean, any with Katharine Hepburn of course, and *The Last Hurrah*, which is a John Ford film about a dying politician; *Guess Who's Coming to Dinner*, which is a bit creaky as a film, but Tracy gives a great performance in it; *Captains Courageous*, for which he won the Oscar. The list is long.

I've wondered if the desire to perform becoming the desire to act – as opposed to, say, the desire to sing – was all wrapped up in my and ma's shared love of Spencer Tracy. I loved the cinema and thanks to Albert Finney saw a way forward, a future that might even include me. But my mum loved Spencer Tracy and so if I became like Spencer

Tracy then maybe I was courting that parental love? Perhaps. Perhaps not. Either way, it's one of many answers to this central question that I've pondered since about the age when pondering became a thing. Why do it? Why be an actor?

CHAPTER 6

My favourite comedy in the world is *The Court Jester* starring Danny Kaye. 'The vessel with the pestle has the pellet with the poison. The flagon with the dragon is the brew that is true.' I saw it as a kid and loved it, and even now I'll watch it if I'm feeling down. Although the movie bombed at the box office (these days it's regarded as a classic but at the time it was considered a veritable turkey), there was something about it that clicked with me. *I got it.* Likewise, Bob Hope and Bing Crosby in *Road to Morocco*, and then all the *Road . . .* films afterwards. That sense of improvisation. The badinage that went on between the two of them. These were films that spoke to me.

So it came from there. This desire to act. But it also came from my childhood and all that tragedy I had to deal with. Lana Turner's father was murdered when she was very young, his killer was never found and, as in my case, that event was the catalyst for years of impoverishment. As a result, Turner grew up too fast, she said, and the feeling of loss never left her. I can relate. As the self-sufficient youngest of five, a dab hand at scoring the batter bits, oh, I can relate.

And no, I don't believe that you have to live through tragedy in order to portray it, but it does help clarify things for you, and for me it all added up to what felt like a formidable singleness of purpose. That was my superpower. It set me on the path.

As a result, I think of myself as blessed. I mean, so many people spend their lives with no vision of the future and not knowing what they want to do, whereas I always did know. I never for one second had a moment of doubt. I never thought, *Oh, maybe I might like to be a dentist, or run a garden centre, or become a cobbler.* It was always just, *I want to be Spencer Tracy or Danny Kaye or Cary Grant or Bob Hope. I want to be an actor.*

And from that I was borne forward on a cloud of good luck, the support of others and, I hope, talent – two out of three of those being factors in what happened next, because what happened next was that I got a break. My supportive teacher Bill Dewar told me about an opening at the Dundee Repertory Theatre. The job was a general factotum, running errands and stuff. The post had become available when the previous incumbent left and went to drama school. Would I be interested?

Yes. Just fourteen years old, I put my best togs on and went down to the Rep on Nicoll Street. Walked in the front door. 'I've come to see Mr Henderson,' I said to the lady on the front desk.

'Aye. Well, you've come to the wrong place, laddie,' she said. 'You have to come to the front, but the only way you can get to the front is by coming through the back. You've got to go to the back to get to the front.'

(This, by the way, is Scotland in a nutshell.)

'Okay,' I said, 'Where's the back?'

She said, 'Ah, well that's at the back. Forrester Street, at the back. It's parallel to Nicoll Street. You go in there and then you can come to the front, but you cannot get to the front from the front, you can only get to the front from the back.'

'Okay,' I said, pretty sure I had it by now. I wandered around to the back where I found that it opened out into a close. On one side was the wardrobe and the green room and then above that were the dressing rooms. On the other side was the entrance to the stage.

As I mounted the narrow staircase up towards the main stage and auditorium, I became aware of some kind of fracas going on on the landing above. I would have to cross this landing to get to my meeting, but coming close, I found myself almost in the middle of a fist fight between a rather effete, red-faced, bow-tied individual and a tall, lean, Viking-like blond. The air was blue. I mean, a *lot* of swearing. Not the kind of language I expected to hear in somewhere posh like a theatre. But I recognized the Viking immediately. His name was Nicol Williamson.

Do the most cursory search on Nicol Williamson and you'll see that John Osborne called him 'the greatest actor since Marlon Brando' while Samuel Beckett said that he was 'touched by genius'. You could add 'troubled' and also 'angry' to that, but genius mainly covers it as far as I'm concerned.

At that time he wasn't yet well known, but even from within a loud, expletive-driven blizzard of pummelling fists and trouser legs at half-mast, I recognized him. Why? Because just the week before I had been to the theatre for what might have been the first time ever, a schools' matinee of *Love from a Stranger* that starred Williamson – complete with a shock of snow-white hair – giving what to this day I still think of as being the scariest performance I've ever witnessed. Not only was his character terrifying but at one point he quelled his rather rowdy audience of schoolkids by walking to the front of the stage and saying in the deadliest and quietest voice imaginable. '*When* you have all finished. I will continue. But not. *Not*. Until then.'

And he stood there and he waited. And waited. Until the noise in the auditorium diminished to nothing. And from that point on, you could have heard a pin drop.

Up until then I had thought of the theatre as being a safe, middle-class experience. The whole thing about *going to the theatre* just seemed like something for distracted-looking men in suits accompanied by haughty women in fur stoles. It was Anthony Page, the director, who used to describe the Dundee audience as 'the felties', because the women would always use the occasion to model their very best felt hats, and these were women like my Auntie Cathy who, because she was not exactly my favourite aunt, did nothing to allay my natural suspicion regarding theatre.

But this was different. I looked at Williamson and I thought, *Wow, this guy's something else.* It was very different from watching an actor on the screen. This was being able to feel his presence and energy actually *in the room*, so real and present it felt like you could reach out and touch him.

The room quietened. Of course it did.

'Okay, if you've finished, I'll go on. If you start, I'll go off.'

He meant it too. Not that any of us knew at the time, but Williamson would become famous for walking off stage. Just saying, 'I'm not good tonight,' and buggering off. He did it frequently, and I'll bet there weren't many who would take him to task over it, because Williamson was scary. I mean, that afternoon, he was playing a murderer and we all thought he was going to get off stage and cut our throats.

I was lucky enough to catch Williamson at what turned out to be the most formative and versatile period of his working life. As I say, he went on to be feted as the successor to Brando and played Merlin in John Boorman's *Excalibur*, but at the Dundee Rep I saw him in a truly remarkable run of performances: Konstantin in a Scottish version of *The Seagull*, Clive in Peter Shaffer's *Five Finger Exercise*, Peter Cloag in *Marigold*. In particular I liked his Jack Manningham in the Victorian melodrama *Gaslight*, which was electrifying, just electrifying. That performance more than anything set me on the road to appreciating just what was possible as a stage actor. He had a quality of cutting the air – you could see it part. An uncanny skill. He was the embodiment of theatrical presence.

I think Williamson was a great influence in that way, much more than I realized until relatively recently. Rep required you to do so many different roles – murderer one week, detective the next – and Nicol adapted to each one. He *shone* in each one, was exemplary in every role he played, showing an astonishing range well beyond his years. He, for me, more than any actor of that generation set the bar of what can be achieved as an actor. Added to that, he was also very kind and considerate to a wee fourteen-year-old kid who was just starting out in the world, and for that I'm eternally grateful to him.

From the Rep, Williamson transferred to the Arts Theatre in London, was hugely successful there, and then went to the Royal Court where he worked with Tony Page, originator of 'the felties', doing *Inadmissible Evidence*, which was a huge success. From there he went to America and performed for Nixon among other things. On the one hand he was enormously successful, but he also messed it up for himself, because he was so very volatile. For example, the first night of *The Seagull* at Dundee was attended by a director, Lindsay Anderson, who was casting what became his first major movie, *This Sporting Life*, which ended up not only making him a huge name in British film but also making a star of Richard Harris, who got the lead.

Thing was, Williamson really fancied himself for the Richard Harris role, but for whatever reason, Lindsay practically ignored him that night, both at the theatre and then during the party afterwards. Williamson left the party, and in his drunken and rejected state announced he was going to end it all by jumping in the Tay. Which he did. Except that the Tay was out and so he landed safely in the mud.

So yes, knowing what I know now, it's not at all surprising that my second-ever encounter with him should see him involved in fisticuffs. As I edged my way around the fighting men, I was greeted by a third guy who looked exceedingly amused at my bewildered and slightly terrified expression. 'It's all right, darling,' he drawled, 'they're just a little overexcited after a night on the bevy and no sleep. Not to worry . . .'

I thought to myself, *Wow, this is great, I've just walked past two guys fighting and this other guy calls me darling. This is brilliant.*

The darling guy turned out to be the actor Gawn Grainger, who had made his professional debut at the Rep in 1961. Grainger, who I'm happy to say is still with us, and at the time of writing is the grand old age of eighty-three, went on to marry – and is still married to – Zoë Wanamaker. He directed me to see John Henderson, the head of the Rep, who was a lovely, lovely Kiwi.

'Do you like music?' said John Henderson. He was behind his desk. I stood there like a kid called up before the head, only a wee bit more nervous.

And I went, 'Yeah, yeah.'

He said, 'Do you know classical music?'

The previous week, our music teacher, in an effort to instil some form of culture into the assembled Dundonian oiks he called a class-room, had played the trumpet march from *Aida* by Verdi, and not only had I found it genuinely uplifting at the time, it was also the only piece of classical music that came to mind at such short notice.

I said, 'Verdi. I like Verdi.'

'You like Verdi?'

'Oh yes,' I said, 'particularly the trumpet march from *Aida*.'

He looked at me and, like a superhero with X-ray vision, saw right through me. But at the same time I think it amused him. He took a shine to me. And he gave me a job.

The job was assistant to the assistant. The assistant was a woman called Bunty, who in addition to running the Rep ran me ragged. If a deck needed swabbing, or an errand needed running or a drink needed making, then you either asked Brian or you asked Bunty who delegated the job to Brian.

My first task, and indeed it became one of my regular duties, was to convey the takings from the night before to the British Linen Bank in the High Street. I thought it was extraordinary then, and still think it's extraordinary, that they would entrust a fourteen-year-old kid who they didn't know from Adam with such an important job, but that was the Rep for you. It was all hands on deck (provided that deck had first been swabbed by Brian).

Looking back, the Rep was a proper through-the-looking-glass experience for me. Perhaps one of the greatest transitions I've ever made. It was a different world, like nothing I'd experienced before. I'd travelled far and wide in the realm of my own imagination but other than that I was not what you might call a worldly kid; my hori-zons were limited. Here, there were no limits. This was where the act of self-expression found its first outlet, a place of raw emotion and boundless creativity. Had I ever met a gay man before? Well, yes, is the answer, I probably had. But not to my knowledge, and certainly not an open-and-out gay man. In those days, it was still illegal, but in Nicoll Street that didn't apply, and this, I immediately discovered, was emblematic of what was truly great about the place. All were welcome here. All were equal. It's why the theatre soon became my natural home and has remained so ever since. In being accepted at the Rep I understood that I'd never really been accepted elsewhere until that moment. All of a sudden, I was this rough-speaking yet oddly arty urchin from the Dundee backstreets, and to the actors and staff of the Rep I was an exotic creature. Little did they know that a mere bus ride away there were thousands of kids who sounded like me. Didn't matter. Those kids were out there. I was in here. Somehow, I had crossed between the two very different worlds, and only I, this hybrid plant, was able to do it. I just knew that as soon as I walked through that door, it felt like a huge weight was off my shoulders. I had an unbelievable sense of homecoming. A sense that this – *this* – was my bliss.

CHAPTER 7

My time at Dundee Rep was full of incident, packed with craziness and creativity, punctuated by wild tempers flaring. And for my entire stay, I was thinking, *This is the stuff of life. This is where I'm supposed to be.*

I soon graduated from taking the money to the bank and mopping the stage at 6 p.m. to moving scenery and then, just when I'd mastered the art of picking up one bit of cardboard and moving it to a different place, I found myself entrusted with 'propping', a dark art that involved helping the assistant stage manager to source props. At Christmastime this would involve going to Fife's to procure bananas.

We had this crazy guy called Campbell Godley who starred in the annual panto. He was billed as one of Scotland's premier actors, but actually he wasn't all that good. I'm not just saying that. He really was notorious for being not very good. There was a production of, I think, *Othello*, at the Glasgow Citizens Theatre, during which Godley fell off the stage at one point. 'Lord Brabantio,' he called from his newly acquired position on the floor, 'helpeth me up.'

To Fife's I would go with Campbell and helpeth him collect bananas for the panto. In due course, I was promoted to other stage-managing tasks. They put me on the book, which involved prompting and triggering sound cues and stuff, so for instance if the characters were like, 'Hark, I hear the sound of a car approaching,' it would be my job to press the button that made the car noise.

The problem being that I was hopeless. They'd be on page twenty-three and I'd still be on page twelve, far too interested in watching the performers at work to flip the pages of the text.

'Hark, I hear the sound a car approaching. Hark, I say. HARK.'

Once I got a tap on the shoulder: 'Telephone.'

'What? For me?'

'No,' they hissed. 'On the stage. The bloody telephone.'

How on earth I wasn't sacked, I have no idea.

Doing *The Merchant of Venice*, we had what's known as a 'warmer' light, which 'warmed' the curtain just prior to the show starting. The sequence would be: house lights to half, house lights out, warmer out, curtain up.

On the first night I went through the sequence and then wound the curtain, the curtain went up, and Antonia started, 'In sooth, I know not why I am so sad. It wearies me; you say it wearies you. But how I caught it, found it, or came by it . . .'

And then suddenly I heard, 'Oh, for fuck's sake.'

'What? What?'

I'd left the safety curtain down. The actors were on stage, doing their thing, and the safety curtain was still in place.

There was this one guy who was a little too fond of the drink. Let's call him Bobby, for that was indeed his name. Bobby was playing the priest in *Hamlet*, and during the scene in which Ophelia's being buried we watched, horrified, as he first slurred, then swayed and slightly tottered before finally pitching forward into the grave – right on top of poor Hannah Gordon, who was playing Ophelia.

'Ow!' was what we heard as Hannah felt the full force of Bobby's drunken priest on top of her. Myself and another stagehand had the task of clambering under the stage to prise him free. 'Oh, I've disgraced myself,' he moaned theatrically and way too loudly, for up above the show was, of course, going on. 'I'm finished,' he wailed. 'Oh, I'm finished. I'm finished.'

Desperately we tried to shut him up. 'Bobby, come on, we've got you. You'll be fine. Let's get you out of here.'

'No, no, no. Unhand me. I don't want to go. I'm just going to stay here – here in the dark and dusty bowels of the stage, where I belong.'

It was a far better performance than the one he gave above.

Oh, and then there was Lynn Redgrave, who of course was acting royalty, being one of the Redgraves. She had just left the Central School of Speech and Drama and was being talked up as a big name of the future; indeed, she had a role in *Tom Jones* just ahead of her, as well a star-making part in *Georgy Girl* a few years later, in 1966. But first she came to us, where she turned out to be as chaotic as she was sweet and funny.

Lynn was playing Portia in *The Merchant of Venice* – Portia in a blond wig. She came to the stage management office after the first night in a bit of a flap. 'I've lost my wig. I can't find my wig. It's gone. It's gone. My wig's gone.'

I was given the job of finding Lynn's wig and located it in the waste-paper basket by her dressing table. She'd whipped off the wig after the performance, tossed it to one side, and it had fallen into the bin.

It was in a mess, so somebody suggested I spruce it up with rollers, which I did, and then returned it to her. 'Oh, thank you very much,

Brian. Where was it?' she asked but had already lost interest in the answer and was off someplace else before I could reply.

The next night, same thing. A panicked Lynn Redgrave. 'Oh my God, I've lost my wig.'

Off I went to the wastepaper basket and found it. God only knows how the wig got in such a terrible state during its short journey from Lynn's head to the bin, but it needed reshaping again. Out came the rollers.

The same thing next night, and the next. Pretty much every night of the run, in fact, although I think she may have missed the bin on one or two occasions.

And if you're asking yourself, *Why didn't they just move the bin?* Or tell Lynn Redgrave not to throw her wig in it? Then, yes. Good point. But that was the Dundee Rep for you. That was Lynn Redgrave for you.

At the end of the run, she came to me and so graciously said, 'Brian, will you please, please thank the hairdressing department for the wonderful work they did on my wig.'

'I will,' I assured her. There was, of course, no such thing as a hairdressing department. There was just Brian and his incredible wig-renovation department.

But I was always there to get that wig, because I lived and breathed the Rep. I slept there often, in a little nook I had created for myself beneath the stage. A proper home from home – except that I didn't really have a home elsewhere. My mother would eventually recover from her illness to become the funny and eccentric character I've already described, but back then she was still in the grip of her mental health problems. She was, as we say in Scotland, a very poor soul. She lost a tremendous amount of weight and was given to wandering off. It was only when I stayed at Bette's that I could guarantee myself a proper meal. Hardly surprising, then, that one Christmas I was really quite ill with anaemia. The thing was that I just didn't want to miss a moment. There was always something happening at the theatre. There were too many great people around. Great actors and actresses at whose feet I could learn simply by watching, by being within their orbit.

I would play tiny parts. My first proper role was Joseph in an A.A. Milne play called *Dover Road*. Joseph was supposed to be in his forties, and I was only fifteen or sixteen, but that wasn't the worst of my troubles. At one point, I had to serve dinner – fish in white sauce – and every night it felt as though I was taking my life in my hands when I served that dinner. One evening the fish slipped clean off the plate, so I scooped it up off the stage as quickly and discreetly as possible, doing what I thought was a fairly good job of covering for my mistake just as I'd seen the professionals do. The problem was, I now had white sauce all down my front – sauce that I managed to transfer to the costume of Jeffry Wickham when I served the fish to his character. The fact that he was wearing a black dinner jacket at the time didn't exactly help matters.

Not that I was discouraged by the experience. I went on to play Corporal Flight in *Simple Spymen*. I played the paper boy in *Picnic*, complete with an American accent (my first American accent, and very much not my last).

I mentioned DC Thomson. As well as the *Beano* and the *Dandy* they published all sorts: the *Romeo*, the *People's Friend*, the *People's Journal*, and no doubt plenty of other periodicals with the word 'people' in the title. If you lived in Dundee back then you'd know someone who worked for DC Thomson, and I was no exception; my friend, George Rosie, a subeditor with an interest in drama, roped me in to help mount a production of the Dylan Thomas play *Under Milk Wood*.

Milk Wood has a huge cast, and unfortunately for George, very few of the people who had pledged to join bothered to turn up, and so with Dylan Thomas's 'play for voices' struck dumb, we ended up doing Edward Albee's *The Zoo Story*.

It was through that DC Thomson connection that I went to a party in Baxter Park Terrace one night. I say 'party', but in fact I'd been working at the Rep, arrived late and found that things had very much wound down. The place was in a somnambulant, post-blowout fug, and I had to pick my way carefully through snoozing bodies sprawled on the floor.

In one particular room lay a couple of guys, slumbering gently. 'Who's that?' I asked.

'Oh, that's this Liverpool pop group. That guy's called . . . um, he's called Harrison, and the other guy's called Starr,' came the reply.

It was 1962, the decade already finding its feet. But for me, that was the beginning of the 1960s. It was the beginning of *my* 1960s, anyway. The overture, if you like, and it all came through my work at the Rep. I can't stress enough what an incredible, life-changing experience it was. I had adopted the theatre and it had adopted me. It was my home, my family, my bread, my butter. I lived and breathed it.

So you can imagine how I felt the day it burned down.

The first of June 1963 was when it happened, the day of my seventeenth birthday. We'd done a run-through of a Henry James play for which I was either stage manager or assistant stage manager, can't remember which, and we'd all gone off to lunch.

Me, I used to go for bridie and chips at Wilson's on Reform Street. A bridie, more correctly but rarely known as a Forfar bridie, is the Dundee equivalent of a Cornish pasty. If it had one hole in it then it was a plain meat bridie. Two holes, a meat and onion bridie. I was no doubt savouring the two-hole version when I heard the sirens which were followed by someone bursting into Wilson's and saying, 'I think the Rep's on fire!'

I was out of there in seconds. My first thought was, *It can't be on fire, it's just been redecorated.* But redecoration is no defence against fire apparently, because there it was with smoke billowing out of it, flames licking at the windowsills and a huddle of shell-shocked staff on the street forlornly watching it burn.

It turned out to have been an electrical problem. Nobody was hurt. That was the main thing. There had been a handful of workers in the box office but they got out sharpish.

We all gathered later in the afternoon at somebody's house and I remember thinking how we were all like lost children. Later I attempted to survey the still-smouldering building. I'm not sure why. Just to see the damage, I suppose. I had sneaked past the police guard without incident but came unstuck when I encountered a fire officer inside. 'Out you go, laddie,' he waved me off. 'It's not safe for you in here.' Meekly, I left.

I never saw it again, the Rep. They moved to another place up in the Lochee Road, and stayed there until they relocated to what is the current building on Tay Street, which is a beautiful little theatre. All of which happened without me, because the silver lining in the whole terrible fire episode – at least as far as I was concerned personally – was that I had moved on. Sad as it was, the burning down of the Rep symbolized that chapter of my life closing in order to make way for a new one. I was about to take advantage of the great social mobility that the decade offered. I was going to study acting in London.

CHAPTER 8

The way it happened was that while at the Rep a director called Bill Davis, who later went on to play Cigarette Smoking Man in *The X-Files*, had invited me to a voice class. The teacher, Kristin Linklater, hailed from the London Academy of Music and Dramatic Art, LAMDA. Intrigued, I decided to give the voice class a go.

Thanks to the Rep, I kind of knew about LAMDA. One of the great things about being there was watching actors come and go and getting a sense of the different kinds of training available. This is a bit of a crude generalization, but the way I saw it back then was that there were actors who had a certain *mien* about them, a self-confidence. These actors were very much performance-based. The text was there, but it was about using text as the means to show off, rather than as a way of telling the tale. I came to see these actors as being emblematic of the RADA way.

Other actors would be a little bit more about the text, more about the structure of the piece. They seemed to have a methodology of working, they seemed to know their way around a text. They were the performers I found myself drawn to the most. They tended to have studied at LAMDA.

Kristin didn't disappoint. She herself was an absolute inspiration, and the voice class, during which I learned to talk from the solar plexus and control my breathing, was a revelation. That was it. That sealed the deal. I applied to LAMDA. Under the direction and tutelage of Susan Williamson, an actress in the company and a LAMDA alumna, I did two audition pieces: Edmund the Bastard from *King Lear* and the Gentleman Caller from *The Glass Menagerie* by Tennessee Williams, went back for a second interview and got a place.

And then, without much of a backward glance – because after all, I had no home life to speak of, and my real home, my proper home, the Rep, had burnt down – aged seventeen, I packed my bags and left to go live in bedsitter land. Putney, to be precise, where I moved into a double room in the Cromwell Road that I shared with a fellow student, David Sparks. I grasped that social mobility I'm talking about with both hands, benefitting from a Scottish Education Authority grant that not only paid for my fees, but gave me an allowance of £11 a week, which in 1963 was enough to pay my rent, my food, my books and ... well, that was about all I needed, because without wanting to sound like a terrible swot, I really was there to learn, not to party, and the fact that we started at 9 a.m. and finished at 9 p.m. suited me down to the ground. A flabby, pimply youth in unwashed clothes, I was – but a very happy one.

Entering LAMDA in Earl's Court, I had an advantage over many of my fellow pupils because I knew the theatre well, whereas it was a bit of a mystery to many of my fellow students. What I wasn't truly aware of, I must be honest, was how prestigious a school it was. (For one thing, the principal was the great, extraordinary and eccentric Michael McOwen, who had directed the first West End production of Eugene O'Neill's *Mourning Becomes Electra*.) I just knew that there was something healthy about it, something enquiring. And I liked the fact that it wasn't built along competitive lines, because I'm not at all competitive (although secretly I am). I didn't want to go to a school where I was having to compete. I just wanted to learn the job. I wanted somewhere with structure.

My first pal in class was a guy called Matthew Guinness. The first time I clapped eyes on him it was summer, and he was wearing a heavy tweed jacket, corduroy shirt, woollen tie and corduroy trousers. I'm sure he looked very smart, but it was not the kind of gear you want to be wearing in an overheated poetry class in drama school.

But that's how I got to know him. We were both a little *outside* of things in that way, not quite aligned with the agile young men and women we studied alongside. We had dance class together and became partners, where our lack of agility became even more apparent, not that we cared too much.

Something I soon discovered about Matthew was that his father wasn't perhaps as kind as he might have been. This wouldn't normally be worthy of comment but for the fact that his father was Alec Guinness. It's well documented that Alec was strict with Matthew growing up, and I saw first hand the hold that he had over him. If Alec visited the school, Matthew would go red and begin to perspire. 'Dad's in,' he'd say in cowed and awestruck tones.

I mean, of course if your father is Alec Guinness, one of the finest actors ever to grace a screen, then you're going to feel that you have a lot to live up to. After all, you do indeed have a lot to live up to. But I don't think that Alec did much to help Matthew in that regard. From what I could see he was really quite tough and critical.

I remember we were both at the Lyceum in Edinburgh where Matthew played the Little Monk in *Galileo*. I walked into the loo and he was sitting in there in his brown cassock, clutching a bottle of whisky.

'Dad in?' I said.

'Yeah.'

Matthew was a good actor and went on to appear in Mike Leigh's *Nuts in May* in 1976, and then Ridley Scott's debut, *The Duellists*, in 1977, but I'm not sure that he has ever really escaped his father's very long shadow.

Martin Shaw was in my year, too. Anna Calder-Marshall, who became a great friend, was in the year below, as was Maureen Lipman. There were some wonderful American actors, too, from whom I learned a great deal, in particular how they were so at ease with themselves. Stacy Keach, for example, had this incredible, amazing ease about himself. The same with Andrew Robinson, who is still one of my best friends, who went on to play Scorpio in *Dirty Harry*. Andrew's a really interesting character. His father was killed in the war and his mother became a drunk. We had problematic mothers in common.

I'd always had an American inclination that wasn't really on the menu at drama school, so by bringing in this American ethos, Andrew and Stacy helped fulfil a need in me. I was exposed to a different set of rules from those practised at the school.

It was also a time that I came into contact with Peter Brook, who had been instrumental in opening the then-new LAMDA Theatre. I got a job in the bookshop and used the opportunity to watch the great director in his natural habitat. He was working with Glenda Jackson and Alexis Kanner at the time, and they did a version of *Hamlet* that featured Hamlet on a swing rope. Brook had Ophelia one side of the stage, his mother on the other and Hamlet swinging between the two of them. It was extraordinary. It floored me. Toto, we're not in Kansas any more. Bobby falling into Ophelia's grave at Dundee Rep, this was not.

Much later, in 1985 in New York, I got to work with Glenda on Eugene O'Neill's *Strange Interlude*, an epic, five-hour piece in nine acts – so long it had a dinner interval in the middle. For the run of that and then *Rat in the Skull* afterwards, I had rented a one-bedroom apartment from a friend of mine, Linda Thorson, who was the original Tara King in the TV series *The Avengers*.

Linda was lovely, of course, her outstanding generosity marred only by the fact that her flat was in a parlous state of repair and probably, in retrospect, should have been condemned. Upon waking up one morning, I looked down from my fold-out bed and thought, I can't remember a carpet being there. And why is the carpet moving?

Cockroaches. The floor was covered in them. Hundreds of them.

Under cover of darkness the roaches would assemble. I went a bit mad with the roach spray one day and then had a talk with them. 'Now listen, guys. I don't want to keep killing you all, because I'm sure you've got a purpose, and I really can't afford the spray. So what I'm going to do is, when I come home at night, I'll rattle the keys very loudly, so you'll know that I'm coming in, okay? The deal is that you can have the apartment during the day, but when I come home at night, I don't want to see you.'

That's what I did. I used to rattle the keys and I'd hear this clicking and scuttling from the other side of the door, the unmistakeable sound that cockroaches make when they're upholding their side of a bargain. I'd go into the apartment and sure enough, not a roach to be seen.

Linda's flat didn't have much in the way of furniture, and I wanted a chest of drawers for my clothes. I found one in the Michael Chekhov acting studios, but it needed lugging down the stairs, and so, with great difficulty, holding it on one foot and bouncing it down the steps, I manoeuvred it down to street level and got it out onto the pavement – sorry, sidewalk – and then stood there looking at it for a second. It was a handsome piece. It was going to look nice in Linda's flat. I wondered if the roaches would approve.

Next, I started looking for a cab. They're ten a penny in New York, of course, but I needed the bigger size, the checker cab, in which to fit my chest of drawers, so I found myself craning my neck looking up and down the street for one. This involved inching away from the chest of drawers a little. Only a little.

Then I saw it. A checker cab. I hailed it over, let it draw up to the kerb, gestured behind myself at the chest of drawers and then turned only to see that . . .

It was gone.

Thanks to *Succession* I live in New York almost full-time nowadays, but that was my introduction: cockroaches and stolen chests of drawers.

And nine acts of Eugene O'Neill.

Glenda always had a strict, patrician air about her. We – Ted Petherbridge, Jimmy Hazeldine and myself – had to force her to take her own curtain call during *Strange Interlude* at the Duke of York's Theatre in London. One night, Ray Davies of the Kinks came to the show. Ray was a friend of Jimmy, who played Sam in the show. Afterwards, Glenda, Ray, Jimmy and I went to eat at a restaurant across the road.

Ray Davies, as you probably know, has a reputation for being somewhat blunt. A little insensitive, perhaps. Sure enough . . .

'Here, what's that thing you do with your head?' he asked Glenda.

Ted Petherbridge and I looked at one another. *Uh-oh.*

'My head?' replied Glenda.

Oblivious to the icy blast, Davies plunged on. 'Well, you do this funny thing with your head.' He turned to us. 'Haven't you guys noticed it? That thing she does?'

We shrugged and shook our own heads like we had not the foggiest idea what he meant. (We knew perfectly well what he meant.)

'I don't know what you're talking about,' replied Glenda.

'All right, all right,' said Davies. 'It's just that . . .'

And finally he became aware that he was being insensitive.

'. . . you do a funny thing with . . .'

She glared at him.

'. . . your head.'

And with that he changed the subject.

He was right, though. Glenda did do a thing with her head, except it wasn't a 'funny' thing, it was just a thing. A kind of nodding movement she did. An actorly tic. Many actors have them, vocal or physical. Jennifer Aniston coughs before she delivers a line. Richard Gere goes to deliver a line then stops and stares off into the middle distance. Jeff Goldblum stammers. George Clooney tilts his head and smiles. Me, I have the habit of beating out the rhythm to a scene on my thigh, or slightly trembling my hand. You don't see it so much on film, but you might catch it in the theatre.

She was great, though, Glenda was. And back during those LAMDA days her work with Brook could often be astonishing. During *The Theatre of Cruelty* at LAMDA, she performed a wordless piece where, as Jacqueline Kennedy, she stripped down to nothing, got into the bath and then emerged as Christine Keeler – a transformation she achieved without words, or clothes.

I never really got to know either her or Brook at that time, though. I subsequently knew both of them reasonably well, but at that point they were just these extraordinary theatrical creatures, and they were part of the fabric of my LAMDA experience, a time when it was simply incredible to be a student. Not only was I getting to see the likes of Brook and Glenda Jackson at work, but we used to go to dress rehearsals at the National Theatre where I'd see Olivier as *Othello*. I watched the dress rehearsal of Peter O'Toole's *Hamlet* there. One afternoon, I saw *Hay Fever* directed by Noël Coward with the wonderful Edith Evans playing Judith Bliss, who was just astonishing, a great comedienne. Another time we got to see Joan Plowright and Rosemary Harris, both astounding as Helena and Sonya respectively in Olivier's *Uncle Vanya*.

To see Olivier walk on stage, this extraordinary, exotic creature. To see O'Toole in his pomp. To see one of Maggie Smith's greatest performances as Desdemona, so still and with such crystal beauty. Witnessing this kind of magic, some of the most famed theatrical works of the era, was inspiring and motivating. It sucked you in and made you yearn to be a part of it. With each successive performance I saw, I knew that I was in the best place for me. Where I wanted and needed to be.

It was for that reason that I never really bought into the sex and drugs and rock 'n' roll side of things, neither at LAMDA nor in the years afterwards. As a perennial outsider, I wasn't exactly being press-ganged to join, but neither did I apply anyway, because my thing then was about trying to keep body and soul together as I learned my profession. I knew that I was just a latchkey kid from Dundee who had somehow found himself at one of the best drama schools in the United Kingdom. Oh, I can fuck things up with the best of them. But I wasn't going to fuck that up.

CHAPTER 9

Still. The temptation to fuck things up was certainly present. At the Central School of Speech and Drama in North London, there existed a whole cadre of guys who prided themselves on taking intoxication to extreme. (Me, I was fifty before I tried my first puff of marijuana. Well, that's not entirely true, but the experience was such that I would have to wait until fifty before I tried it again.)

Among the Central crowd was Bruce Robinson who later wrote and directed *Withnail and I* and based Withnail on Vivian MacKerrell, who was probably the most dissolute of that bunch. Vivian apparently really did drink lighter fluid, just as Withnail does in the film, although unlike Withnail who survived unscathed, he went blind for several days as a result.

Some of them managed to ride it out, go on and forge careers. Mickey Feast, for example, who was last seen in *Game of Thrones*. Or David O'Hara, who's graced *Braveheart*, *The Departed* and *Harry Potter*. They have their problems, though. I worked with O'Hara at Stratford, and he's immensely talented, but he was drunk a couple of times on stage. Once we were in a bar just opposite the Old Vic and he kicked over a table full of bottles and glasses, creating quite a ruckus. Afterwards I said, 'You know, that kind of thing went out ten years ago. Do you really want to be carrying the flag for that?'

Other weren't so lucky. Michael Elphick was a Central guy who ended up dying of the drink. For his part, MacKerrell ended up boozing his whole life. At fifty, having survived throat cancer but in a terrible physical state, he was admitted to a care home where he drank a bottle of liquid tranquilliser then contracted pneumonia and later died.

My friend Nigel Terry, another of the Central alumni, was also dogged by alcohol his entire life. Unlike MacKerrell, whose credits you could count on the fingers of one hand, Nigel enjoyed great success on the stage and in film. A real maverick type, he played Arthur in *Excalibur*, alongside Nicol Williamson, and was Caravaggio in the Derek Jarman film. With alcohol he tended to binge. For a while he might stop altogether, but then he'd buy himself a crate of vodka, lock himself in his room and drink the lot.

I moved in with him at one point. Although this was in the 1980s, shortly after he'd done *Excalibur*, his house looked like it hadn't seen a lick of paint since Harry S. Truman was president, and he was showing no signs of wanting to spruce it up.

'Look, Nige,' I said to him one day. 'Brush. Paint. Wall. Use brush to put paint on wall. Wall . . . much nicer.'

'Oh, really?' he said, amazed.

Nigel was the first birth registered in Bristol after the war. As a boy, he'd had a problem with his legs that meant he'd had to have them broken and re-set over a period of years, and as a result he was very dependent on his parents. When it came to the house, they were trying to help him in more guerrilla, stealth-like ways, by turning up and actually doing stuff, and as I arrived home from rehearsals one afternoon, that's exactly what they were doing: his dad was involved in some tiling. His mum was sewing something.

Of King Arthur, there was no sign.

'Oh hello, Brian, how are you?' said Mrs Terry.

'Oh, I'm fine, thank you, Mrs Terry,' I said, 'Where's Nige?'

'Oh, he's not here, he's not come home yet.'

I said, 'Oh, okay . . .'

I trod the stairs and was making my way along the landing to my room when I noticed that the door to his bedroom was closed.

The bugger's in there, I thought. I know he's in there. I dumped my stuff down and knocked on the door. 'Nige?'

No reply.

I opened the door and there he was, lying in bed in an overcoat, facing the wall in an almost foetal position, his hands covering his head.

'Nigel?' I said softly.

He turned in bed and fixed me with those soulful eyes, catnip to the ladies. 'I wish they'd go away,' he moaned.

Which said it all. It said it all about his dependency. How overwhelmed and guilty he felt. His inability to face up to problems that stretched back to his childhood.

I didn't see him for a while. Not until years and years later when I played King Agamemnon in *Troy*, which was a traumatic experience for personal reasons I'll detail later but professionally great, because not only was I reunited with Nigel, but – talking of legendary drinkers – I got to work with Peter O'Toole for the first and only time in a staging of *The Iliad*.

I was a great admirer of O'Toole. Not only had I loved him on stage and adored his films, especially *Lawrence of Arabia*, of course – what a performance – but I'd read his book, *Loitering with Intent*, so I was feeling a bit star-struck. To make matters worse, my very first scene on my very first day involved killing O'Toole, who was playing King Priam. You didn't know that King Agamemnon kills King Priam in *The Iliad*? Well, he does in this version. This, after all, is a world where Orlando Bloom can beat Brendan Gleeson in a fight. Orlando Bloom?

Even though it was my first scene, Agamemnon killing Priam happens right at the end of the film, but that's the vagaries of film-making for you. In TV on something like *Succession* we do things more or less in the order they appear on screen. Film? Not so much.

So I was in my dressing room on standby – Shepperton, this was – in full make-up and costume, mentally preparing. *Come on now, Brian. This is no time to feel star-struck, not when you're King Agamemnon in a big old Hollywood production.* Trying to remind myself of what my mum always said when she thought I was getting a bit serious about my work, 'Och, Brian, it's only a fillum.'

But then again, this is Peter O'Toole. Lawrence. The Murphy in Murphy's War. *You saw him do* Hamlet *when you were at LAMDA. Peter O'Toole, and you've got to kill him.*

I sat there for most of the day, until finally, about 3.30 p.m., they called me to go and do the killing.

I arrived on set to find them struggling with a technical issue. The idea was that I, Agamemnon, stab Priam in the back – symbolism! – and you see the blade come out of his stomach, but they were having problems getting the fake blade to come out of O'Toole's stomach. That meant a lot of waiting. I was close to O'Toole now. Close enough to appreciate the imperious lived-in sculpture of his face. Close enough to fully appreciate that when he talks it's with a kind of wounded nobility, even when he's just shooting the shit with the crew.

Eventually I got to stab him. We went through it a few times. Stab. I say the lines. He dies. Stab. I say the lines. He dies. The blade worked perfectly each time, and then we wrapped, the scene finished, and he dusted himself down, looked at me and said, 'So. Brian. How are your nerves now?'

I goggled at him. 'How did you know?'

'Oh yes,' he said, sagely, 'I can tell.'

And I thought, *You can tell because you're Peter O'Toole, and for the past forty or so years, people like me have been losing their shit when they meet you.*

'There's just a slight giveaway in your behaviour,' he added knowingly.

'It's because it's you,' I managed. 'I still think of myself as this kid seeing you as Lawrence, so to be here now on a set playing Agamemnon and you're playing Priam and I have to kill you . . .'

He just nodded, like, *I know*, gathered his bloodstained robes about him and left the set. In his wake, I felt as though I'd been anointed.

Becket was another one of his I loved. Richard Burton was in that, and I'm sure there are some stories from that set. After all, the myth of the drunk actors hangs over us all. Actors like Wilfred Lawson, who famously was sitting in the theatre, turned to the lady in the seat next to him, and said, 'You'll love this next bit, this is where I come on.'

The same Wilfred Lawson was in Michael Elliott's production of *Peer Gynt*, playing the Button-moulder. Lawson liked to hide his whisky in the toilet cistern and get his shot, but one thing we know about boozing is that it's not an exact science, so one night he overdid it, fell over on stage and didn't get up. He played the whole of the Button-moulder scene lying on the stage.

Michael Caine was no fan of the imbibing actor. I wouldn't describe Michael as my favourite, but he's Michael Caine. An institution. And being an institution will always beat having range. Caine was, and probably still is, very dismissive of the drunken-actor brigade, and one of his targets, of course, was Richard Harris, another famous drunk who became a friend. Harris used to say, 'Jesus fucking Christ. Michael fucking Caine. This thing with the eye – the eye doesn't move. What fucking bollocks,' which was a reference to something Caine did in an acting video, the idea being that in close-ups you should always focus on just one eye of the other actor, so that your own eyes don't move around. I won't give my own view on this technique, but put it this way, Harris was right.

Why is it so prevalent? The drinking? So endemic. I think there's a sense that the drunkenness is often about the fact that actors don't fit in. Spencer Tracy was a drunk. He loved his profession and was good at it, but he also felt an element of shame that it wasn't a proper job for a man, added to which he had had guilt issues over his relationship with his wife and his son, who was deaf. He was tremendously tormented and the drink assuaged that.

Burton, I suspect, was similar. His talent was discovered by a mentor. He went to Oxford. And yet on the other hand he was the son of a miner, and he came from that community where drink was a way of life, a means of dealing with life down the pit.

That for Burton was as much his inheritance, for better or for worse, as it was a way of keeping one foot in Wales. It meant he could wear tights and flounce about on stage with a clean conscience that he hadn't forgotten his roots, that he was still a rough-hewn man of the valleys. Drinking and mining is manly. Acting is not.

Trevor Howard was a great drunk. Eric Portman. Jimmy Villiers. Ronnie Fraser. John Hurt was another one, of course. I did a TV thing with him, *Red Fox*, and we were filming in France, where there was always a bottle of wine on the table. I said to one of the French crew, 'Listen, we can't have bottles of booze hanging around. He's an alcoholic,' and the guy looked at me as though I'd just informed him of an alien invasion. *Qu'est-ce que c'est? What is this? Al-co-hole-eek?* They don't believe in alcoholism in France. They refuse to countenance its existence. Meanwhile, Johnny Hurt was helping himself to the vino like a man with three arms. 'This is wonderful. I've got wine. Oh, I do love working in Paris. It's just such a perfect place to be.'

Later we did *Rob Roy* together. We were all staying at the Spean Bridge Hotel in the Highlands where one night Johnny was getting progressively more drunk. Also present: a rugby team. John Hurt at his drunkest and most acid-tongued and a rugby team in the same bar is a fairly combustible mix and, sure enough, he began baiting them, allowing for a lull in the festivities before he spoke. 'You're all after each other's bottoms, aren't you?' he drawled, loudly, barely raising his head from his drink. I'll tell you this: Johnny Hurt knew how to kill a buzz.

They all stopped talking. 'That's what you're doing, isn't it?' he growled, with no regard for either political correctness, his own safety or mine. 'Rugby. I mean, it's a sort of substitute, isn't it?'

I coughed and stood up. 'Johnny, it's time to say goodnight,' I announced and then turned to the team. 'Gentlemen, good night, Johnny's saying goodnight,' and to the great relief of everybody in the bar, I was able to usher him out. Next morning, he had no memory of even having been in the bar, let alone taunting the rugby team.

But I'm blessed. I can handle it. Maybe I just never needed drink as a way of compensating the way others do. I've always used drink to relax and unwind and occasionally as a means of drowning my sorrows rather than as I suspect the way others do, as a way of escaping themselves, a method used to compensate for being so in touch with their feminine side.

There was a whole club culture around it. The Kismet, that was one. Gerry's Club was another. Gerry's was notorious as a place to go and get drunk after a show. I was a member of the Buckstone Club which was behind Haymarket, and went there with Michael Gambon one night in 1970 to celebrate the birth of my first son, Alan. Gambon was getting me drunker and drunker. After our session, we staggered out, and he watched me get into my car but said nothing. He also saw that I hadn't put on my car lights and said nothing (this, by the way, is typical Gambon).

What he didn't see, of course, was the fact that not long after leaving him and driving away from the club, the police were on to me. I didn't see them either. It was simply the case that when I eventually pulled in at home, they appeared, one of them opened the driver's door of my car, and I fell out.

(I say none of this with any sense of pride, by the way. Nor am I intending to make light of drink-driving. But there you are. It shouldn't have happened, but it did. I paid my £28 fine and served my year's ban.)

Anyway. Years after *Troy*, I was doing a film in Bucharest. Back at my hotel, I fell asleep and woke up only to see that *Troy* was being shown on TV. In practically the first scene I saw Nigel Terry and also my other friend, John Shrapnel. I watched for a few minutes and was about to switch off before King Agamemnon arrived (don't like to see myself) when, no word of a lie, my phone rang and it was John Shrapnel – John who was on the television.

It took me a moment or so to process it. 'John,' I managed at last, 'This is bizarre, you're on the television. You and Nigel.'

He said, 'I'm calling about Nigel, he's in a bad way.'

'Really?'

He said, 'Yeah, yeah, I spoke to him. He thinks he's got prostate cancer.'

I said, 'Oh Christ.'

And he said, 'Oh yeah, and he's really worried.'

I spoke to Nigel after that call and helped to calm him down. But it wasn't the cancer that got my amazing friend Nigel Terry in the end. It was emphysema that took him in 2015. He was sixty-nine. One way or another, his addictions were always going to kill him.

CHAPTER 10

At LAMDA I concentrated on my focus, not something I find easy. Ask my family now, and they'll tell you that one of my biggest problems is my absence. Physically not being there, at home, of course. There's been an awful lot of that over the years, it being very much a feature of the job. But also being present yet absent at the same time. Not really 'in the room', as it were. Spending too much time with dreams.

We had a great teacher called Vivian Matalon, a TV and stage director who was very tough, very rigorous about text. A student of Sanford Meisner, he came from that Stanislavsky place of asking about motivation. Why are you here? What are you doing on stage? He was all about understanding the intention of the writer and trying to become his or her conduit. To do that, I had to get Brian Cox out of the way, because having been dragged up in the streets of Dundee, Brian Cox was very strong, very forceful, the owner of an extremely robust survival mechanism. At LAMDA I had to drop the habit of survival and just be, and in that sense, it wasn't just learning about being an actor, it was learning about being a human being and doing so in the context of the world in which I lived as well as the career I was pursuing. It was only two years, but it was such a fermenting time for me. Learning. Following my bliss. Dealing with my own arrogance and vanity.

Vivian used to put the boot in. I remember we were doing a play called *Dark of the Moon* with me as the Witch Boy, which involved a great scene at the end. At the same time, I was also playing another, lesser, character earlier on. I was sitting in the wings at the beginning of the show when Vivian said to me, 'What are you doing?'

'I'm just thinking about what's coming up at the end – my big scene,' I told him.

He scowled. 'Don't worry about that. Worry about the part you've got to play now. That's your problem, Brian: you're always thinking that way instead of dealing with the now.'

I knew exactly what he meant. My tendency was to cut to the destination rather than paying attention to the journey. What Vivian taught me then, and subsequently, was that the actor's responsibility is to give equally, wherever and whatever you're doing. This goes back to my conversation with Nigel Hawthorne, and we'll circle back to it again in due course, but years later, after having had a great theatrical career and won all kinds of awards, my way ahead looked like following one of two paths: either I fell into the pattern of being one of those British actors who went to the Garrick, played in the West End and remained part of the London theatrical firmament, or I took myself off to the States to try and make my living as a character actor.

Now, I'm a member of the Garrick, but the stereotypical life that came with the membership wasn't what I wanted, so I took the latter option. I went from being a lead actor on the London stage to a supporting turn in Hollywood, and I did it with a big smile on my face.

In a way, every actor's a character actor, but to me the whole idea of leading actors is the Gary Coopers and the John Waynes, and I knew that simply wasn't my ballpark; besides, I'm too short. Instead I wanted the experience of doing the work and I wasn't really interested in how good the script was or how artistically credible the movie seemed, because what I'd noticed and what I was influenced by were the wonderful character actors from the 1930s and 1940s. The ones who had a way of creating an arc for themselves, no matter how big or small their role. I was fascinated by the idea of creating a character that in the normal scheme of things would just disappear in the *mise-en-scène*.

Who else but Spencer Tracy was a great influence on me in that regard. Although Tracy was primarily a leading actor, he was a consummate support. He had that ability to be so present that you were following what he was thinking and doing and feeling, and that was what was interesting to me about going to work in the cinema.

I'm getting ahead of myself. The point being that Vivian helped instil in me a sense of focus that doesn't come naturally to me, and for that I'm eternally grateful. I've always been lucky in that I've enjoyed the benefits of having some great mentors and he was among the first.

After LAMDA, I met the wonderful late Tom Fleming, who invited me to the Lyceum in Edinburgh. Tom, a familiar voice to millions of Scots, thanks to his stentorian commentaries at numerous royal events for the BBC, had recently set up a company at the Lyceum, making me practically a founder member. And if I want to feel every single one of my seventy-five years on this planet, I need only remember that in 2015, the great Bill Paterson and I helped celebrate the fiftieth anniversary of the Lyceum with a production of *Waiting for Godot*.

It was at the Lyceum that I played Dromio in *The Comedy of Errors*. John Thaw was in town at the time, starring in a play called *The Square* at the Traverse Theatre. One afternoon we were at John's digs, where for some reason he decided to make an afternoon of it.

John, at the time, was another one who was fond of the drink. The fact that he was great pals with Nicol Williamson said it all.

So anyway, on this particular afternoon, John had a case of wine and he endeavoured to make short work of it. He was determined to get me plastered, and in short order, I was drunk as a skunk. Worse, I had to go on stage that night. Staggering to the theatre, I first encountered the actor, Paul Chapman. Two of him, in fact. 'You're drunk,' they both said.

'No, no, I'm not drunk,' I told them. 'I'm fine. I'm fine.'

I was supposed to walk on stage and say, 'Hello, Master.' Only when I eventually heard my cue, I stumbled on and slurred, 'Hello . . . M . . . M . . . Master,' in slow motion, as though this were *The Comedy of Errors* as directed by Sam Peckinpah. Paul was on stage, too, both of him. They looked at me. I looked at them, and we both knew it was going to be a very long and hard performance indeed.

And that – thank you very much, John Thaw – was the one and only time I have ever been drunk on stage. Years later, I did an episode of *Inspector Morse* with him, and it was all very professional. As the star of the show he had a huge amount on his shoulders and so I decided it best not to mention the *Comedy of Errors* incident. Such, ladies and gentlemen, is my famed diplomacy at work.

But wait. I've lied. John Thaw wasn't the only time I've ever been drunk on stage. It wasn't even the only time at the Lyceum. I'm shuddering now to think of it, but we did a panto of *Rumpelstiltskin* in which I essayed the dual role of White Witch and dalek. As the White Witch, I looked like a Michelin man. As a dalek I looked like, well, a dalek.

Call me an entitled and pretentious diva if you wish, but it was never my ambition to dress up like a bloated witch or Doctor Who's least imposing enemy. After some nights of being forced to do so, I could take no more. New Year's was approaching. New Year's Day, I sought solace in a bottle. How wasted did I get? So wasted that I went to Stockbridge and threw my house keys in the river.

Of course, moments after having done it, I realized what a monumentally stupid thing it was to have done. I trudged to a friend's house to drown the sorrows I'd accrued while drowning my sorrows. Eventually, I crashed out and the next morning made my way to the theatre, where I arrived, still drunk and hung-over, went into make-up, got into my 'Michelin Man meets White Witch' costume, stumbled on stage and promptly fell over.

Beached on stage, there I remained. Rendered immobile by the costume and alcohol, more the latter than the former, I lay there for both the matinee and the evening show. It left them one White Witch short, of course, but they struggled gamely on. Presumably I slept for a while so I don't remember much, but I do recall that when it came to the dalek, all they did was bring my costume on, plonk it down on the stage and leave it there. I dimly remember looking at the dalek and thinking *I should be in that dalek. That should be me.*

Not my finest hour, needless to say.

Believe it or not, the Lyceum wasn't all drunken shame. One great thing was that I met the director Peter Dews, another mentor, you might say. Back in 1960, on a TV that had a wire coat hanger for an aerial, I didn't just watch, I *devoured*, a fifteen-part BBC series called *Age of Kings*, which was all of Shakespeare's history plays (two Richards and three Henrys) presented in sequential order. I was particularly struck by Sean Connery as Hotspur. He was a complete unknown then, of course, but as a fellow Scot I was very excited and inspired by him.

The *Age of Kings* director – in fact he won a BAFTA for it – was Peter Dews. My future benefactor, Tom Fleming, was also in the cast and he got along with Dews enough to invite him to the Lyceum in Edinburgh to direct a version of Brecht's *Galileo*.

Here's where I come into the story, because after a period of gritting my teeth through various tiny parts and understudy roles, I was cast as Andrea Sarti and did well enough that Dews took me to one side. 'Are you all right, luvvie?' he said. Dews was a Yorkshireman. Cut him, he bled *Yawkshire*. 'I'm going to Birmingham Rep and I'd like you to come,' he said. 'What would you like to play?'

'Um, Hamlet?' I said.

'Hamlet. Of course,' he said. 'And what about Iago?'

'Sure,' I said.

'Mercutio?'

'Yes,' I said

'Bolingbroke?'

'Of course.'

'What about Peer Gynt?'

'Uh, fine.'

'Right, well we'll see, we'll see. We'll see what we can do.'

CHAPTER 11

So it was that when my time at the Lyceum drew to a close, I transferred to Birmingham Rep, and true to his word Peter Dews saw to it that, over the next two years, I played Iago, Mercutio, Bolingbroke, Orlando and Peer Gynt, all before my twenty-second birthday. The only one on my shopping list I didn't do was Hamlet.

Regarding Shakespeare, I had realized very quickly that the theatre journey is defined by a series of stepping stones, and while a stone or two may be reserved for Shaw and a couple for Ibsen and Chekhov, the majority belong to the Bard. Going way back to the likes of Irving and on to Gielgud, Olivier and Richardson, there's simply no getting around the fact that if you want to prove yourself in the theatre, you need to do your Shakespeare.

Back then, I could have done without him, because my thing was always films. On top of which, when I did eventually click with theatre, I much preferred Ibsen. But still, you can't avoid Shakespeare. As a kid I'd seen Olivier in *Hamlet*, *Richard III* and *Henry V* – all at the cinema – while an incredible thing that John Henderson at the Dundee Rep had done was play me recordings of famous actors performing the same Shakespearean speech.

As a result of this grounding – not to mention the Illustrated

Classics and what I saw on TV – my understanding of Shakespeare was sufficiently advanced that when Peter Dews asked me for my shopping list of dream roles, it was overwhelmingly Shakespearean. What I didn't realize until I joined him in Birmingham was that I had never really understood Shakespeare properly.

It took Dews to change that. He showed me the allegory in Shakespeare. How each play is about one thing but also about another. He broke down the psychology, particularly the motivational elements of the characters. He understood that, and because he was a very practical, hands-on director and fancied himself as an actor, he always used to demonstrate, too.

That could be good.

But it could also be bad.

Playing Mercutio in *Romeo and Juliet*, I had the famous Queen Mab speech. Dews would tell me, 'You know, I played Mercutio at Bradford Civic. I were a fat Mercutio.' What's more, he kept demonstrating what he meant, doing the whole Queen Mab speech in broad *Yarkshire*, time after time, until on one occasion, having become mightily fed up, I said to him, 'You'd like me to do it *exactly* like that, would you? Are you sure? *Exactly* like that?'

'Aye, I would. Do it like that, lad.'

So I did it – I did it in broad Yorkshire.

As I did so, I became aware of a space being created around me. Slowly, the other actors drew away, backing right into the wings until I found myself alone on stage, shivering in a blast of ice emanating from the auditorium. Dews was jowly and I watched the saggy skin quiver angrily as he stood from his seat and stormed to the stage. 'Don't ever do that again, luvvie,' he said sternly. 'It's more than your life's worth.'

Lesson learned. I never did anything like that again.

While at Birmingham I met Michael Gambon for the first time. Gambon's an interesting thing. As well as being very fond of his Irish roots, he's astonishingly talented, very funny and completely irreverent. But he's got a dark interior, as you might have surmised from the drink-driving story I told earlier.

Mainly, he's irreverent, though. During our time in *Othello* together, he would get up to all kinds of naughtiness. He'd be doing the mad scene and mouth things to me. He might go, 'I love you, Iago, I love you,' just to make me laugh. I used to get so angry with him. Another of his tricks was to suddenly stop acting in the middle of a scene. I'd come off stage and go, 'What the fuck? What's going on?'

'Oh, I was bored,' he'd declaim airily. 'I got bored.'

'Bored you may be, but I was the guy opposite you and I wasn't bored.'

He said, 'Yes, well. I was. I was bored.'

He could be frustrating like that. Dews used to lose it with him. 'All I ever get from you is dumb insolence, Gambon, dumb insolence.'

But that was Gambon for you. He was notorious. If he saw the opportunity for some mischief, he just couldn't help himself. The famous story about him is that while at the National he was working with Olivier, who at one point had to sweep onto the stage wearing a huge flowing cloak. During rehearsals, another actor stood on Olivier's cloak, completely ruining the entrance, and Olivier got more and more irate. 'If I find out who's been standing on my cloak, their fucking life won't be worth living,' he apparently seethed at one point.

Gambon let it slip that it was an actor called Peter Cellier who was standing on the cloak, and sure enough Peter was on the receiving end of a bollocking, but Peter was a lovely, mild-mannered guy – no way would he have stood on Olivier's cloak. The true culprit, of course, was Gambon. The same Gambon who once took the actor Terence Rigby up in a two-seater aircraft, supposedly to cure his fear of flying, and then pretended to have a heart attack. The same Gambon who used to adorn his dressing-room mirror with a photo of Robert De Niro, signed, 'Dear Mike, I admire your work, love always, Bob,' that he'd written himself.

Mind you, even Gambon was prone to nerves. On an earlier occasion he'd sat next to Olivier and spotted a wallet with the word 'Norge' on it.

'Hamlet,' blurted Gambon, nervously.

'I beg your pardon,' said the world's greatest living actor.

'Did they give you that wallet when you played Hamlet?' managed Gambon.

'What?' snapped Olivier.

'When you played Hamlet,' said Gambon. 'You know, in Norway.'

'I played Hamlet in Denmark where it is set, and I don't know what the fuck you're talking about,' snapped Olivier. 'And it's not my fucking wallet.'

At Birmingham, Gambon had a disagreement with the guy with whom he was supposed to be sharing a dressing room. For some reason, Gambon was the one who had to move out of the dressing room, so he came to share mine. It was a tiny space, and I used to have to sit behind the door at my make-up table. After one particular performance I was being visited by the producer of a TV series, *The Borderers*, Peter Graham Scott. The summer before I had agreed to do the part with a previous producer and anticipated it being a step on from Birmingham. 'Michael, listen,' I said, ahead of the meet. 'I've got this guy coming after the show. Do you think you could shift out as soon as you can, because I've got to greet him and there's not enough room to swing a cat in here.'

He said, 'That's fine, Brian. I'll do that. No problem.'

Whether by accident or design, Gambon didn't get out quickly enough, and when he opened the door to a knock, there stood the director who, upon edging his way into the tiny room, said, 'Oh, I think you're wonderful. Absolutely brilliant. I'd like to offer you a part in *The Borderers*.'

'Oh,' said Gambon, 'But . . .'

And he closed the door to reveal me, sitting at the make-up table, looking pale and frazzled. 'Hello, Brian,' said the director and with that, turned and left, leaving Gambon with his job offer – a job offer that he promptly accepted, going on to make a decent critical impression with his part in the television series. To rub salt into the wound, I had just persuaded my agent, a lovely man called Larry Dalziel, who's no longer with us, to take Gambon on as a client, and one of his first jobs was to do this deal for *The Borderers*.

They asked me about it, of course. It's not as though my friend and my agent completely stole *The Borderers* part from me, but I agreed it was okay, because after all, Gambon was married with a kid and probably more in need of the work, whereas I was just a single man at the time.

A state of affairs that was soon to change.

CHAPTER 12

Since we've got Sir Laurence Olivier effing and jeffing in the previous chapter, this seems as good a place as any – before talking about my romantic life – to recount a couple more encounters with him, beginning with the time I was still at the Lyceum, when he summoned me to London for an audition for the National Theatre.

Peter Dews had already made his Birmingham offer at this point, but even so, this was Sir Laurence Olivier and the National Theatre. Suitably excited, I replied that of course I'd love to come.

In those days, you could take a late-night flight from Edinburgh to Heathrow leaving at about 11 p.m. for something like thirty shillings. So I was all set, bags packed, with plans made to stay with my friend, George, in Camberwell, the idea being to leave right after the show I was in at the time. I'd arrived at the theatre when the stage doorman, Jimmy, said to me, 'Oh, Brian, I've found this wee note for you. It had slipped down the back of your cubbyhole. It's a note from somebody called Laurence Oliver.'

Of course, it wasn't from 'Laurence Oliver' at all. It wasn't even from Sir Laurence Olivier. It was from the National's casting director on his behalf, and it was telling me that Sir Laurence was indisposed and would like to postpone our meeting.

Oh, for fuck's sake, thought I. What do I do now?

I did the show and went to the pub afterwards, the Shakespeare, just across the road, where I sat with my bag mulling over whether to go ahead and get the plane or stay in Edinburgh. In the end I couldn't be bothered to make the journey and went home.

The next morning was 28th October 1965. I woke up and there was a *Sunday Post* through the letterbox. On it was a 'Stop Press'. The flight that I was due to catch the night before had run into deep fog at Heathrow and crashed into the tarmac, killing everybody on board. It remains to this day one of Scotland's worst aviation disasters.

I was the lucky one. Pretty shaken up by it as well. But of course I had Laurence Olivier to thank for the fact that I hadn't got on that flight, and I still tell people that he saved my life.

I eventually got to see him in one of the Nissen huts that passed for offices at the National Theatre in those days. Olivier in person was quite different to the Olivier of stage and screen, the definitive Hamlet, the Prince to Marilyn Monroe's Showgirl. He was actually quite modest and self-effacing. His managerial air was more 'bank' than 'football'. As I walked in that day, he was engaged in trying to tape a card across where somebody had tried to break in by smashing a window.

I told him my story of having missed the doomed flight thanks to his postponement but he was fairly nonplussed, perhaps preoccupied with the attempted burglary. 'Oh, that's good. That's excellent.'

We got talking, and I had to come clean. I said to him, 'You know, Sir Laurence, I've actually been offered Birmingham Rep.'

He said, 'Really?'

I said, 'Yes, I've been offered a whole string of roles at Birmingham Rep.'

He said, 'Oh, well, then what the fuck are you doing here? That's what you should do. You should go to Birmingham Rep, because I can tell you now that you'll only understudy here.'

It turned out that he had special affection for Birmingham Rep, having started his career there, so he really couldn't have been nicer about the whole situation. I left that day with a lovely feeling of having my decision vindicated by perhaps the greatest authority in the land.

The next time I came into contact with him was almost two decades later, when I was in his TV adaptation of *King Lear*, directed by Michael Elliott (a year before Elliott's death). Olivier was Lear, of course, and although I was supposed to play Cornwall, I couldn't make the dates, so I ended up playing Burgundy in just one scene near the beginning.

Olivier by this time was pretty old. Just six years later he would die. And even though the production department were doing all they could to alleviate the pressure on him, he was finding it very tiring.

'Ah, baby, I'm so tired,' he would say during breaks in filming. 'I really do find this part so exhausting. I mean, it's such a big part.'

The thing was that the previous Sunday, Jonathan Miller's production of *King Lear* had been on TV with Michael Hordern as Lear. 'I'm so tired,' repeated Olivier, 'it's quite a demanding role, you know. I mean, it really is. Did anyone see Michael Hordern . . .'

And then he'd be interrupted. Somebody would come and say, 'Sir Laurence, we need to—'

'Oh, why, what do you want now? Ah, okay. Thanks. I've got to get up.'

And then he'd come back, sit down again and say, 'Yes, it's really tiring. I find it so difficult. I have to lie down in the afternoon these days, you know. I'm all right after a good sleep. I feel a lot better but, oh, it's a lot. It's a lot, this role. Did anyone see Michael Hordern on TV the other—'

And then, again, he was called away.

He came back, sat down, and muttering almost to himself, said, 'You know, we have a wonderful cast. I think I'm incredibly lucky to be playing this part now at my age, such a great director in Michael, the wonderful Michael Elliott. Leo McKern. Who could hope for better? Johnny Hurt as the Fool.' He stopped, and it was as though something had only just occurred to him. 'I don't know my lines,' he said. 'I don't know a fucking word of this part. Did anybody see Michael Hordern—?'

I said, 'Well, yes, I saw it.'

'Ah,' said Olivier, glumly, 'he knew his lines. He knew all of his lines. But I tell you this . . .'

And suddenly it was as if Olivier was a different person, pushing his chest out to exclaim, *'I'm still a better fucking actor than he is any day.'*

Wow, I was really struck by that. By the same insecurity that I talked about in the prologue, that lurks in us all (apart from Steven Seagal), and also that he still had this oomph in him, this rage, an urge to fight. Incredible.

CHAPTER 13

The 23rd of March 1968 was when I became a married man.

I'd met Caroline in the June of 1967, during what was my West End debut, *As You Like It*, which we'd brought to London on tour from the Birmingham Rep. I was playing Orlando in another of my dream-list roles, and I'd not long celebrated my twenty-first birthday.

There was a girl in the play called Charlotte whose friend Caroline came to a show one night, and being beautiful and blonde (her, I mean, not me), she caught my eye, and I made enquiries. Charlotte did a bit of matchmaking and within days of meeting, Caroline and I were an item. A few days later we were living together. It really was that quick.

Despite Peter Dews telling me, 'Oh, luvvie, don't get married. You're too young. Just remember, when Albert Finney got married, he got his first string of bad notices,' Caroline and I tied the knot in Birmingham Registry Office, then went on to the Albany Hotel for the reception. Everybody from the Birmingham Rep was there, including Gambon, of course, and although it was early, not to mention the fact that we all had an afternoon performance of *Othello* to do, they all began to get progressively more drunk.

All apart from me, of course. I had the matinee and then an

evening performance of *Romeo and Juliet*, in which I was playing Mercutio, so it was, frankly, more than my life was worth to get pissed. Also, I'd learned my lesson in *Rumpelstiltskin*. Instead I was tasked with getting everybody out of the hotel and to the theatre, which was only a short walk from the hotel.

After I'd herded them all out of the hotel, I deposited my bride in the honeymoon suite and checked the reception room, to see if the company had left anything behind. They had. Gambon. Somewhat inebriated, he'd got himself stuck behind one of the large double doors of the reception room. I managed to get him out onto the walkway towards the theatre. As soon as we were out in the open and the fresh air hit him, his inebriation deepened.

He started moving. Very, very slowly.

'Michael,' I said, 'we've got to go . . . the show starts in twenty minutes'.

He looked up at me. 'Oh, but it's such a wonderful day. It's such a beautiful day. I mean, you've had a wonderful time, I've had a wonderful time. We've both had a wonderful time.'

'Yes, but now we have to do the show.'

His brow furrowed. 'Oh, really? Why?'

'Michael, don't be stupid, of course we've got to do the show.'

After what seemed like an eternity we arrived at the theatre and into our shared dressing room.

This particular production of *Othello* was set at the time of the Crimea, so my own make-up as Iago was little more than a moustache. I pasted that on and then looked at Gambon, who, slowly, like a man awakening from half a century of deep sleep, was beginning to prepare by attempting to pull on a pair of braces that he needed for his outfit. I watched the tortuously slow process as he tried to hook the braces over his shoulders but missed and pinged himself in the face.

He recoiled. 'Ow. What was that?'

He tried a second time. Once again he pinged himself with the braces and once more he pulled a face as though he were under attack from some unseen entity.

'Brian,' he wailed, panic beginning to set in. 'Brian, what's happening? Something keeps hitting me in the bloody face.'

'Michael,' I replied, in my most consoling, reassuring voice. 'There's nothing to worry about. You're simply hitting yourself in the face with your own braces. It's fine.'

He stared at me as though I were mad, before it dawned on him. 'Oh, thank God. Bloody braces.'

'Beginners,' came the call, which was the cue to make our way to the stage. I checked for Gambon who had by now managed to get his braces on, thankfully without flaying the flesh from his face. However . . .

'Michael, you haven't got any make-up on.'

'What?'

I said, 'You're white. You haven't got any make-up on.'

'Oh, bloody hell.' He gathered a bunch of make-up sticks and melted them on one of his dressing table light bulbs. He literally shoved the make-up onto his face, and I tried vainly to blend it on his skin. By the time I'd finished he looked like he'd had an accident with a chocolate pastry, but it would have to do.

We hurried to the stage. At which point it suddenly became awfully apparent that *everybody* was drunk. Everybody, that was, apart from me and one other performer, an actress who complained bitterly. 'I'm going to report this to Equity,' apparently unmoved by the emotion of my recent nuptials. 'I've never seen so many drunk actors.'

It was too much for me. At one point I was due to perform a song but my drunken fellow cast members sat on me so I couldn't sing. I don't know if you're familiar with *Othello*, but there's no point at which the other characters sit on Iago. Next thing you know, one of the actors stood on a table only to fall off and lie comatose on the stage. We had to do the play with him lying at our feet until a stagehand crept on and dragged him off. God knows what the audience thought.

And that was my wedding day.

Caroline turned out to be as amazing with money as I am crap with it, and it was thanks to her canny investment eye that the houses we bought together earned more than we did. Sadly, her heart lay in acting, and despite her talent, that side of things didn't go well for her. Also, it also pains me to admit that I wasn't always as faithful as I might have been.

'I wondered why you'd got better as a lover. I could tell you'd been practising,' said Caroline after one particular disclosure.

No names, no pack drill, obviously. But if I'm going to admit to my imperfections then now's as good a time as any. The fact is that there's something of a hothouse atmosphere to any theatre or film production, and it's almost always the case that a show throws up its fair share of 'ship romances', especially among the more youthful cast members. It's so easy to fall in love in that kind of environment, even though you know deep down that you're not really in love at all, and that it's all to do with the world you inhabit, where you're working together on a day-to-day basis, playing people who are not yourselves. It's part and parcel of doing what we do.

Even so, having said all that and admitting what I've admitted, I'm actually the type of person who sticks with things, and despite what I've said about the affairs, I think we'd still be married if Caroline hadn't left me. The thing is that ever since childhood I've wanted stability and structure. I looked for it in my family life, and I looked for it in my career. For a while, I even found it.

CHAPTER 14

I always looked for parent figures in my work because of that need for stability. I think it was also to do with my whole thing about being at school but not really 'being at school', a situation that, whether through choice or circumstance, created a childhood lacking in mentorship. As a result, I was drawn to people who would empower me in a way that I wasn't empowered by my contemporaries. Actors of experience, rather than actors my age who were having the same problems as I was.

In that regard, the two major influences of my early career were the Scottish actors Duncan Macrae and Fulton Mackay, both of whom were wonderful, extraordinary men. In my final year at the Edinburgh Lyceum in 1966 I appeared in *The Birdies* with them both and fell under their spell. To see the two of them play scenes together was incredible, and watching them, I began to appreciate what I realized was a uniquely Scottish method of performance. I'd been so Anglicized in my grounding and subsequent training that I hadn't really seen it before, but here it was: an almost balletic physicality that both Mackay and Macrae brought to the stage. The way they could go from something very rooted to something quite fantastical and do it within milliseconds. I just loved that and incorporated it into my own work.

Having observed them, I subsequently became aware of this same physicality elsewhere. I saw it in a wonderful actor called Callum Mill and I recognized it in Stanley Baxter. Most of these guys were alumni of the Citizens Theatre in Glasgow; they'd all come out of the army and ended up in this one extraordinary working-class theatre in the middle of the Gorbals, where the great director Sir Tyrone Guthrie – a son of Tunbridge Wells who nevertheless had an affinity for the Scots – worked on them in order to accentuate their inbuilt Scottishness.

Macrae you might know from *The Prisoner* or *Casino Royale*, both of which appeared after his death in 1967. He was a skinny, almost odd-looking man, but he had a kind of weird energy that meant you could hardly take your eyes off him. A legacy, I'm sure, of Guthrie's tutelage. He was the first truly sensational Scottish actor I ever met – the first whose sheer extraordinariness reached out to me.

Inspired as I was by him, I never really kept in touch with Macrae, and I wasn't as close to him as I was to Fulton Mackay. Fulton almost adopted me. He became like a surrogate father: my mentor, my guru, my tutor, my coach, my confidante, and above all my friend. He once said to me, 'Brian, Brian, Brian. You're always worried about being a star. You don't have to worry about any of that. Just say your prayers and be a good actor.'

And it was perhaps the best advice I've ever been given, a foundation upon which my entire career was subsequently built, because I *was* ambitious, no point in denying it, and I did have my sights set on a certain kind of stardom. But Fulton could see that those urges would not serve me well in the long run; that I was forcing myself into a real-life role for which I was not entirely suited. I was an actor, not a star. And what Fulton showed me was that there was no greater or higher ambition than simply being a good actor. His words reminded me not to worry about career and worry about craft instead. To work on what talent I had and try to make it a better, greater talent. To be better at my job.

Subsequent to his time as a serving soldier in India, Fulton had trained at RADA, where he was a contemporary of Robert Shaw. He then returned to his native Glasgow and joined the Citizens Theatre. Not only was he a fine companion and an extraordinary, exemplary actor from whom I was honoured to learn, but he also instilled in me the values of the theatre, of text and the visions of certain directors. He was a great thinker, philosopher and painter. Just to be in his orbit was to develop and grow.

And yet, for all he had to teach me, his own world was often in a state of disarray. Mostly his problem was one of identity. When Fulton was two years old his mother died of diabetes and his father sent him and his brother to live with aunties and cousins in a house in Clydebank. For Fulton, this was a great hurt that he carried throughout his life. The fact that he would come home from school and instead of his own name on the front door it was the name of his cousins meant that, 'I always felt disenfranchised in some way. That name on the door reminded me that my life was dependent on the kindness of strangers,' as he said to me one day.

I remember him calling me shortly before he died and saying he'd made a breakthrough in one of his therapy sessions.

'What's that, then, Fulton?'

'I can speak in an English accent, Brian,' he said. 'I feel liberated.'

I don't mind saying, I felt pretty crushed by that sentiment. This, after all, was an actor who had helped me locate the Scot within myself and bring it to the fore. And yet the whole time he himself had been feeling this pressure to somehow *be* English. So much so that he felt liberated by the ability to ape an English accent. That was the word he used. *Liberated*.

But then you realize how deep that fissure goes in terms of nationhood, in terms of identity, in terms of 'where do I come from, where do I fit in?' A lot of people don't think about that, they don't even bother about it, they're fine. But it mattered to Fulton. It fed into what had been troubling him his entire life.

It irritates me enormously that he is so associated with his character Mr Mackay in *Porridge*. I love it in one sense, because *Porridge* is often repeated so I get to see my old pal, and of course he's brilliant in it. The episode with the pineapple chunks is one of the funniest single episodes of a TV sitcom ever, no doubt about it. Even so, there's a lingering frustration that comes with watching it, because I know that Fulton didn't want to get sidelined into stock characters. I know it went deep with him. His lack of family. His feelings of rootlessness. He was such a great actor; he could do anything, and he's superb in, say, *Gumshoe*, or *Britannia Hospital* or *Defence of the Realm*. There was a lot more to him than *Porridge*.

Another of his favourite sayings was, 'We follow our mercenary calling and draw our wages.' And although it's a piece of wisdom I have often warmed my own hands on, having done more than my fair share of turn-up-and-get-paid jobs, I'm not sure Fulton fully believed it. I think he wanted a little more to his legacy than he eventually ended up with.

Fulton was married to Sheila Manahan for many, many years, and together they were an incredibly welcoming, inclusive couple, first to me and then to Caroline. We would often go to their house for Sunday lunch and end up staying for hours. They were a happy couple, although at the same time you'd have to say that their relationship had, shall we say, 'complexities', which I won't go into here. Fulton developed cancer of the oesophagus, which could have been treated, but he decided – much against medical advice and the wishes of those around him – to have an operation to remove it. I saw him in hospital at the time, and he had a typically Presbyterian attitude. 'Cut it out. Cut it out.'

So they did. And who knows? Perhaps, had he not developed sepsis, the operation might have been successful.

As it was, he did indeed develop sepsis. And on 6th June 1987, about three weeks after his op, he died.

I was devastated. Divorced by then, I suddenly, and for the first time since my father had died, felt truly alone. At the same time, it prompted in me a change of course and a search for new purpose that ultimately took me to Moscow. But I'll come to that.

Tragically, within a year of Fulton's death, Sheila, who had been recovering from colon cancer, also died. It was another terrible blow. To me they were the two most beautiful people in the world. They were like my real family, my surrogate parents in many ways. Sadly, their marital issues dogged them to the end, and it was tragic to see the relationship of two people who had been such great friends end in what were somewhat ignominious circumstances. Among other things, it brought home to me the simple fact that nobody gets out of here alive, but the one thing you *can* do is to try to make a good death. I've seen people make good deaths and I've seen people who haven't. Among the other changes wrought in my life by the passing of Fulton and Sheila, I found that I was asking myself that one question. *How do you do that? How do you make a good death?*

CHAPTER 15

Leaving drama school, you have to do Actor Stuff, and one of those things was to join Equity. Applying to join, I found there was already a Brian Cox registered. You have two choices when that happens. Either you change your name or you go down the second route, which was what I did, penning a letter to the guy and sending it via Equity. 'Dear Mr Brian Cox, We are both actors with the same name, but I was wondering, as you have not worked in some time, if I could use the name Brian Cox?'

Weeks later, I received a letter that said, 'Dear Mr Brian Cox. We are both actors with the same name but I was wondering, as you have not worked in some time . . .'

Yes. The 'other Brian Cox' was me, and I had written to myself. Apparently, I had joined Equity at Dundee Rep only to promptly forget.

Another thing I did was to get myself the agent I mentioned earlier: Larry Dalziel. Larry was Scots, which was a benefit. Better still, Larry liked me (top tip: get yourself an agent who seems to actively like you), and he got me a job with a director called John Gorrie, playing a character in *The Wednesday Play* for the good old BBC.

The piece was called *A Knight in Tarnished Armour*. It was about a boy who works for a private detective and lives in a fantasy world. The kid meets a Glaswegian bully boy in the park, played by yours truly. Needless to say it wasn't a leading role, but it was a decent part, and a good opportunity for me to show my wares. Mostly it meant that my new agent Larry was earning his ten per cent.

I ended up doing a fair bit of TV, spending so much time at the BBC Television Centre in White City that it became like another home to me. They used it for filming *Top of the Pops* so you'd get all these crazy kids running around, while at the same time the BBC was still doing classic plays like *Hedda Gabler*. For me it brought back memories of being a kid and going to my cousin Lizzie Carroll's house on Balmore Street in Dundee on Sunday nights to watch the telly: Rod Steiger doing *Death of a Salesman*. The young Sean Connery in *Requiem for a Heavyweight*. This was before the days of ITV – as in, ITV *did not yet exist* – so there was only one channel, it was the BBC, and it was dedicated to getting the best possible drama to the maximum number of people. True, when you look back on those plays they were pretty clunky, and the experience of watching them required a concentration that wasn't necessarily conducive to a relaxing night in front of the TV, but I still think I was fortunate to be alive and watching that kind of thing on the box. I mean, I wouldn't say that I feel sorry for today's broadcast TV audience, fed a diet of reality shows and decorating challenges, because that would sound paternal and culturally snobbish, so I definitely wouldn't say how fucking sorry I feel for today's audiences being fed a diet of reality shows and decorating challenges. No way.

A lot of those plays were live. Not my *Wednesday Play*, though, although we recorded it 'as live'. We had to run through it several times before they filmed it. Meanwhile, I wasn't just haunting the

BBC Television Centre. For the newly formed Thames TV I did *Redcap* with John Thaw, he of the drunken afternoon, and what I remember about that is that we did it down on the Thames, and there was a guy playing one of the soldiers called David Jones, who eventually became David Bowie. A skinny kid, and not a particularly good actor. He made a better pop star, that much is for certain.

Later on, in 1971, I appeared with Sir Ralph Richardson, Tom Courtenay, Thora Hird and Trevor Peacock in a television adaptation of *She Stoops to Conquer* by Oliver Goldsmith, directed by Michael Elliott. Sir Ralph thought the cast was too deferential. 'Treat me as a fly on the wall,' he insisted in his own lordly fashion. 'Just ignore me.'

Over lunch, he told me, 'Brian, I'm a bit tired. I'm not sure I'm going to rehearse this afternoon. I think I'm going to hide.' He proceeded to cover his face with his hands and held them there.

When we were called back, Sir Ralph remained in a large wing chair, indifferent to our imprecations. Nothing would shift him. Even when Michael approached him, Sir Ralph retorted, 'Go away, I'm hiding.'

Richardson did no further work that afternoon, but he wasn't being awkward. He was simply so good at his job that he could afford to entertain the cast. Off stage, he cultivated eccentricity – sitting a parrot on his shoulder while riding a motorcycle – but he could still act his socks off.

Sir Ralph had something in common with all the great actors who still worked at an age when people in other professions have collected their carriage clocks. They brought experience, but they never stopped learning. They were not young, but their curiosity kept their minds young.

Richardson last played at the National in 1983, aged eighty. Sir

John Gielgud, who worked into his nineties, was similar. He had total recall of every moment in his life. I remember him recounting in detail how he celebrated VE Day with George Bernard Shaw, but his sense of the past was sharply related to the present.

It is a strange thing for people like me who were born in the late 1940s and early 1950s to be picking up our pensions. For years, we baby boomers called the shots. We invented the teenager and still consider ourselves young, even if our creaking backs, locked fingers and crunching knees serve as troubling daily reminders that age is catching up on us. Mick Jagger is still on that energy high, although I'm sure his joints are a little stiffer these days.

As for the work, well, there have always been decent roles for older men. Women often complained of being overlooked after a certain age. To make it worse, while a wrinkly sixty-year-old man might get a leading role, his love interest would be played by an actress likely to be mistaken for his daughter. That is much less the case now: Judi Dench has carved out a new career, as have her fellow dames, Helen Mirren and Maggie Smith. My friend Gemma Jones once said to me, 'I'm getting older. Am I still going to be working?' She's since been in the *Harry Potter* series, along with the *Bridget Jones* films, *Spooks* and Woody Allen's *You Will Meet a Tall Dark Stranger*. You can never know.

CHAPTER 16

So, I mentioned Michael Elliott. Michael is the father of Marianne Elliott, who produced stage productions of *War Horse* and *The Curious Incident of the Dog in the Night-Time*. He's also probably the finest theatre director I've ever come across, and along with Fulton the biggest overall influence on my career.

I met him partly through an Ibsen translator called Michael Meyer, and partly through Fulton, who would always be quoting Elliott. Fulton's admiration for Elliott had already fully rubbed off on me by the time I first worked with him, which was on TV in 1968, a film called *The Year of the Sex Olympics*, written by Nigel Kneale who also wrote *Quatermass* among other things. A science fiction piece, *The Year of the Sex Olympics* proved to be pretty prophetic about reality TV. I played a character called Lasar Opie, a TV producer who slouched in a large chair and controlled television events with a somewhat Machiavellian air. One thing I remember very clearly about it was that we were rehearsing when Bobby Kennedy was shot. (Which reminds me, I was still at LAMDA, having a drink in the Earls Court Tavern when JFK was assassinated. A fellow student rushed in and gave us the news, and we ran to the paper stand just outside Earls Court station where the terrible news was confirmed by the *Evening Standard*.)

Leonard Rossiter was in *The Year of the Sex Olympics*. What a gifted actor. Another of those unfairly associated with his sitcom work, in his case *Rising Damp* and *Reginald Perrin*. He had quite extraordinary comic intensity on stage, and that was very much a facet of his offstage life as well. A very driven guy, quite eccentric with it – almost hyper, you might say. Put it this way, it came as no surprise to learn that he was a champion squash player. All that explosive energy needed to go somewhere.

At the time he lived in Fulham, as did I, and I'd just left the gym one morning when quite unexpectedly I spotted him in a shop doorway. He was leaning in the recess looking a bit knackered.

'Leonard, are you okay?'

'Oh, I'm fine, thank you, Brian,' he said, straightening, 'absolutely fine. Couldn't be better, actually. I've just walked to Hampstead and back.'

'*What?*' I said, because Hampstead to Fulham and back is a trek.

'Oh yes, yes,' he said, 'I've become obsessed with Macready.'

William Charles Macready, this was. Macready was a nineteenth-century actor famous for his public rivalry with the US actor Edwin Forrest, which at one point sparked off the famous Astor Place Riot in New York. Macready was also a well-known walker, and Leonard, it turned out, had taken to recreating some of his most famous perambulations, that particular one – Fulham to Hampstead and back – included.

Leonard was also a Tory. A Liverpudlian, working-class Tory. And, like a satisfied customer at Fawlty Towers, you don't encounter many of those. We should have had him stuffed, as Basil would say.

As it was, Leonard died a typically eccentric death. He'd been playing Inspector Truscott in *Loot*, came in for the interval one night, sat down, said, 'Well, I think the first half went well,' and then died, just like that, of an asymptomatic heart complaint.

Anyway. Michael Elliott and I hit it off during the making of *Sex Olympics*, and it began a long relationship that lasted right up until his death in 1984. He recognized in me a particular kind of actor in the mould of Leo McKern and Albert Finney – what you might call character-leading actors. To have your card punched by a director of Michael's stature was quite something, and I was only too happy to follow wherever he wanted to go. Sure enough, after *Sex Olympics* the next thing I did with him was to play Ulfheim in Ibsen's *When We Dead Awaken* at the Assembly Hall in Edinburgh. I adored Ibsen, I adored the play and I adored Michael. He was so very freeing, so encouraging. As an artist, he was obsessed, and his zealot-like passion was infectious. He had the knack of pushing me in certain directions – taking me to places that would deepen the work, and it was through him that I developed my love of 'the text' and understood how you as an actor are there to bring the text to life, to be a conduit for the writer.

There are so few directors for whom the text is paramount. Most of them seem to care only about lighting and camera angles, elements of style that are of course crucial to the work but by no means its entirety. Michael, who also shared my love of Ibsen, had a searing intelligence and he brought that to bear on whatever text he worked on. *When We Dead Awaken* was a big success. We went to Manchester on the back of that, and Michael became part of a triumvirate of directors of the Royal Exchange Theatre. Mostly, he moved between stage and TV. We did *She Stoops to Conquer* in 1971 for TV, *The Cocktail Party* on stage in 1975, and he directed the *King Lear* that I mentioned before, when Sir Laurence Olivier had his amazing outburst.

The last thing I did with him was an incredible production of *Moby-Dick*. He came to me and said, 'Look, Pat McGoohan is supposed to be playing Ahab in this production of *Moby-Dick* that I'm about to do. But he's jumped ship.'

'Captain Ahab has jumped ship?' I said.

Michael was in no mood to even acknowledge my joke, let alone play along with it. 'Yes, that's what I just said. He doesn't want to strap his leg up.'

I said, 'What do you mean, "strap his leg up"?'

'Well, he has a peg leg, Captain Ahab. It's uncomfortable for the actor, and Pat McGoohan doesn't want to do it. Would you take over?'

So I went up to Manchester for *Moby-Dick*, and my goodness it was the most astonishing piece of work, an incredible tribute to Michael's mania. Our whale ship, the *Pequod*, was constructed on stage. We sailed in it and then we fought the whale, and we did all the rowing and all the harpooning – all of it beautifully designed and intricately choreographed.

But exhausting. Totally exhausting. Absolutely and utterly draining on every level – most especially whatever level deals with having one's leg strapped up for four hours straight.

After each performance it would take about twenty minutes to get the circulation back into my leg. This created a problem, because we did a 4 p.m. matinee, and because the play was four hours and we were supposed to go back on for the evening, that didn't give me enough time to unstrap the leg, get a bit of feeling back into it and then strap it up again.

I said, 'Michael, I can't go on at eight o'clock. I've got to give my leg a rest,' and so Michael had to come in every night and give a little speech in order to delay the beginning of the evening performance. For that reason we actually welcomed in the new year. It's the only show where I've done a curtain call and wished the audience a happy Hogmanay.

Caroline came up with the kids, Alan and Margaret, and I'd love to say that it was a nice bit of family time together but the truth was that I was in a terrible state. My voice was suffering, my leg was in constant agony and I was permanently exhausted. When I wasn't on stage I was sleeping. I would literally get in a taxi on Saturday night after the evening performance and sleep until the Monday afternoon, at which point I'd return to the theatre for physical therapy.

It was worth it, though. The show was a massive success, critically and commercially. In a couple of chapters' time, I'll be saying that the worst kind of theatre director is the sort who gets too carried away with his or her production values, but if there's always an exception that proves the rule then *Moby-Dick* was it. The vast ship set was incredible, a genuine spectacle, sails and ropes everywhere. We had this amazing *coup de théâtre* effect where at the end of the play the floor of the ship rose up, so it looked as though the whale had appeared from beneath us. The crew would hold me up and I'd throw the harpoon, at which point the whole thing fell down and what was left was Queequeg's coffin with Ishmael, played by my friend Nigel Terry, clinging to it, and that was the end of the play.

As Ahab I had a bit where I nail the doubloons to the mast. I'd jump up on the guard rail and do this speech. Well, on the first night I did all that and my peg leg fell off. Other actors grabbed the leg and were surreptitiously trying to screw it back in as I soldiered on with my speech, until, eventually, I said, as Ahab, 'Leave it boys, leave it,' and ended up swinging off stage, Tarzan-like. A good bit of improv, if I do say so myself.

Michael was there, of course, sitting in the first tier, at eye level. I could always tell it was him because he had these sticky-out ears, and they were red from the light behind them. He was looking at me and I was looking at him and we were both thinking, *Shit*. For all the massive effort and all the creativity and imagination that had gone into the show, we were about to be undone by what was a simple wardrobe malfunction, an errant peg leg.

But of course we weren't. The show was a triumph. Apparently one of the critics had commented, 'I particularly liked the moment when Ahab's peg leg fell off. What we saw in that instant was the total vulnerability of the man. It left a lasting impression.' Ha! If only he knew.

Sadly, the show was to be Michael's last. Since childhood he'd had dwarf kidneys. One was poisoning the other. He'd had a series of transplants and rejections, until at fifty-three – two months after *Moby-Dick* had finished, in fact – he died.

A brilliant man. Absolutely brilliant. Really, truly inspiring. And I was very distressed by his passing because he was a linchpin for me. Plus I felt that our journey together was only just beginning. As a young actor I had learned from him. I had benefited from his patronage. I miss him still.

CHAPTER 17

I was already an admirer of Lindsay Anderson, to the extent that I loved *This Sporting Life*, and I had encountered him that night at the Dundee Rep when Nicol Williamson launched himself into the riverbed of the Tay, but I first met him properly during auditions for the play *In Celebration* at the Royal Court, which he was directing. I got the part.

The play is about brothers who have left their mining town in search of education but return for a fortieth wedding anniversary – only for buried tensions to re-emerge. The miner dad was played by the brilliant Bill Owen (talking of actors defined by their signature sitcom roles), while the three sons were me (youngest), James Bolam (middle) and Alan Bates (eldest).

It's a wonderful show, and there are some great lines in it. I say this as someone who pinches from it all of the time. 'Fed in ignorance, spread in ignorance, dead in ignorance,' is one of them, and the other one is, 'Andrew, Andrew, Andrew, what do we do? How do we all end up? What have we become?' to which the reply is, 'Artists, I suppose,' which is saying, we can't all become artists, we can't all self-actualize. Some of us have to be miners.

Me, Bates and Bolam were the three amigos on that show, and we stayed friends for a good few years afterwards. Less so Jimmy, but Alan and I kept in touch right up to his passing. He was a wonderful, lovely man, very funny, but also slightly troubled by his own bisexuality. People were always urging him to come out, but he never would.

Jimmy Bolam is a very down-to-earth Geordie. He'd done *The Knack* and plenty of work at the Court, but of course what he's most remembered for is *The Likely Lads*. He'll hate me for saying this, but I'm going to anyway. We were buying flowers from a little flower stall outside the Royal Court one day, I can't remember why. The cheery flower seller recognized Bolam and said to him, 'Hey up, there goes a Likely Lad.'

Jimmy glowered at him. 'You can stuff your fucking flowers,' he snapped, and rammed them back at the seller before storming off.

That was Jimmy. We did a film of *In Celebration* – same cast as the stage show – and he would say to me, 'You're getting a lot of close-ups aren't you? I've watched the rushes. You're very popular . . .'

Well, he was kind of right. As with Michael Elliott before, I'd hit it off with Lindsay, and what I came to learn about him was that he thought of himself as being in the tradition of Jonathan Swift, a satirist, holding a mirror up to life, a polemicist for the state of the nation, and with *If . . .*, *O Lucky Man!* (my favourite), and then later *Britannia Hospital*, he truly showed that he had no equal in that regard.

Although he's best known as a film director (perhaps even *the* quintessential British director of his era), and he was a true cineaste, he was also a brilliant stage director, the reason being that he was excellent with craft. And it was because of that that he joined Michael Elliott in forming my view of how a director should work. Half a century later, he continues to do so.

For me, Lindsay's most important quality was his ability to combine the visual with an understanding of the complexities of the text (see a theme developing?). Directors, most of whom I consider pests, love to give actors notes, and most of the time I will bear these notes politely, with a smile, before being equally as polite as I go about doing what I intended to do in the first place. At the time of writing, for example, I'm working on the third season of *Succession*, and the cast, as embedded and veteran a unit as you could find, are still getting notes from newcomer directors. Kieran Culkin the other day was asked to *slow down*. Now, this is an actor who's calibrated the patterns of his character's delivery over the course of two previous seasons. In that sense at least, the work is done, and unless the writing calls for it he won't be changing it anytime soon. He's not going to suddenly *slow down* just because you've given him a note.

But that's directors for you. As I've said, as a rule, they have little appreciation for text but will behave as if they do, when in fact they're far more at home holding endless discussions about lighting. Their interest is in the shots, the cinematic element, and they often fail to realize that the cinematic element is informed by the text; that you come up with even greater cinema if you can relate the visual to what is written.

It can be similar in the theatre when directors get carried away with lavish design. As in film, it's the furniture of the piece that excites them, rather than the piece itself.

But Lindsay? Not like that at all. He was an artist for whom the dance of dialogue and action was paramount. A text man through and through.

Lindsay gave me an insight into the craft of acting. It was through him that I learned to *be* a character rather than describing or acting it (important note: *being* a character, not *becoming* one). Through Lindsay, in other words, I moved closer to the more naturalistic styles that I had come to admire on screen. He showed me the dangers of 'attitudinizing', which is obfuscating the art of playing from moment to moment and allowing the action, the moment itself, to define the attitude of the performance, never the other way around.

So it was with *In Celebration*. In an early scene the idea was that I would come into the living room through the kitchen and call to somebody in the house. In the living room I would place my overnight bag down on the sofa, walk over to a door, call up the stairs and then after a moment or so my father (that was Bill Owen's character) would appear.

So one day in rehearsals, that is what I did.

When I had finished, Lindsay told me to do it again, but this time, slower.

I did as he asked.

'No, again,' he told me. 'But do it slower this time.'

I did it, as asked, but slowly. To me it was as though I were doing it in slow motion. It felt as though I was taking *way* too much time over this simple aspect of performance. For about an hour and a half we rehearsed this one sequence that would eventually take up less than two minutes of stage time.

'Brian,' said Lindsay, finding within himself a way to communicate what I was doing wrong in his eyes. 'How long is it since your character has been in this room? What in this room is familiar to you? What is unfamiliar? What for you, as Steven, has gone on in this room with your brothers when you were a child? Enter it again and take into account all of these factors.'

And then he gave me the classic note. He said, 'Brian, don't just do something, stand there.'

'What?'

'I said, "Just stand there. Don't *do* anything."'

I tried it again, taking his notes on board (for once). I found myself looking around the room and imagining pictures on the sideboard depicting important family events, weddings, christenings, graduations. The table by the sofa would be full of my dad's novels, the ones mentioned later in the play as 'terrible westerns written by English blokes from Dorset'. It was rehearsals, so these things weren't actually there, but what Lindsay was wanting me to do was use my imagination, and use it I did.

I used it so much, in fact, that eventually, he said to me, 'Now, now, Brian, you really are being a little indulgent here. There is no need for a five-hour drama, a minute will suffice.'

Which is better than *slow down* for Kieran Culkin, a far more meaningful and helpful note because it actually related to the text. In one incisive intervention, Lindsay took my natural volatility and moulded it into something involatile. As a result, it was the first time that I felt truly connected as an actor; the first time I understood about economy and the specifics of what you want the audience to see and what you don't want them to see. This particular role called for exactly that kind of economy, and as a result of Lindsay's direction, I found the stillness of the character, this guy who did very little but exuded volumes-full, and received some great reviews.

It was a fantastic learning experience, one that taught me about understanding range and how private one could be in acting, even on stage, how you could let the audience come to you rather than go to them. I don't think I even realized it up until then, in the sense that I'd never put my finger on it, but I'd always had a problem with a certain type of English actor who is all front foot, all out there. 'Oh,

now is the *wintah* of our discontent. Made *glo-horious summah . . .*'
More about that later, no doubt.

Lindsay had white hair and often wore a bemused look, an ironic half-smile playing about his lips. His family were Scots, but Raj Scots, and he had that streak of Scottish puritanism about him. Funny, mercurial, but with an implacability about him, as well as a very clearly defined sense of being a misfit. He was rather tortured by the fact that he was gay but never openly so, and this gave him an unreachable, distant aspect. He had a long relationship with the writer Gavin Lambert, who he'd met at school, and together they had created *Sight & Sound* magazine, which is still going strong. Gavin was openly gay, and had had an affair with Nicholas Ray, as well as a long, platonic relationship with Natalie Wood. But while Gavin was honest about his homosexuality, Lindsay couldn't deal with his. In his book, *Mainly About Lindsay Anderson*, Gavin talks about how he feels that Lindsay would have been better off if he'd come out, but while it's fair to say that such circumstances hone an artistic edge, there was indeed something riven in Lindsay, a kind of dignified longing, probably a longing for a relationship that he could never find, and the people he became obsessed with were people who were never going to reciprocate that.

This was most apparent in his relationships with his leading men. He'd form what were almost infatuations. He'd had it with Richard Harris. He had it with Malcolm McDowell and Alan Bates, and also with an actor called Frank Grimes, known among the cognoscenti as Grim Franks.

The two of them did a production of *Hamlet* together. Batesy said, 'Hey, Brian, we've got to go and see this *Hamlet*. Can you see Grim Franks playing Hamlet? I can't, can you?'

Well, really, I couldn't. So we went down to Stratford. Of course it wasn't very good and afterwards backstage we just said, 'Oh, well done,' and offered up some general platitudes, but I think Lindsay got the wind up that we didn't like it, and because he'd always loved Alan, it was me who took the brunt of his ire.

I wasn't involved with his last satire, *Britannia Hospital*, in 1982. By then he and I had lost touch, possibly as a result of the infamous Grim Franks *Hamlet* incident. Batesy was involved in that trip, too, of course, but as I say, Lindsay always did love Batesy and sure enough found him a part in *Britannia Hospital*. Fulton was in it, too. In fact, practically everyone was in *Britannia Hospital*, including Leonard Rossiter, and even Mark Hamill who played Luke Skywalker in *Star Wars*.

Just not me.

Perhaps as a result of sour grapes, I thought the film was rather silly at the time. However, I saw it again the other day and revised my opinion. Even if it's not quite up to *O Lucky Man!* or *This Sporting Life*, it's still Lindsay fulfilling his own Swiftian brief, and it's still more brilliant than what he did next, when he started making films he would never have considered before. He shot some kind of documentary with the pop group Wham! that was by all accounts rather troubled, and then he did a film with Bette Davis and Lillian Gish, *The Whales of August,* which is a nice film, but even he never really considered it a true Lindsay Anderson film. It just didn't have that edge.

The last time I saw him was in 1991 when he came to see a production of George Bernard Shaw's *The Philanderer* that I was directing in Hampstead. (Oh yes. For all his talk about directors being pests he is indeed the poacher who turned gamekeeper.) *The Philanderer* was an interesting one. Shaw had discarded the ending after a friend, Lady Colin Campbell, told him to, so traditionally the play was performed with the replacement act. Meanwhile, the first one was considered lost, until it was found by the biographer Michael Holroyd and performed by us.

Clive Owen was starring in it, and it went really well. Clive was good and his opposite number was Eleanor David who was even better, although unpredictable.

'Clive, you know, she's running you ragged a little,' I told him.

And he went, 'Oh,' and had to slightly up his game.

Anyway, we'll have more about my directing exploits later. I mention *The Philanderer* because Lindsay came to that but was looking very frail. He had a heart condition, and it had clearly taken its toll on his overall health. Three years later, in 1994, he went for a swim at the beach and suffered a heart attack so massive that it threw him clean across the pebbles. It was the death of a consummate artist, someone who had a profound effect on me, and I value my time with him enormously.

CHAPTER 18

As we're talking directors, I did *25th Hour* with Spike Lee in 2002, and he's simply one of the best directors I've ever worked with. People associate him with African American subject matter, which is fine and fair enough, but they don't realize that he's a consummate cineaste. His knowledge of the cinema is second to none.

What's more, I've never known a director be so diplomatic. Ed Norton was in the film and he's a nice lad but a bit of a pain in the arse because he fancies himself as a writer-director. He and I had this scene set in the bar owned by my character. Spike set it up immaculately, but Ed came in and was saying, 'Now, I've done some work on the script and I've got a few ideas and I'd like you to think about them. I've rewritten a few things in there . . .'

Spike was like, 'Oh, good, let me see.' He had a look at Ed's notes and then said, 'Well that's very interesting. Okay, so what we're going to do now is . . .' and put Ed very firmly in his place.

It was done beautifully. Seamless. It was taking Ed's points on board but making sure Ed knew that we were doing things his way. And the fact that he did it without upsetting Ed, who after all does have a reputation for being a little volatile, was really quite an achievement.

That's an amazing gift Spike has, and it transfers to the screen. I rewatched *Do the Right Thing* recently. I hadn't seen it in years, but it's a flawless movie and absolutely timeless in the sense that it's as relevant now as when it was made, possibly even more so.

There's a skill right there, to be able to hone something as brilliant as that. For me it comes from, firstly, that diplomacy he has, which allows him to get the best out of the people round him; secondly, his incredible filmic knowledge and literacy when it comes to the medium; and thirdly, his vision, which is immense. It's a shame that he's pigeonholed as a black film-maker because to me he's one of the great film-makers of any ethnicity, and I'd put him up there with Bergman, Hitchcock or Antonioni.

He's also been very canny with money by making a lot of commercials, which is a pretty lucrative business. Presumably having that kind of money behind him allows him to concentrate on doing the kind of films he wants to make, and as a result barely an Oscars ceremony passes by without an appearance from a Spike Lee joint.

As we're on the subject, *25th Hour* was written by David Benioff, who of course went on to be showrunner for *Game of Thrones*. I'm often asked if I was offered a role in *Game of Thrones* – reason being that every other bugger was – and the answer is, yes, I was supposed to be a king called Robert Baratheon, who apparently died when he was gored by a boar in the first season. I know very little about *Game of Thrones* so I can't tell you whether or not he was an important character, and I'm not going to google it just in case he was, because I turned it down.

Why? Well, *Game of Thrones* went on to be a huge success and everybody involved earned an absolute fortune, of course. But when it was originally offered the money was not all that great, shall we say. Plus I was going to be killed off fairly early on, so I wouldn't have had any of the benefits of the long-term effects of a successful series where your wages go up with each passing season. So I passed on it, and Mark Addy was gored by the boar instead. (I lied. I did google it.)

The money thing is par for the course. There's always been a tendency for American productions to treat British actors differently from American actors. In other words, to get them cheap. When I first went to America, I discovered the problem with British agents, which is that they always see the other person's point of view. In America they don't give a shit about the other person's point of view. They just protect their clients. They're like *Goodfellas*: 'Fuck you, pay me.' British agents, on the other hand, are like, 'Well, they can't really afford that sort of money, Brian, they haven't got that much. So do you think you could do it for less?'

It used to drive me up the wall. I'd be like, 'I don't want to know about the other side. I'm not interested in their problems. I'm only interested in doing the deal,' which is how US agents operate, and although it sounds mercenary it's also healthy because it's no-nonsense, everybody knows where they stand.

So anyway, with a *Game of Thrones*, or any show like it, there's a risk element. You could sign up to do a *Game of Thrones* and it gets cancelled, and you don't know why it gets cancelled because you thought it was great, but there you are.

I did a series for the BBC called *The Game* in 2014, which I thought was excellent. Written by a guy called Toby Whithouse who had written *Bridget Jones's Diary* and *Being Human*, it was a spy thriller set in the 1970s. Tom Hughes played the lead. He was good. Johnny Aris was in it, and Johnny I've known since he was a child. His dad was Ben Aris, a wonderful actor who died of leukaemia, sadly, and

Johnny was at school with my son, so I've known him since he was twelve. Vicky Hamilton, who I love as an actress, was in it, too.

In other words, it was a very happy job. What's more, it brought me back home, which was great because I'm always looking for opportunities to return to the UK. Unfortunately, there's nothing enticing financially, but there is in terms of the quality of work and *The Game* was something I thought was great.

But they canned it. It was one of those where a new set of bosses come in, and being very keen to assert themselves, go, 'Oh, it's not my show, so we'll cancel it.'

Another case in point was *The Straits*, which I did in 2012. Also a series. See, when you get older, like when you get to my age, you're looking for . . . well, I hesitate to say security because that sounds as though I'm selling insurance, but maybe continuity. You're after something that you might be able to do for a few years, that'll keep you level and on the straight and narrow, so that you're not out there on the hustings going, 'Gi' us a job.'

And when I look at these series, like *The Game* or *The Straits*, I'll always be thinking, *Oh yeah, there's potential, I can do that, that might go to a second or even third series.* That's what's reassuring about *Succession*. Hopefully we'll do a fourth series, and that'll probably be it, but it will have been a great run.

The Straits was a sort of *Sopranos* set in Australia and I played the head of the household, Harry Montebello. The idea was that he was originally from London but had gone on the run and ended up Down Under, where he'd settled down. So far, so great, and I loved working in Australia. Not the first time I'd been there – I went in the mid-1980s to chaperone Alan, who was making *Young Sherlock Holmes* – but it was the first time I'd been in this particular bit,

Cairns, close to where James Cameron filmed *Avatar*. It's a beautiful area in the heart of crocodile country where you can watch a crocodile wandering along the main street at any given moment. Literally. You just see these prehistoric creatures mooching around like they own the place, which they do, because anybody with any sense clears out sharpish.

But the power of my love for Australia was not enough to fuel the future of *The Straits*. Nor was the fact that *The Straits* was rather good, even if I do say so myself. No, the powers that be decided to cancel it after one season. Just as *The Game* was lost, so *The Straits* were sunk.

But, like my mum always said, 'If it's not for you, Brian, it'll go by you,' and I suppose that if either *The Game* or *The Straits* had taken off then I wouldn't have ended up with Logan Roy, so I can't complain. Just that at the time it feels like a bit of a knock-back.

Harry Potter. That's another one they ask me about. Harry fucking Potter. I think someone had a burning cross held up for me not to be in *Harry Potter*, because all my pals were in it. I think the part I *might* have played was the one that Brendan Gleeson got, Mad-Eye Moody, but Brendan was more in fashion than I was at that point, and that's very much the way of the world in my business, so he got it. Also, he's much better than I would have been.

Meanwhile, I turned my nose up at the part of the Governor in the *Pirates of the Caribbean* franchise, a role that was eventually played by Jonathan Pryce. The guy who directed *Pirates* was Gore Verbinski, with whom I made *The Ring*, and he's a lovely chap but I think I blotted my copybook by turning down the Governor. It would have been a money-spinner, but of all the parts in that film it was the most thankless, plus I would have ended up doing it for film after film and missed out on all the other nice things I've done. Another thing with *Pirates of the Caribbean* is that it's very much the 'Johnny Depp as Jack Sparrow' show, and Depp, personable though I'm sure he is, is *so* overblown, *so* overrated. I mean, *Edward Scissorhands*. Let's face it, if you come on with hands like that and pale, scarred-face make-up, you don't have to do anything. And he didn't. And subsequently, he's done even less. But people love him. Or they did love him. They don't love him so much these days, of course. If Johnny Depp went for Jack Sparrow now, they'd give it to Brendan Gleeson.

So no – no regrets about *Pirates*, I don't think.

All of which are digressions from the main digression, which was to mention one or two of the directors I've worked with. And that brings me on to Woody Allen, for whom I made *Match Point* in 2005.

Woody Allen is a legend in the world of cinema and, I have to admit, I was pretty star-struck upon meeting him. I mean, I've talked about O'Toole, and that was a major moment for me in terms of being star-struck, a round ten on the struck scale. Then you've got Richard Harris. I was pretty awestruck to meet him because *This Sporting Life* is a major movie in my life. Alan Bates, of course. I was lucky to be close friends with them both. Oh, and I once met Claudette Colbert who came to see me in a play on the West End. She came with Rex Harrison, who I wasn't star-struck by at all – don't ask me why – but Claudette kind of blew me away. She was a huge star in the 1930s and 1940s and lived to the ripe old age of ninety-two. As a cineaste, I was just bowled over to meet her. Who else? Olivier, without question. Gielgud, without question, Ralph Richardson, without question.

And Woody Allen.

A controversial character these days, of course, but I have to speak as I find, although I appreciate I only had a short time with him. On set he mooches around looking exactly like Woody Allen, complete with the floppy bucket hat. He talks and behaves how you expect Woody Allen to talk and behave – exactly as you *want* him to talk and behave, and he's funny and sweet, and really genuinely shy, and he fully admits he is uncomfortable socializing with actors, for two reasons: (a) he hates wasting their time, and (b) he really doesn't like disappointing them, even though he's not at all disappointing and indeed that self-deprecation is just another facet of Woody Allen that you find thrilling.

In short, Woody Allen is Woody Allen. Cut him, he bleeds Woody Allen.

The thing about his films is that you do them for the prestige, because they do not pay well at all. I mean, they pay something, but you don't ever think of a Woody Allen film as a great payday because it's absolutely not. The trade-off is that it's Woody Allen.

Woody would play chess with himself in between takes. He'd just sit there with a chessboard, his only opponent, himself. He'd always sit reading the *New York Times*' sports pages with his glasses up on his forehead, and I remember once the clapperboard boy went past and accidentally hit the clapperboard, and Woody jumped and said, 'Action,' which was very funny, but also very revealing, showing how he was so completely in another world.

Match Point was filmed in London, and we got to see the famed Woody Allen efficiency at work. I remember we shot down in a big house in Eaton Square in Belgravia, and we finished ridiculously early, about 3.30 p.m., when Woody just said, 'Well, I think that's it, I don't need to do any more, let's go home.'

And we did, and let me tell you, that is virtually unheard of in films. In fact, the whole shoot would have been perfect if not for the behaviour of Jonathan Rhys Meyers, who lost us a day at the Royal Opera House. I wasn't there for much of it, but I heard that he turned up worse for wear and couldn't act, and while of course I feel sorry for anybody who has those kinds of problems – alcohol, in case you haven't read about it in the papers – it cost the production a lot of money. It's not cheap to rent the Royal Opera House for the day.

Scarlett Johansson was also on that show. Scarlett. Divine, funny, smart, wonderful. I loved her. As well as *Match Point*, I did a film called *Her* with her in which she replaced Samantha Morton. She's so real and down to earth. And she was delightful with Woody. I mean, they had a real simpatico relationship. She would send him up constantly, always on his case, but very funny and very loving with it.

I took her out for the day. I said to my friend, Ian McNeice, 'I'm going to go out for the day with Scarlett Johansson.'

He went, '*What?*'

I said, 'Why don't you join us? I'm just showing her around . . .'

Needless to say, he made up a trio; we took Scarlett around the Tate Modern, and it was an absolute gift of a day.

As for Mia, things have clearly been very difficult and painful for her, and probably affected her own career. I met her years ago. I spent an evening with her and André Previn way back in the 1960s, and she was very sweet and very gamine. I liked her. So, I don't know. Nothing is ever as cut and dried as we'd like it to be.

CHAPTER 19

During the early 1970s, I continued to work in TV. I did *Z-Cars*, for example, a two-parter called *The Shooter*. I also did *Doomwatch*. A little digression here is that my friend Ian Bannen was in the feature film adaptation of *Doomwatch*. I knew Ian quite well, and in fact was working with him when he died, on a film called *Strictly Sinatra* in 2001 starring Ian Hart, directed by Oscar-winner Peter Capaldi. (You didn't know Peter Capaldi was an Oscar winner? Indeed he is. Peter won the Best Live Action Short Oscar for *Franz Kafka's It's a Wonderful Life* in 1993.)

One weekend Ian and his wife Marilyn went off on a jaunt to the Highlands, there was a bit of a storm and the car turned over on one of those single-track 'passing place' roads. Ian was killed. It was shocking. A total tragedy and the end of a lovely man and a brilliant actor with a great CV.

The show goes on, though. It really does. Alun Armstrong had to come in and take over, and all of Ian's bits were re-shot, so the public never saw him do his version of Presley's 'In the Ghetto', which I can say, having been there, was really quite something.

And then, in 1971, I made my feature film debut in *Nicholas and Alexandra*.

It was directed by Franklin J. Schaffner, who was then a very big deal thanks to 1968's *Planet of the Apes* and a best director Oscar for *Patton* in 1970, and it was produced by the very legendary Sam Spiegel who had produced, oh, little things like *On the Waterfront, The Bridge on the River Kwai, Lawrence of Arabia* . . . and a whole load more.

So a big deal, then. I mean, the reason you might not have heard of *Nicholas and Alexandra* is because it's fair to say that it didn't turn out too well, being a little less than the sum of its parts. But at the time? On paper? A very big deal.

I was doing a play up in Harrogate, which meant long train journeys from up north to London taking about five hours apiece. For the audition, I took the train, met Schaffner and then Spiegel. I did my audition, which was for the part of Kerensky. All seemed well, and I returned to Harrogate, but then got a call to return for a second audition.

'I can't go back. I'm here.'

Well, they really want to see you again.

So, I dragged myself out of bed at 5 a.m. knowing that I had to get a 6.30 a.m. train down to London, do my business then get a 1 p.m. train back in order to perform that evening. I got up, got the train, got into London about 11.30, got to the meeting at about 11.50. There they all were: the casting director, Schaffner and Sam Spiegel, who was absolutely the epitome of the cigar-chomping Hollywood exec. They all looked at me, and Spiegel said, 'What are you doing here?'

I said, 'Well, you called me.'

He said, 'Oh no, we've already decided, you're fine, you're in the picture.'

And I went, 'Oh, okay,' and I was about to leave when I said, 'So, Mr Spiegel, is it Kerensky or is it Trotsky?' And he looked at me and said, 'Kerensky? Trotsky? You're in the picture.'

And that was it. Ten or so hours in order to meet Sam Spiegel for ten seconds and get the part – not of Kerensky, as it turned out, but Trotsky.

We shot in Spain. It was the first time I'd been on a plane since that occasion I told you about, when Sir Laurence Olivier saved my life. Olivier was also in *Nicholas and Alexandra*, but his bit of the film had nothing to do with our bit, and so our paths didn't cross on that occasion.

Schaffner was another cigar-chomper. He'd remove the cigar and say things like, 'I think that what this scene requires is what we call in the trade, motion picture intensity.' And then he'd wink. Who knows what he meant? Perhaps he knew full well how dodgy the script was, because the dialogue was banal in the extreme. There was one bit where James Hazeldine, who was playing Stalin, had to say, 'My name's Stalin, Joseph Stalin.'

And in reply, Michael Bryant, as Lenin, said, 'Lenin!'

James's response. 'Yes! I know. I've read all of your books.'

We were just in hysterics doing this stuff.

Steven Berkoff was in it, too. I'd met him when I worked at Dundee, when he'd come up for something or other. I was his stage manager, and he ended up meeting my mum. He'd say, 'I always remember meeting your mum. I liked your mum.'

Berkoff was a sweet guy but a tricky character. He was cursed with that whole British thing of not quite knowing where he fitted in, which meant that he was getting a reputation as either 'eccentric' or 'difficult' depending on your point of view or how much money you might stand to lose. Steven was playing the character AN Bolshevik, which was how it appeared on the page. But he wasn't happy with such an anonymous moniker, so they provided him with a name, Pankratrov, except that we called him Wankitoff, which didn't help his mood. Meanwhile, Peter O'Toole was supposed to play Rasputin, but at the last moment the deal fell through and O'Toole bailed out, so Berkoff saw his chance. 'They can't get a Rasputin,' he growled. 'I think it's an opportunity for me . . .'

After that he was always trying to catch Sam Spiegel's attention but Sam would just ignore him. Berkoff would be fuming. 'I can't get that man's attention. What do I have to do?'

It then transpired that Tom Baker was being lined up to play Rasputin – Baker's first major role.

'What the fuck do they want bloody Tom Baker for?' raged Berkoff. 'I'm a perfect Rasputin.'

And actually, he was right. Put a wig on him and he would have been a good Rasputin.

But still, shooting that film was another major through-the-looking-glass moment for me. You had Schaffner and Spiegel and a real who's who in the cast list, while the director of photography was Freddie Young – who'd worked with Lean on *Lawrence*, *Doctor Zhivago* and *Ryan's Daughter* – a complete hero of mine.

Even so, the film, when it eventually came out, didn't do well, but I never really thought about that. I didn't have that kind of ambition at the time and, if I'm honest, I still don't. I just wanted to do the work. My film work didn't suddenly take off as a result of *Nicholas and Alexandra*. But that hardly mattered to me. Why?

Because although I had grown up loving the cinema, I was now consumed by the theatre. It was on the stage that I found my bliss.

CHAPTER 20

My acting life has been a series of stepping stones. Lindsay Anderson and Michael Elliott set me on a path and then developed it. They told me that acting is not all about emoting, which was what I was good at. I mean, I could wake people up with my temper if I wanted to, but I realized it was not the key thing. The key thing was finessing it. If I were to rewatch *The Year of the Sex Olympics* now, for instance (which, for the record, I have no intention of doing), I'm sure that I would see a far more restrained, naturalistic performance – more of a 'back foot' performance – than I had been used to giving in the theatre. I brought that into my television work, but also, thanks to the 'don't just do something, stand there' lesson, into my theatre work as well. Years later, I would see that I had inadvertently taken the credo *too much* to heart, when the friendly advice of a young Indian girl helped add another dimension to my work. We'll get to that in due course.

For the time being, I was beginning to get to grips with the distinction between stage and screen acting. It's the same root, but it grows up into different branches and then it flowers. So, on the stage, you have to project, you have to take it from the root and bring it out. To me, the greatest-ever English stage actor is Paul

Scofield, by a mile. He had that incredible ability to never lose his reality while at the same time being extraordinary and doing the most incredible things. I'll give you an example. I used to watch Scofield rehearse *Uncle Vanya* at the Royal Court. I was working on a play of my own upstairs, and I would come down and go in the back of the circle to watch Scofield go through his paces. There was a scene where Vanya goes dry in the throat and requests a drink of water, and every time I watched him do it, I forgot that he was acting. I thought that he, Paul Scofield, genuinely wanted a drink of water. That was his ability.

You get that sometimes. An actor will just pop a line. One of my favourites is Prunella Scales in *Fawlty Towers*, when she says, 'Don't mind him. He's from Barcelona,' and it tells you *everything* – everything about him and her, about the relationship between the two and what separates them. And the way she delivers it is just iconic. It's wonderful when you see an actor nail a phrase so completely that you think to yourself, *Nobody will ever be able to say that again*. I like to think I might have got close to that myself, perhaps with Lecter (or Lecktor as he was in my version) and I'm pretty certain that I've cornered the market in fuck-offs with Logan Roy, but I'll never – *never* – be quite as iconic as Prunella Scales in *Fawlty Towers*.

Then there's the physicality, of course. During *She Stoops to Conquer*, Trevor Peacock asked the director, 'Look, please can you film the *whole* of me for this bit?' And I knew what he meant, because the story was told by the whole body. Look at Laurel and Hardy, for example. You almost always see their entire bodies. On film, as opposed to stage, you have to construct your frame to tell the story. You have to learn how big you can be on camera, and how you'll come across depending on its position. Film allows you to give more detail to your performance, but it also robs you of certain other tricks. At the Royal Court, for example, we did a lot of what we called 'down-staging'. Up-staging is where you're up and taking the attention, but down-staging is where you might put your back to the audience and get them thinking, *What's going on over there?* because you've excluded them.

The theatre is all about the rehearsal, but in television or film, you have no prep time, you have to be in the moment; you have to walk on that set and do your thing. It means you have to be completely focused, and that comes from developing the skill of how to be present in the job, how to define and then inhabit the character. That's why directors become pests when they start coming up with their notes. They're saying, 'We can shape this. We can do this differently.'

You as the actor are going, 'No, it's already there because I've already established who this guy is. Respect my ability.'

And how do you do that? How do you define and create that character? Each one is different, of course, but as a rule you have to have that thing that makes the audience want to lean forward. Get them asking questions of the character. 'What is his or her secret? *What* are they? *Who* are they?' A character like Logan is a gift in this respect, because Logan is complex. He's not Rupert Murdoch, he's not Conrad Black, he's Logan Roy, his own entity, and he's much more interesting.

The other day, I was asked, 'Would you ever fancy playing Donald Trump?'

'No,' I said.

'Why not?'

'It's such a bad script.'

There's no dimension to it. That's the problem with Trump. There's nothing to be investigated, which would make him unrewarding to play. Logan Roy is more interesting because he's a darker character, but he's got other elements which are surprising too. That's the great reward of him. He does villainous things but he's not really a villain. And another thing that interests me about him is that we have this in common: we're both disappointed in how the human experiment has turned out. We share a certain disgust, which in his case manifests itself in his attitude to his kids, in whom he's trying to instil a sense of self-worth. He's saying, 'I want my kids to be themselves, instead of these bottle-fed individuals.'

It's an interesting dilemma of our times, the whole thing of entitlement and how that destroys people. Logan's never had that, there's never a sense of entitlement to him because he's earned everything he has, and he sees the tragedy of his children not having that foundation in their own lives. That's why Kendall is such a fuck-up. It's because he doesn't know where he fits in, so he's constantly trying to get rid of his father while at the same time loving his father. Logan knows that Kendall is a fuck-up, just as he knows that Connor is a space cadet and that Shiv can't keep her mouth shut. Roman is the interesting one, of course. He's still forming and developing as a character, and Logan can see that there's actually something that's quite considerable in his youngest child.

As actors these are dimensions you create for yourself. When I first went to the States, I knew that I was going to earn my wage as a character actor, and what I really wanted to do was create characters similar to those that I loved from the old films. These days, the supporting parts are often very flat. They're flotsam and jetsam. But in the old movies, the characters just zing at you, no matter how small the part. They have a totality about them. So that was important to me, to give the characters an arc, some definition. A friend of mine describes it as displacing the air. A character walks on and the air is displaced for a moment because of what is presented to the audience. And that was my challenge as an actor. I wanted to displace the air.

CHAPTER 21

The Royal Court had been refurbished and reopened in 1952, at which point George Devine was appointed artistic director and the English Stage Company was formed. Wanting to promote new writers, Devine's third production was John Osborne's *Look Back in Anger*, directed by Tony Richardson, who then went on to make the movie version, kicking off a directorial career that positioned him as one of the top British directors.

Meanwhile, back at the Court, *Look Back in Anger* was followed by *The Entertainer* – also by Osborne, also directed by Richardson and also subject to a film version later on – starring Sir Laurence Olivier. The Royal Court, tucked neatly into Sloane Square, was a crucible of British culture.

Somehow, the new regime at the Royal Court seemed to epitomize that great upheaval of life that we experienced in the 1960s, when suddenly it felt as though anything was possible, when a working-class grunt like me could find himself at one of the country's most prestigious drama schools. This was the trickledown effect of the 'new realism' of John Osborne, and if what I had achieved was an example of that mobility on a micro level, then new realism was an example of it writ large – a living, breathing case of theatrical culture not just catching up with the 1960s climate, but helping to drive it. Here I was, part of that tradition, bringing with me my movie world ways, self-schooled in Spencer Tracy, Marlon Brando, James Dean, Peter O'Toole, and finding that rather than those two worlds being at odds, they actually rather complemented one another. Growing into my career, I watched as theatre and cinema had created that almost symbiotic relationship, where plays at the Royal Court went on to become major and, as we now acknowledge, classic British films of the era – documents, if you will, of life in that time. And just as the way had been paved for Lindsay, Tony Richardson, Albert Finney, Richard Harris and Tom Courtenay, so I trod that path, too. Talk about being in the right place at the right time: coming into the world of theatre in the 1960s at the Dundee Rep, I was unaware of the seismic changes about to take place in society and thus oblivious to how they might affect me. I was conscious only of a gap between who I was and what I wanted to be, wondering if I'd ever be able to marry the two together. As it happened, as luck would have it, society solved that problem for me.

My own relationship with the Court stretches over . . . well, almost my entire career. Having auditioned five times until I got in, I did a production a year with them for four years from 1969. At first, the artistic director was Bill Gaskill, after which it was a triumvirate of Bill, Lindsay and Tony Page, but of course my first production was *In Celebration* for Lindsay in 1969, after which I was in a Sunday night production of a play by Robert Holman, *The Big Romance*, directed by Roger Williams, followed by John Osborne's adaptation of Ibsen's *Hedda Gabler*, directed by Tony Page, and after that, in 1973, David Storey's *Cromwell*, again directed by Page, with Albert Finney, Jarlath Conroy, Pete Postlethwaite, Alun Armstrong and Frances Tomelty – the one with the corpsey cast I mentioned before.

I was back in 1984, when I premiered Ron Hutchison's *Rat in the Skull*, directed by Max Stafford-Clark, with Colum Convey and a young Gary Oldman, for which I won the Society of West End Theatres Award as best actor, and then in 1999 I appeared in Conor McPherson's *Dublin Carol* which was to reopen the newly furnished theatre, although this was delayed so we took it to the Old Vic, until the new year of 2000 when we finally opened at the Royal Court. Lastly, I was in Tom Stoppard's *Rock 'n' Roll* in 2006.

All of which means that I squeezed work from the Court in every decade from 1969 to 2006. It became another second home to me.

Obviously, *In Celebration* was important because it brought me into the realm of Lindsay. After that came Osborne's version of *Hedda Gabler*, in which I played Ejlert Lövborg alongside Denholm Elliott as Judge Brack, and Osborne's then-wife, Jill Bennett, as Hedda, and thus I found myself thrust into yet another new world.

Denholm Elliott, for example, was quite a character. A brilliant actor. I would come on stage as Ejlert Lövborg and he would just look at me, as though to say, 'I think it's time you had a shower.' Literally, a filthy look. It was an incredible bit of performance. With that one facial gesture, he made me feel dirty, like an urchin – and that was great for the role.

For the opening night get-together of *Hedda Gabler* we convened at the Osbornes' house in Chelsea. We walked into the house and Denholm took a look around at the decor, giving it the once-over and then said, 'Oh, look, sublimated pine.'

I'll never forget that remark. Funny how things stick with you. If I think of John Osborne, I think of his house and I'll immediately go to Denholm Elliott saying, 'Oh look, sublimated pine.'

Osborne, then. This genius who had moved from acting to writing and in so doing energized first the Court and then the wider British culture, shining a theatrical light on issues of class. A great man, whose work speaks for itself. Thoughtful and quiet but passionate. I adored *Look Back in Anger*.

His wife, Jill, was a terribly good actress. She did dressage in her spare time and had a suitably elegant air about her, making Hedda Gabler the perfect role for her. She was, I thought, magnificent in it. Later, there was so much bitterness between her and John that it was terrible to see, it really was. I could never work out where that vitriol came from; how two people who'd seemed to be so much in love could reach such an awful state of hatred. Much of it sprang from a sense of being professionally thwarted, no doubt. At the Court, everybody tended to be assigned roles. I was regarded as a rough-but-sensitive type – 'soul in a donkey jacket', that was me – but the trouble with being cast in this way was that it slightly limited the breadth of my newfound imagination. Through Lindsay Anderson's guidance, I had discovered something fundamental about myself, but the Court, because of its dedication to writing of a political and sociological bent, where the actor was merely fodder for that ideological end, was not the place to do it. John Osborne found the same. What happened was that the Court unwittingly played upon the actor's basic feeling of insecurity, the one I mentioned at the top of the book. They were saying that a working-class actor could never play posh, a posh actor could never play working class. They put you in your box and wanted you to stay there.

This is what happened to John. He'd had huge success with *Look Back in Anger* and then *Inadmissible Evidence*, but after that they – and by 'they' I mean the powers that be at the Royal Court – wanted him to write what *they* wanted him to write, rather than what *he* wanted to write. He wrote a version of *Coriolanus*, for example, but they all dismissed it. 'Oh no, he's not writing the plays we want him to write.' You get that sometimes, when decision-making is done by committee. There's this almost feudal thing of needing to keep people in one place, not allowing them to progress, and I think that John Osborne fell victim to that at the Royal Court, despite – or maybe because of – his long association with the theatre. It's like my ex-mother-in-law used to say: 'Well, it just isn't done.'

I said, 'Well, what isn't done?'

'*It* isn't done.'

I said, 'What's *it*?'

'*It* is *it*.'

'And *it* isn't *what*?'

'*Done*. It isn't done. We don't do that.'

Who knows what the fuck it all means? And yet at the same time it makes perfect sense in terms of the mentality we're talking about. I dare say that had I mentioned that conversation to John it would have made sense to him as well.

I used to live in Finlay Street, in the Bishops Park area of London, right by the Fulham football ground, when Caroline and I would throw the New Year's Eve parties I was telling you about, where I'd suddenly decide we needed napkins and pull a famous disappearing act. Just up the road from our house was the Finlay Street School and I remember one evening a bunch of people were smoking outside when I looked up the road to see John standing opposite the school.

I went up to him. 'John, are you okay? Is everything all right?'

'Yes, thank you, Brian,' he said, and then indicated the buildings opposite. 'I went to that school. I hated it. I hated every fucking second of it. In fact, we used to live round the corner, and I hated that too. I can't believe that you live here now. I couldn't wait to get a-fucking-way from this place. It was the worst time of my life when I lived in this area.'

Perhaps that was how he felt: that he'd moved away from his beginnings but not far enough; that whatever happened he was still being held back. I firmly believe that in our profession you have to constantly reinvent yourself, and I think that John, and perhaps Jill, both suffered from living off what they'd achieved, and so, instead of going forward, they'd stopped; they'd just sort of . . . given up. Of course, the fact that they openly hated one another didn't help matters. The name-calling came from both sides and was like a hideous game of oneupmanship, six of one, half a dozen of the other, until eventually they divorced in 1978, when to say it was acrimonious is to understate matters considerably. After that, Jill suffered from depression for the remainder of her life until, in October 1990, she took an overdose. John was so overjoyed at her passing that he wrote a new chapter in his autobiography rejoicing in the fact.

Another suicide was Rachel Roberts who, like Jill, was a great actress who had her fair share of relationship problems. Rachel had starred in *This Sporting Life* for Lindsay, as well as *Saturday Night, Sunday Morning*, with Albert Finney. A famous drunk who had a very turbulent relationship with Rex Harrison, with whom she was absolutely besotted, Rachel died in 1980 by drinking some kind of caustic, bleach-like substance and then falling through a glass partition.

As I say, Lindsay was friends with both Jill and Rachel, and as part of a documentary he made, *Is That All There Is?*, he gathered a load of friends and colleagues to scatter both of their ashes on the Thames.

*

Meanwhile, work in TV continued to pay the bills. I played Stalin in a production called *These Men Are Dangerous: Stalin* for the BBC's *Thirty-Minute Theatre*, as well as Rod in a production of *Combing Down His Yellow Hair*, again for *Thirty-Minute Theatre*. On the stage I was just as – if not even more – busy: *Getting On* by Alan Bennett and *Don't Start Without Me* by Joyce Rayburn at the Garrick.

That same year came the dreadful blow of our stillborn twins, but for the time being at least, Caroline and I remained a couple and I was as busy as I'd ever been, decamping to Nottingham Playhouse. That year, however – as was often the case when my career was going well – I suffered another blow in my personal life.

CHAPTER 22

After leaving the Court in 1973, I spent a season at Nottingham Playhouse, during which I played Berowne in *Love's Labour's Lost*, Sergeant Match in Joe Orton's *What the Butler Saw*, and the title role in Ibsen's *Brand*. Our Christmas show was *The Three Musketeers*, with me as d'Artagnan. Caroline was in that one, too, playing Constance, and along with Alan – then just a wee tot – we stayed in a lovely house in the Park area of Nottingham.

It was during *The Three Musketeers* that I managed to fall off stage, stabbing my sword into a front seat. Upshot: several alarmed but thankfully unharmed audience members nearby. Which reminds me that years later, doing *King Lear* at the National, there came a point in the first scene when I tore off my metal crown and flung it away. On this one occasion it caught in my voluminous costume and instead of going safely into the wings frisbeed directly into the front row.

It was a heavy thing, and for the next few moments I continued with my heart in my mouth, casting surreptitious glances at the front row. There I saw a rather dazed-looking young woman turn to her partner and mouth the words, 'Your shirt's red.'

She was not wrong. The shirt had been white but now was stained with blood. In the next second she realized that the source of the blood was her and that she was bleeding from a nasty cut to the forehead. To paraphrase a famous saying, bloody is the head that gets clonked by the crown.

Bless them, but the couple made a discreet exit and the majority of the audience were oblivious. When the scene finished, I rushed to the nurses' station to check she was okay, as well as to apologize profusely. Thank God it was just a superficial head cut, but even so, there was a lot of blood, and that poor bloke's white shirt was now a distinctly tie-dyed red. Memo to self: it's you who's supposed to suffer for your art, not your audience.

As for the guy? Years later, when performing in Edinburgh, I received a note prior to that evening's performance. It was from him. 'I'm coming tonight. I have a new wife. Is she safe?'

But anyway, it was during that Christmas performance of *The Three Musketeers* that it happened. Not the sword thing. The other thing. As I say, Caroline had played Constance in that production, and there was another girl playing a maid, but for reasons lost to the mists of time they decided to double it so that the girl who played the maid would also play Constance and Caroline lost her part.

She was upset, rightly so, and I was in a difficult position as the leading young man of the production. I tried to use what little leverage I had to fight her corner, but it wasn't enough. Caroline was off the production. She and Alan had to return home to London.

Shortly after that, I began an affair.

One night, my lover (and I hesitate to use the word 'lover', but in lieu of her name I suppose that's what she was) had left the hotel in the middle of the night, about 4 a.m., to return to her digs, when there came a knock on my door.

I couldn't tell you exactly what went through my mind when I opened it to find two policemen standing there. All I know is that I interpreted their visit as more to do with the affair than anything else. Not that I was doing anything illegal, you understand. Something to do with the clandestine nature of things, I suppose. It was just where my mind went.

'Yes?' I said.

'Brian Cox?'

'Yes?'

'Is your mother Mary Ann?'

Nobody knew her as Mary Ann, of course. The world knew her as Molly. Everybody apart from the police at my door, who were sorry to inform me that my mother Mary Ann had died while in Los Angeles.

At first, I thought it might be a mistake because I'd briefly forgotten that Ma had decided to go to America to visit my sister, Irene. As a young woman, Irene had migrated first to Canada and then, in 1964, to Los Angeles, eventually meeting someone and then getting pregnant. Wanting to help with the pregnancy, my ma had gone out to see my sister. The problem was that Irene lived in a place on a very steep hill, and a few days after arriving in LA, my mum had walked up this hill for some reason. On the hill she had the heart attack that killed her.

Later that morning, as I sat downstairs in the hotel, I tried to absorb the news and found myself experiencing a strange and unexpected emotion. It was a sense of . . . well, there's no other word for it, a sense of release. A sensation of freedom that I had never before experienced.

I mean, it goes without saying that I loved my mum. I loved her for her eccentricity but also for her strength. I admired how she'd been through so much in her life. How she'd endured heartbreaking problems with her mental health. How she had been through extreme poverty and emerged, if not exactly unscathed, certainly unbroken.

And I suppose, what with one thing and another, I had not been as attentive as I might have been. I was a struggling young actor, so helping her financially wasn't always possible, but the tragedy of my mother was that while she was all right – in the sense that she was much better than she was at her worst – she never really took care of herself, and maybe I could have done more to help her with that. Either way I had evidently felt some rock of responsibility, unconscious or otherwise, from which I was suddenly released.

But I take comfort in knowing that she was with family when she died. Also, that she had conquered the worst of her troubles, those suicidal ailments that had afflicted her in the wake of my father's death. She had changed over the years, no doubt about it. And the person she was when she died was a far less unpredictable and unstable character than she had been during her darkest hours.

An atypical mother, Ma was also an atypical Catholic. Not for her the traditional Catholic aversion to cremation. She had often talked of going that way.

'Well, Ma, that may not be possible,' we her children, used to say, because back then things were different in the UK; for Catholics in particular cremation was a no-no. But of course because she died in the States, she ended up getting her wish after all. Her send-off took place in LA.

I finally got there later, when I met up with Irene, who was then a new mother – she'd gone into labour the day after Mum's death. She and I were driving down Sierra Madre Boulevard when we passed a garish, bright-pink funeral home. 'That's where Ma ended up,' said Irene.

Ma did eventually make it back to Dundee, though – in an urn. She was parked at the rather flash home of my sister May's great pal, Winnie, who was also very much like a sister to all of us. One evening, Winnie and May were joined by Bette, the three of them all quite tipsy, and they decided it might be an idea to inspect Ma's urn. What happened? Well, they dropped the urn on Winnie's beautiful carpet, spilling mother on the shagpile. Apparently they got quite giggly restoring Ma to her urn, trying to separate her from the bits of flotsam and jetsam of the shagpile.

CHAPTER 23

Early 1976. I was thirty and had been summoned to a meeting. Not just any old meeting. Oh no. This was a meeting called by one of cinema's pre-eminent directors, John Schlesinger.

At that point in his career, Schlesinger had a CV to die for. *A Kind of Loving* in 1962 then *Billy Liar* in 1963, followed by *Darling* in 1965, *Far from the Madding Crowd* in 1967 and then *Midnight Cowboy* in 1969, for which he won the Best Director Oscar. After that, *Sunday Bloody Sunday*, and another Oscar nomination, followed by the rather underrated *The Day of the Locust*.

Film-wise, things would go very badly south for Schlesinger with *Honky Tonk Freeway* in 1981, but he wasn't there yet. At the time that I turned up for our meeting, Schlesinger was based at the Paramount Studios in Hollywood. There my tale begins, for I can distinctly remember gazing at the Hollywood sign through the gates of Paramount Studios and thinking, *This is it. I've made it. I'm about to have a meeting with John Schlesinger. The guy. The director.*

Now, of course, I'd already made *Nicholas and Alexandra*, but this felt different. Getting the part of Trotsky had been a long, drawn-out process conducted entirely in rainy London. But this was Paramount. And for a kid from Dundee who had experienced on a regular basis at the picture houses of Dundee the promise of the Paramount 'mountain' at the commencement of many a great movie, it was somewhat overwhelming in a way that a dreary casting office in Wardour Street certainly wasn't.

I wended my way through countless sound stages and arrived at a newish building boasting spacious, cosy offices and a lady who greeted me with all the enthusiasm of 'seen it, done it, washed the T-shirts' – a living breathing Madame Defarge of the Paramount lot.

'John is in the editing suite. He wants you to join him,' she told me dispassionately.

Here's the thing. Having journeyed from London to Los Angeles, I still had no idea why John Schlesinger should want to see me, but I knew one thing: if John Schlesinger wanted to see me then it had to do with a film John Schlesinger wanted to make, and the films that John Schlesinger made were the sort that come out in January, by which I mean the sort that are made with Oscars in mind and sweep the board accordingly. Just as an aside, I personally hate the way that the timings work. How films released at other times of the year seem to slip the Academy's mind; how you would be forgiven for thinking that the Oscars are awarded only to those films released between Thanksgiving and the new year. I don't like it and I don't understand it, and I feel that I have at times missed out because of it (cough, *Churchill*).

Madame Defarge directed me to another building, which was darker and more secretive in appearance. This was the editing suite. I found my way to a spacious area littered with countless snacks of popcorn, potato chips (that's crisps to the likes of you and me) and coffee dispensers. In one corner of the room sat a man who seemed totally at one with his environment, sipping coffee and dipping a doughnut.

At that moment I realized that my preparation was flawed. True, it had been a hastily called and arranged meeting, but I'd had time at Heathrow, not to mention many hours on an aeroplane, to think about it, and what I realized was that I had no idea what John Schlesinger looked like.

So I went for it. After all, what did I have to lose?

'Mr Schlesinger?'

The guy looked at me. 'Not guilty,' he said, 'John's in there.' With the doughnut he gestured at the editing suite. 'He's trying to make sense out of chaos.'

'Ah,' said I, still wondering what I was doing there. Just then the door of the editing suite opened and a face appeared – a face that had clearly spent a long time, and perhaps, if you were being uncharitable, too long a time under a sunbed. This guy was wearing sunglasses that seemed too big for his face. 'Who are you?' he barked at me. More of an accusation than a question.

'My name is Brian Cox,' I said in reply. It doesn't translate well to the page, but for some reason I'd forgotten how to pronounce my surname so instead of it coming out the regular way, I made a kind of strangulated sound with which no sane person wants to be associated.

'Why are you here?' demanded the over-tanned man.

'To meet John,' I said. (Incidentally, I knew at once that this guy wasn't Schlesinger. For a start, he was American.)

Orange bloke looked at me, said, 'Oh yes, reshoots,' and then quickly disappeared back into the editing suite.

Reshoots.

It suddenly dawned on me. This was why I was there. I was wanted for reshoots. Wow. Finally I was about to begin – as in properly begin – my movie career. *Nicholas and Alexandra* was one thing, certainly not to be sniffed at, but this was John Schlesinger.

'Who was that?' I said to the doughnut guy.

'That was the producer, Bob Evans.'

Back then, Bob Evans wasn't quite the legendary figure that he is now – or should I say was, because he died in 2019. Back then he had been studio executive for *The Godfather* and the *The Godfather Part II* and had produced *Chinatown*, but he still had a long career ahead of him, not to mention a controversial run-in with the law when he was convicted of cocaine trafficking in 1980.

'What's going on?' I asked the doughnut guy.

'The usual director–producer crap. Lots of differing points of view about the cut.'

'What cut? I asked, thinking that whatever the answer was, this is the film for which I'd be doing reshoots. I was racking my brain as to whether I had read anything on John Schlesinger's current project. It was coming to me. Dustin Hoffman. Sir Laurence Olivier. Something to do with a Twix. A Mars Bar.

'*Marathon Man*,' said doughnut guy.

Of course. *Marathon Man*.

Marathon Man would go on to become one of the keynote films of the 1970s, infamous for the legendary scene in which Olivier dentally tortures Dustin Hoffman, as well as the equally-as-legendary story that Hoffman and Olivier's differing acting methods caused a rift during the shoot. Olivier's acting method was to do Olivier. Hoffmann's acting method was, well, 'method', and he apparently stayed in character for the entire production, refusing to sleep among other things. 'My dear boy,' Olivier is famously reputed to have said, 'why don't you just try acting?'

My ma, Molly, aged 22, and my dad, Chic, aged 24 (1927)

Me, aged 4, with Bette (behind on the left) and her pals (1950)

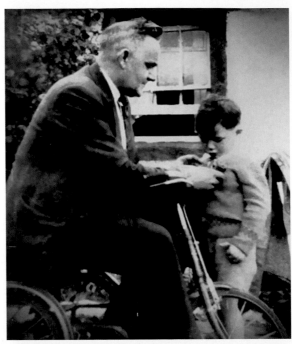

The photograph of my dad sitting on my tricycle that always moves me to tears (1950)

My dad and Irene in his shop (1954)

Me as a teenager
(1959)

The entrance to the
Dundee Rep (1958)

Me, Bette, Charlie, May and Ma (1960)

My Spotlight headshot of me aged 20 (1966)

As Lazer Opie in *The Year of the Sex Olympics* (1968)

With Fulton Mackay, my best friend (1969)

With my son, Alan (1971)

Alan and Caroline (1973)

My daughter, Margaret (1981)

With Margaret and Alan (1977)

The Changeling with Emma Piper (1978)

Ready to stab Sir John Gielgud in *Julius Caesar* (1977)

With my son Alan in
The Devil's Crown (1978)

With Jane Lapotaire in
The Devil's Crown (1978)

There in a nutshell is the principal difference between actors from the UK and those from the US. Personally, I'm not a method actor and don't hold with it. You hear it on US sets a lot. Actors talking about their 'process'. They have to go through this entire rigmarole about acting, the whole method thing of not just 'being' but 'becoming' the character.

I believe that an actor has to be less locked in than that. You have to be free to turn on a dime, and that means giving yourself the freedom to locate your own moment as opposed to somebody who says that I have to create the space that I inhabit and everybody else must kowtow to that.

It was like Daniel Day-Lewis speaking to Emily Watson. That pressure Emily felt when he greeted her in character. She'd have been thinking, *How do I respond to this? How do I respect Dan's 'process'?* And that meant that she didn't feel free to react to him as she felt fit. Now, this was just an introduction, not even a rehearsal, certainly not the real thing. But the ideology carries through right from that moment into the performance. It sets up a precedent.

But it's fine. Who am I to judge? I'll put up with anything as long as the result is good. For example, Jeremy Strong, who plays Kendall in *Succession*. I don't always agree with him regarding the way he prepares or the way he does things, but his 'process' is his business. It's nothing to do with me; as long as it never gets in the way when we actually play the scene then that's fine, and, as it happens, it's always great.

But still. I'm not a big fan of the Strasberg thing, by which I mean Lee Strasberg, who ran the Actors Studio in New York, where he was considered to be the top proponent of the method. Those who studied with him include Dustin Hoffman, Montgomery Clift, James Dean,

Marilyn Monroe, Jane Fonda, Paul Newman, Julie Harris, Al Pacino, Robert De Niro . . . You get the picture. Strasberg leaned heavily on the teachings of Konstantin Stanislavski, who believed that an actor should look into their own emotional memory in order to create their performance, which meant that Strasberg was also very big on emotional memory.

Stanislavski died in 1938, but not before meeting up with the actress-then-coach Stella Adler, in Paris, who had travelled on a mission to 'beard the lion in his Parisian den' and who was surprised to learn that Stanislavski himself had gone off the idea of using the 'emotional memory' technique.

'No, no, that gets in the way of imagination,' Stanislavski had apparently said.

Stella was a founder member of the Group Theatre. The Group Theatre was founded by Harold Clurman in association with Cheryl Crawford and Lee Strasberg.

Taking her revelation back to the Group, Adler encountered resistance from Strasberg who absolutely refused to adapt his system, sticking to the emotional memory concept. Upon hearing that Stanislavski had rejected the notion of it, Strasberg merely shrugged and said, 'Well, then Stanislavski is wrong.'

I, however, agree with Stanislavski and Adler (whose most famous pupil was Marlon Brando, by the way). There is no more powerful tool than the imagination. I learned that from Lindsay Anderson, looking around the invisible room of my childhood home in *In Celebration*. After all, what actually is your 'emotional memory'? It can only serve you in a very narrow way. It doesn't actually broaden your performance because your own emotional memory is by definition quite narrow. You end up having to base it on what you know, or what you think you know, possibly leaning too heavily on the latter. Ultimately, you have to rely on your imagination to avoid coming up blank.

Thankfully the method approach fell out of fashion, partly through the influence of improv and *Saturday Night Live*, when you'd get actors like Bill Murray coming through who had a much looser attitude, who were far less keen to abide by the quite stringent dictates laid down by Strasberg.

However, as usual, we digress. The point being that Olivier and Hoffman apparently were not best suited during the shoot of *Marathon Man* while Schlesinger was, as it turned out, having his fair share of problems attending to the edit.

So just to refresh your memory, we're back in the room. Bob Evans has departed and Jim the coffee-and-doughnuts guy is winning the award for today's friendliest face by some considerable distance.

'The editor's been fired,' he told me. 'He was given the bum's rush, poor guy. Not altogether his fault, but he was in an unenviable position, caught between the obsessiveness of John and the bloody-mindedness of Bob. So I'm now editor and arbiter of their bruised egos.' He gestured with his doughnut. 'But currently on a break. I'm Jim, by the way.'

'Darling?'

He raised an eyebrow. 'Yes, sweetheart?'

'No, *Darling*. You edited *Darling*.'

'Ah, yes,' he nodded.

'And *Far from the Madding Crowd*,' I said.

'Guilty as charged.'

I was about to pick his brains like a true fan when the door to the editing suite suddenly burst open to admit a bald, stocky man of about fifty. This, it quickly transpired, was a somewhat strung-out John Schlesinger. 'Brian? I haven't got a lot of time. Let's go. You hungry? I'm starving. We'll grab a sandwich on the way.'

Moments later, without even bidding goodbye to Jim Clark (the genius Jim Clark –he's dead now, but they called him 'Hollywood's greatest repairman'), John Schlesinger and I were making our way through the alleyways of sound stages. The whole complex seemed to have taken on a new glow in the last twenty minutes. Being with John Schlesinger afforded you respect, it seemed. Passers-by who just moments ago hadn't given me a first glance, let alone a second, now looked at me with smiling, curious, respectful eyes. 'Well done,' they seemed to say. 'Well done.' And in my mind's eye I began to project myriad elaborate scenarios of my new, impending movie career. Perhaps these particular reshoots would require the introduction of a new character, a villain who holds the key to the whole plot, or perhaps the younger brother of the main character, who ultimately saves the day. My imagination was in danger of hitting overdrive.

After a brief stop to grab a sandwich for Mr Schlesinger at one of those portable kiosks that you see all over the studios complex, we arrived back in his office where Madame Defarge greeted us with a possibly uncharacteristic volley of smiles. Another omen, I thought, as we finally settled into the cosiness of John's office.

This was it. Now he was going to tell me.

He began to eat his sandwich. 'Well, Brian, I've heard a lot of great things about you. Great things.'

'Great,' I said.

'I believe you're joining the National Theatre.'

I was genuinely unsure how to reply. Would it be a good thing if I was joining the National Theatre, in his eyes? Or a bad thing? Besides which, it hadn't yet been finalized.

'Oh no, they want you. They definitely want you. Peter Hall says he thinks you have a great future in the theatre.'

'Oh, that's nice,' I said. *What a great way to hear the news.*

'And it's to that end I wanted to see you,' said Schlesinger. 'I'm to direct *Julius Caesar* at the National, opening in early spring next year, but I've lost my Brutus. The actor who was to play it has . . . declined. Both Peter Hall and Gillian Diamond, the casting director, believe you would be perfect in the role. What do you say?'

Well, what can you say? You swallow your disappointment that you're not going to be making a film with John Schlesinger and you bloody well say yes, that's what you say.

CHAPTER 24

So, as Schlesinger had revealed, in 1976 I joined the National Theatre for its inaugural season headed by Peter Hall – Sir Peter Hall as he later became.

These days, of course, Hall is regarded as a titan of the British theatre, and rightly so. He founded the Royal Shakespeare Company; he introduced UK audiences to Pinter and Beckett, and now, having joined the National Theatre as artistic director, he had the job of overseeing the huge, and I mean *huge*, transition from its old home at the Old Vic to London's South Bank.

Here's where it gets interesting, because Marlowe's *Tamburlaine the Great* was due to open the new National Theatre, starring Albert Finney in the lead and me as Theridamas. One of the reasons I wanted to go to the National in the first place was Albert. As I've recounted, he had effectively changed my life as a kid; latterly, I had worked with him at the Royal Court on *Cromwell*, and despite feeling the sharp edge of his tongue on that occasion, I loved him still.

Him going to the National and playing in *Tamburlaine*, itself a rarely performed piece, was quite a gesture on his part. In 1976 he was a big property in film, having led an incredible ensemble cast as Poirot in the 1974 version of *Murder on the Orient Express*, and it's to his eternal credit that rather than sit around counting his money and reprising what had clearly been a popular role, he decided to take a complete break from films, put his money where his mouth was and support the UK arts scene by going to the National.

No doubt he ended up wishing he'd gone off and made another Poirot.

Things went badly right from the beginning. For a start, the Peter–Albert, director–star dynamic fostered a somewhat too-macho atmosphere. Albert was big and boisterous. He smoked cigars and drank Dom Perignon. 'Have a glass, lad,' was one of his favourite sayings. What Peter needed to do – and what he *should* have been doing as director – was steering Albert away from that side of himself. Instead he exacerbated it. The two were blowing metaphorical smoke into each other's faces. They'd go, 'All right, Peter?' 'All right, Albert?' in this pretend-confrontational way, like a joke but not a joke – a big-dick, alpha-male competition that clearly met some need in them but as far as I could tell achieved nothing that was of any benefit to the piece. The two of them had worked together at Stratford and maybe it had been okay then. Perhaps that was why they considered themselves the *Tamburlaine* dream team, capable of raising the curtain on the new Southbank complex. Just that it didn't quite work out that way because, for all the posturing, there was simply no creative spark.

Hall, of course, had a lot on his plate. The Southbank building was a purpose-built affair and there were all kinds of strikes and delays when it came to the construction. Thus, he was pulled in two different directions: the creative side of him, which was the reason why he'd got into the game in the first place, presumably, clashed with the logistical nightmare of opening the Southbank. Frequently the rehearsals for *Tamburlaine* would be interrupted as he was dragged into crisis meetings. The stagehands were in revolt and Peter had to deal with that.

It was a huge job. And, thinking about it, perhaps I was a little selfish in that I thought almost wholly in terms of his relationship to *Tamburlaine*, rather than the wider problems he had to deal with. I perhaps talked about him a little unkindly. Yet there was no denying that he had lost connection. He would do this thing in rehearsals of never looking at the stage. He would constantly have his head down looking at the text, surrounded by a cloud of cigar smoke. I'd stand there doing . . . well, let's just call it a rude gesture and he'd never even notice. I wouldn't have minded, just that this was 'the great Peter Hall', and I didn't think he was so great.

As a result, we never really got into the guts of the play. I remember on one occasion Albert attempted to deliver a rabble-rousing speech to the cast. 'Look, lads, we're like magicians, we've got to pull the rabbit out of the hat.'

It was Oliver Cotton who remarked, 'You've got to get the rabbit into the hat in the first place.'

We rehearsed and rehearsed. For seven months in all. We broke and came back and there was one particular actor, John Nettleton, who they forgot to recall. He wandered in one day. 'John, where have you been?'

'Well, I've been at home waiting for my call. Nobody's phoned.'

They'd forgotten about him.

That was just the normal rehearsals. Technical rehearsals were even more chaotic. We had this elderly actor called John Gill in the company, a character actor who'd been around for many years. Most of the real meat of his part had been cut – probably for time reasons, I can't remember – but there remained a bit where we literally had to tie him up and hang him on a wooden frame with his legs pulled apart. At which point we had to shoot little cannons at him.

Anyway, he was up there for a while as we were firing stuff at him and they were trying to figure out the special effects. They had blood squibs attached to him but they weren't working properly. At one point, it looked as though he was shitting blood because the blood was staining his crotch, which of course we thought was hilarious. John was being very patient about it all as the various tech staff fussed around him and the actors continued firing stuff at him, until after about an hour and a half he finally lost his rag. 'That's it, that's it. I've had enough. I've had enough. You cut my part. You cut everything I'm in. You're laughing at my crotch. You're ridiculing me.'

Which was true. We were. I mean, he was tied to this thing with fake blood spreading from his crotch. I defy anybody not to see the funny side of that.

And Peter Hall. I'll never forget this. He sort of put it on John as though it was entirely John's fault that he was up there, complaining with a soggy crotch. Hall sighed and said to him, 'John, I can't talk to you like this if you're up there doing that.' Which only made matters worse.

And this was an example of the difficulty Peter was having in engaging with the actors. Over the years, I began to feel a little bit more empathetic towards him. I mean, there was one side of him that was actually quite jolly. I remember seeing him at a party and thinking, *Perhaps this is what Peter's really like. Perhaps I was too judgemental at the time*. But looking back with the hindsight of time and tide, I'm a little more empathetic. Not sympathetic, just a bit more empathetic.

Basically, then, a shitfest. A complete nightmare, from start to finish. I might even say that it was the worst experience I'd ever had with a major theatre company.

I might say that – were it not for the fact that it was followed by *Julius Caesar*. And, oh my God, *Julius Caesar*.

CHAPTER 25

John Schlesinger's *Julius Caesar* was a misbegotten nightmare if ever there was one. In the play, the assassination occurs at the beginning of act three. In our version the entire production was a bloodbath.

And yet, like Caesar's reign, it had all started so promisingly. After all, my meeting with Schlesinger had gone sufficiently well that I was genuinely excited to be working with him; we had the great Sir John Gielgud as Julius Caesar, having nudged ahead of Sir Ralph Richardson to get the part; and the first read-through had been extraordinary.

The problems began as rehearsal commenced. Gielgud was not alone in his detestation of the new National Theatre. The complex has three theatres: the Olivier, the Lyttleton and the Dorfman. Of these, the Olivier is the most prestigious, or is supposed to be, but I never liked it, thinking it an ill-conceived space designed by committee. The famous revolving stage, intended to revolutionize the staging, never worked in all the time I was there, nor for a long time afterwards. Frankly I wouldn't be surprised if they still had problems with it. Plus there was the fact that there was very little wood; it was all concrete. Thus there was no resonance. Everything about it was quite dead.

Gielgud felt the same. He'd sit in the wings saying, 'I keep waiting for my flight to be called,' while at other times, he'd place a fluttery hand to his forehead and moan, 'Oh, boys, you're so good, you're so very good. But don't shout. Please, don't shout.'

Schlesinger, too, made noises about disliking the NT, but the bigger issue where he was concerned was a lack of confidence in his own theatrical skills. As a film director? Unsurpassed. Among the best in the world. Riding the crest of a critical and commercial wave that most movie directors can only ever dream of.

But as a theatre director? As a director of classics? Despite the fact that he was by no means a rank amateur in this realm, having directed *Timon of Athens* for the Royal Shakespeare Company, as well as *I and Albert* at the Piccadilly Theatre, Schlesinger exhibited a somewhat nervous, uptight air around *Julius Caesar*.

'I need to understand this,' he would fret, 'I really need to understand this.'

Yes, we thought to ourselves. Understanding *Julius Caesar* would indeed be an advantage when it comes to directing it.

We found ourselves having to spell it out for him. Schlesinger had been to Oxford, but he either had no classical background or was hiding it. We would have to talk him through scenes, spelling out the rationale behind each gesture, intonation and inflection. It felt as though we were in a constant process of bringing him up to speed, and that in turn meant cutting into our momentum, slowing us down to a snail's pace.

He had some strange ideas. In the last act we had Gielgud as a Caesar ghost, or should I say ghosts *plural* because Schlesinger had identically dressed actors wearing Gielgud masks. The problem was that Gielgud was quite tall, so you had a tall Caesar and then a smaller Caesar and then a little Caesar. You remember that 'class system' sketch? John Cleese looking down on Ronnie Barker, who's looking down on Ronnie Corbett? Like that. Except that *Julius Caesar* is not a comedy, so the effect was ludicrous.

'I feel like a Russian doll,' observed Gielgud, who was proving that his reputation as a master of the waspish aside was well deserved.

There was so much corpsing. So many times when the whole cast was just creased up, unable to control ourselves. It wasn't that we were unprofessional (well, a bit), just that the whole thing had the air of a school production.

On one occasion we, as an ensemble, were processing onto the stage towards the Soothsayer to be warned about the Ides of March. Gielgud naturally was leading the procession. Most of the cast following behind. There had been some laughter in the wings which had developed into hysteria as we approached the stage. Oliver Cotton, who was playing Decius Brutus, had to break ranks, run to the front of the procession and present a petition to Caesar. Oliver was desperately trying to control himself, clutching the file of papers he had to present to Gielgud. 'Guys, come on,' was his plaintive cry to the rest of the uncontrollable conspirators. As he approached Gielgud he was still carrying the file under his arm, but Oliver was shaking so much that the contents of the file slipped out onto the stage floor.

He reached Gielgud saying, 'Trebonius doth desire you to o'er-read this his humble suit.' He opened the file . . . empty, no papers.

At this Oliver let out a release of repressed laughter, which sounded more like a cry for help. 'Aargh.'

Gielgud responded, totally out of character 'No, Oliver . . . *please.*'

This completely finished the rest of us. How we recovered . . . I have absolutely no idea.

*

Opening night, we did the show. Afterwards I had a dressing room full of family, friends and agents. I'd like to say that we were celebrating a great show but more likely, we were commiserating, metaphorically wiping our brows with relief that, while bad, the show hadn't been *that* bad. We had at least completed it.

Suddenly, in stormed Schlesinger. He looked like an angry, irate man on a mission, and blow me down if his ire wasn't directed at me.

'Well,' he raged at me, as the rest of the assembled company looked on, 'we had them and then you lost them.'

I looked behind myself. Poked a finger into my own chest. 'What? Me?'

'Yes, you.'

'What about me?'

'You were far too slow.'

'But you told me. You *told* me to go slower.'

He said, 'Well, it was far too slow, and we lost them. *You* lost them.' And off he stormed.

So that was a bit depressing, to say the least. Worse was to come. I went home to my flat in Bishops Park, determined not to read any of the following morning's reviews. Waking up the next day, there was a knock at the door from a bike messenger bearing a card from Peter Hall.

Inside the card, it said, 'Brian, I don't care what they say, I still believe in you. Yours, Peter.'

I stared at it.

What did they say?

I had no idea, of course. Hall's card sent the imagination firing off in all kinds of hideous directions. God, it was the cruellest card ever, because as anybody who's ever had feedback on a creative endeavour knows, it's not the *good* bit that you concentrate on. And as far as that note went, any expression of belief in me was overshadowed by the word 'still', and even more so by the words 'I don't care what they say'. So overshadowed, in fact, that the good bit might as well not have existed at all. Hall could just as easily have scribbled the words, 'Shite reviews, Bri! Suck it up, sunshine!'

Even so, I decided that I was going to stick to my word and continue to avoid all the reviews. That afternoon we were due to perform a matinee. I made my way to the theatre and, to avoid going in through the stage door and risk encountering those who had not had the foresight to avoid the reviews, I went in through the underground garage and then a series of lifts, making my way to the dressing room unaccosted, until . . .

'Bernard Levin is in the afternoon. Get him. Get Levin. Do you hear me?'

It was Schlesinger. He was screaming at me. It was like one of those horror films where the final girl is trying to escape from the killer, with me as the girl, rattling the door to my dressing room, desperately trying to get in, and Schlesinger the killer, approaching from the other end of the corridor.

'Get him. Get Levin,' I heard as the door finally opened and I made it into my dressing room, slamming the door behind me.

God, what's going on? I thought to myself. I half expected Schlesinger to start hammering on the door demanding to be let in. *Get Levin. Get Levin* – what did 'get Levin' even mean? But thankfully he had taken his temper elsewhere. As I decompressed after what was a frankly baffling encounter, I found my initial confusion turning to irritation and then anger. Yes, the whole thing was a bloody disaster but it was hardly my fault. I'm willing to bet he hadn't gone psycho on Gielgud.

Suitably enraged, I went on stage that night and charged through my Brutus at exactly the pace I would have intended to do it in the first place, were it not for his stupid note, and as a result cut about twenty minutes out of the show. What's more, Bernard Levin gave us a rave review. I had indeed 'got Levin'.

But the rest of the reviews? They absolutely shredded us. 'Gang of youths mug old man on Southbank.' That was one of them. Another was, 'Plot to kill off the best verse speaker in the English language.'

Et tu, critics?

CHAPTER 26

While at the National, I took part in a workshop performance that was attended by none other than Princess Margaret. God, it was rough, and it was painfully evident from her dismissive reaction afterwards that it completely went over her head and that she absolutely hated it.

She was so dismissive, in fact, that she completely pretended not to remember me.

Did I forget to mention that I got touched up by Princess Margaret once? This is going back to 1969, during the stage play of *In Celebration* with Alan Bates and Lindsay. We were at the Royal Court where one night we were informed that Margaret and her husband, Lord Snowdon, were in to see the show that night.

After the show, which happened to coincide with my birthday, we all trooped into Alan Bates's dressing room – the number-one dressing room at the Royal Court. It's now become the TIE, the Theatre in Education department. Back then it was a vast room, replete with a huge bay window, a big rest area and sofa plus an alcove for the dressing table.

So anyway, we – by which I mean the cast and various VIPs, including Princess Madge and Lord Snowdon – were all gathered in this huge dressing room. I had arrived late, having had a quick hair-wash after the show (because that was my habit). I wore a red shirt given to me as a birthday present by Lindsay, and I was slightly damp from my hair-wash but otherwise looked very swish as I was introduced to her Royal Highness in a corner area of the room.

A corner area which was rather shielded from the rest of the room.

'I thought you were so wonderfully hooded,' she said to me. 'I really wanted to know more about you, because you were so hooded in your performance.'

Hooded, I thought.

'I didn't know who you were,' she continued, 'but I *wanted* to know who you were, and as a result I was transfixed by you for the whole evening.' She paused to take a sip from her drink. 'You certainly made a very profound impression on me.'

'Thank you, ma'am, thank you,' I said, with suitable deference. The conversation duly moved on to the fact that it was my birthday and that I'd been given this present by Lindsay Anderson. This shirt. This lovely red shirt.

'Oh yes,' she said admiringly, 'it really *is* a lovely shirt, isn't it? And with that she put a hand to my chest, just at the base of my throat, undid one button and slid her hand inside the shirt.

Christ, I thought, *Princess Margaret is feeling me up. One day I'm going to be writing about this in my memoirs.*

No, that's a lie. I didn't think that. In actual fact, what I thought was this.

Nothing.

I froze. I froze because Princess Margaret was feeling me up. No, *trying* to feel me up. Her hand was inside my shirt and travelling in the direction of my left nipple yet Princess Margaret was just chatting away as though this was something she had done a hundred times before. As though tweaking actors' nipples was all in a day's work for her.

Suddenly, Jimmy Bolam was there. Now, I'm not saying that I wasn't pleased to see Jimmy, but what's a nice way of putting it? He's unpredictable – maybe not the first person you'd go to for a sensible, considered response in a situation like that. It was entirely within his gift to take a bad situation and make it considerably worse.

Sure enough, that's what he did. He said, 'Ooh.'

Oh God, I thought. *Why is Jimmy making that strange sound?* At this point he was standing with his back to the room, creating a barrier between me, Princess Margaret and everybody else. The 'everybody else' don't forget, included Lord Snowdon, her husband.

'Ooh.'

He did it again. And with the whole terrible surreality of the situation threatening to engulf me, I eventually found some semblance of composure and blurted out, 'Oh, ma'am, I have to return to my dressing room. I've left something there, and they start locking up soon . . .'

And with that, I beat a hasty retreat, bowing and scraping and sliding past Jimmy Bolam to head for the door and out to safety.

That was of course a very intimate brush with Royalty, but not my only encounter. In 1966, during *Galileo* at the Lyceum in Edinburgh, we had a Royal Command Performance, which meant that the Queen was in attendance. Tom Fleming, who was playing Galileo, was very nervous and we had a hilarious malfunction when a tape snapped during our version of 'God Save the Queen'. You had to be there, but I will treasure Tom Fleming's reaction, the sound he made, '*Oh*,' for the rest of my days.

I'm pretty ambivalent about my CBE. After all, I'm not, as you may have guessed, the most 'establishment' of people, and so I accepted it for sentimental reasons. My sister, Bette, is a great royalist and I knew she'd be pleased with the association.

On top of that, it's a good day out. You get to visit Buckingham Palace Gardens and meet the Queen – for the second time, in my case – and I found the whole pomp and circumstance of the occasion interesting, especially from a theatrical point of view. As an actor, that sort of stuff is undeniably appealing.

The ambivalence is because the thing I can't bear about the so-called United Kingdom – which hopefully will not be united for much longer – is the fact that we're still such a feudal society. We dress it up, of course, but there's always been a them-and-us mentality in the United Kingdom. Wittingly or unwittingly, we maintain and support a system that exists to put people in their place and keep them there, and it all springs from the notion of the union and the Queen, the royal family and all the pageantry, which at the end of the day, I'm sorry, I happen to think is bollocks.

That's why, for a while, the United States of America seemed like such a free, egalitarian place. The whole idea of 'the American dream' was rooted in the idea that anybody could 'make it'. But not in the UK. Our class system is too embedded, so that those at the top can continue to benefit while those at the bottom are destined to always struggle.

So yes, I'm conflicted, you might say, while also being aware that I'll never be offered a knighthood, especially not since I've attached myself to Scottish independence. Yes, I know they gave one to Sean Connery, so in theory it's not out of the question, but I'd still refuse (sorry, Bette) and at least I'd be in good company if I did. Albert

Finney refused a knighthood. Paul Scofield refused one ('I don't mind if it's a CBE at the end of my name, but I have no ambition to be *Sir* Paul Scofield, thank you very much,' he is reputed to have said), although, of course, if I did turn it down, which I would, my wife Nicole would kill me. I'm sure she'd love to be Lady Cox.

CHAPTER 27

My time at the National Theatre, marked chiefly by artistic frustration, ran parallel to the world of theatre in general, where the concept of 'directors' theatre' was beginning to wear thin with actors for obvious reasons. Not only that, but it had robbed me of my mojo, if by 'mojo' we mean passion, enthusiasm and that spark for work that gets you up in the morning.

Thank God, then, for Peter Gill and his workshops at the Riverside Studios, where my passion for stage acting was reignited. There I joined a troupe of actors including Anna Massey, Antony Sher, Penelope Wilton and Lindsay Duncan, and from the workshops came a series of productions, including *The Changeling*, in which I played De Flores. By the end of my time working on *The Changeling*, I felt, if not quite like a new man, then certainly like a new actor, and yet . . . and yet . . . I still hadn't quite made my mark.

After that, I made a three-part TV adaptation of *Thérèse Raquin*, by Emile Zola. It's a steamy tale of marital dissatisfaction in which the eponymous Thérèse embarks on a sordid affair with one of her husband's friends, Laurent, which has tragic consequences.

Kate Nelligan was Thérèse, Kenneth Cranham played Camille, her cuckolded husband, and I was Laurent, the lover. Back in those days

I tended to play a certain type on TV. I was the guy who turned up in a cop show playing a sort of 'heavy with a heart' character, a lion who needed the thorn plucking from its paw. If you needed a guy just out of prison and trying to go straight? I was your man.

Playing Laurent, therefore, marked something of a welcome departure for me. Meanwhile, as Thérèse, Kate Nelligan was extraordinary. A Canadian actress, Kate did a fair bit of work in film: *Prince of Tides*, *Wolf*, *Frankie and Johnny*, *The Cider House Rules*. But she was better known on TV and especially on stage where she was David Hare's muse for a while.

We were shooting way down in the West Country, rowing a boat on the river Avon. The idea was that I should throw Cranham out of the boat, *mwah-ha-ha*. Kate was directing proceedings as I rowed us to water shallow enough that I could chuck Ken into it without killing him but deep enough that it would look convincing. 'Left oar, right oar, left oar . . .' Kate was saying.

'Listen, if you shout at me about my rowing I shall end up in the reeds,' I replied, and this became a metaphor for our relationship from then on. I called her Eskimo Nell and she called me the Pict, and for our time on the show that was our catchphrase. 'Left oar, right oar . . . we shall end up in the reeds!'

One time we had to do a sex scene. Being a little more risqué than your usual TV drama, *Thérèse Raquin* included a number of such scenes, but this was our first and possibly the most steamy. The director was Simon Langton, and whether through embarrassment or some clever psychological ploy known only to him, he had not mentioned the fact that we would have to take our clothes off. We knew about it when we signed up, of course. But other than those initial discussions the subject had simply not arisen. In rehearsals, I waited for Simon to say, 'Right, you'll have to take your clothes off at this bit,' but he never did, and then, when shooting commenced, I similarly expected him to broach the subject. 'Right, Brian and Kate, tomorrow we'll be shooting the love scene and you'll have to take your clothes off.'

Still nothing. I was thinking, *Well, I'm not going to say it if he's not going to say it.*

Anyway, come the night. Bad turn of phrase, but you know what I mean. In those days we frontloaded with rehearsal for about two weeks or so and then shot quite quickly over a period of days, which did tend to mean that the shoots went on until the early hours of the morning. Sure enough, it was one of those days and it was about 1 a.m. when we eventually got to this scene.

Assembled by the bed, and in the absence of any direction from our leader, I said to Kate, 'Kate, let's just start, see what happens,' and she agreed.

We got into bed. Simon appeared. 'Ah, you have your clothes on.'

They're famed for their powers of observation, are directors.

'Yes, we have,' I told him.

'Well, you're supposed to make love.'

'Yes.'

'Then your clothes should not be on.'

'You didn't tell us. I mean, if you want us to take our clothes off, we'll take our clothes off, but you have to tell us.'

'You're making love. People don't make love with their clothes on.'

'Yes, they do.'

'No, they don't.'

'Yes, they do. Sometimes they do.'

'No, they don't. Not all their clothes anyway. There have to be some clothes missing.'

'Not necessarily.'

'Look, Brian, I don't care what you get up to in your private life. All I care about is Thérèse and Laurent, and Thérèse and Laurent don't have their clothes on.'

I'd known the scene was approaching and so, to gird my loins, so to speak, I'd been swigging from a large bottle of vodka and orange, and whether that had anything to do with my arguments concerning lovemaking and the sartorial aspects thereof, I shall leave you to decide.

Anyway, I began to disrobe until eventually all that covered my modesty was a bed sheet. Kate went somewhere private, returning with a retinue of dressers clustered around her, giving her the look of Ophelia in *Hamlet*. I joined her in the bed. She wore nothing on top, but down below she wore a pair of strange tights which were cut off at the knee.

Next, she began to oversee the arrangement of her monitor. Throughout filming Kate was very Joan Crawford-esque about her monitor; she always liked to know where it was so that she could check everything was okay. And tonight was no different.

Except tonight *was* different, because as I positioned myself on top of her and we waited for Simon to call action, she said, 'Can you check the monitor?'

'Why?'

'Can you just check it?'

'It's here. You can see for yourself.'

'No, no, can *you* look? I don't want to see it. Will you do it for me?' Her legs were up at this stage, her knees on either side of me. Why on earth she should be unwilling to gaze upon this scene in the monitor I could not possibly fathom.

I looked across. Something wasn't quite right. Kate had a large wedge-like shape around her thighs.

'Kate, there's something wrong with your tights.'

Between you and me, I wasn't entirely sure exactly why she was wearing these tights. I could only assume that it was some kind of modesty issue, but courtesy forbade me from asking.

'What do you mean?'

'Well, it looks as though you've got some kind of growth on your leg.'

Which I immediately realized was not exactly the most elegant way to express what I was trying to say. Courteous, I may have been. Diplomatic, not.

'A growth?'

'It's your tights. I think they're sort of rolling back down your thighs.'

Things were getting a bit strange by now. But as we were holding up the shoot and it was 1 a.m. and everybody wanted to go home, Eskimo Nell evidently decided that modesty be damned and so, without warning, she yanked down the infernal tights to remove them completely.

Keywords there being 'without warning'. The suddenness of the motion, not to mention its vigour, caught me by surprise and I had no chance to get myself, and more importantly my private parts, out of the danger zone.

'Ow,' I cried.

God knows what those tights were made of. Some kind of military-strength fabric, bulletproof, even. I don't know. All I know is that all of a sudden my eyes were watering and I was experiencing a hideous, painful sensation in my nether regions. A sensation I can only describe as burning.

'Oh, Brian, I'm so, so sorry,' said Kate, knowing that she had inadvertently caused me pain but unaware of its exact nature because, yes, as it later transpired, the tights had given me a truly unique and memorable friction burn. A friction burn right on the end of my willy.

If getting an end-of-willy burn at 1 a.m. was the worst of that show then it was more than made up for by the fact that I met Kate and, of course, my great friend Alan Rickman.

Alan, who as I'm sure you know, passed in 2016, was one of the sweetest, kindest, nicest and most incredibly smart men I've ever met. Prior to acting he'd been a graphic designer and he brought the considered, laser-like precision of that profession to his work.

Thérèse Raquin was I think his first TV job, and of course he was wonderful in it as he would be in everything throughout his entire career. Later we worked together on the stage, and I'll never forget that he took me to one side one day and said, 'Brian, I really, really think, (beat) if I think about it at all, (beat) that you're being . . . very . . . very . . . well, I would say . . . you're being rather . . . slow in picking up your cues.'

I looked at him in wonderment. 'Alan,' I said, 'do you realize how long it took you to say that? You call me slow. You – *you* are the master. I mean, you're brilliant at it, but you're the master of slow and, quite frankly, I could benefit from you being a little quicker here and there.'

Around this time, I appeared in an episode of *Hammer House of Horror*. This was one of my 'heavy' roles, and because it was 1980 and the trend was for male perms, I was sporting the full Martin Shaw.

My particular episode of *Hammer House of Horror* starred Peter Cushing so, lucky me, I got to work with one of cinema's great gentlemen, a man who could boast of having worked with Laurel and Hardy among many, many others.

'I don't like the word horror,' he told me. He was a vegetarian and always wore gloves. 'I don't even think of them as horror films. To me they are just fantasies.'

In the episode he starred as a sinister pet shop owner. The front of the shop was just your everyday, average pet shop, but at the back were tigers and panthers and it was my job as his just-out-of-jail and newly employed assistant to look after the big cats. They brought in the animals from Chipperfield's Circus: a cougar, a black panther and a tiger.

We were shooting a scene where I feed the animals. My character's in a cubicle with the panther, and I had to approach a large electrical console and activate a lever, at which point sparks were supposed to come shooting out. For safety reasons there was a sheet of glass between me and the panther. I was on one side, with the lever and the sparks, and the panther was on the other, but thanks to the magic of film it looked as though we were in the room together.

As ever when filming these things, there were 'issues'. Firstly, the fact that the sparks were not quite doing what they were supposed to do: either they were a bit wimpy, indoor-firework strength or they were way too strong and I was in danger of getting burnt. No prizes for guessing which of the two options the director, Alan Gibson, preferred. After various tests we managed to find a happy medium whereby Alan was happy and my perm would stay intact.

That, however, wasn't the only problem . . .

'Brian, would you mind if we move the glass?'

'Why do you need to move the glass?' I said, eyeing the panther nervously.

'We're getting a bit of reflection off the glass.'

'But isn't the glass supposed to stop the panther eating me?'

There was laughter. 'Don't worry, Brian,' they scoffed, 'the trainer's here. He'll stop the panther eating you. Either way, you'll only be in there for a matter of moments without the glass protecting you. Don't worry.'

We went again. I did my bit, went over to the console and pulled the lever.

Bang.

Sparks flew everywhere. Sparks went right up the panther's jacksy and the panther went nuts.

It's not everybody who can say that their job allows them this degree of experience, but I'm now able to state with some authority exactly what happens when you shoot special effects up the backside of a panther. To be specific, two things will happen: one, the panther will go berserk. Two, the crew will show a turn of speed hitherto undreamed of. I mean, these guys were fast. I was still standing there, frozen to the spot, my hand on the lever, when I looked around to see that the room was deserted. So much for 'don't worry, the trainer's here. He'll stop the panther eating you.' The only living things left were me, the berserk panther and – thank God for small mercies – the trainer.

'It's all right, it's all right. Very carefully now, slowly release the handle and back away. You'll be fine. You'll be fine.'

The panther was placated. I was neither mauled nor eaten and lived to fight another day. But I learned a very valuable lesson that afternoon. When the crew say, 'Can we move the glass?' You say no. The glass stays.

CHAPTER 28

Jonathan Lynn is a writer-director-producer who co-created *Yes Minister* and directed *Clue*, *Nuns on the Run* and *My Cousin Vinny* among others, but back in 1980 he was the director of the Cambridge Theatre Company, from where he invited me to play the lead in his production of *Macbeth*. The idea was that there should be a tour of England, just a short one, nothing spectacular, followed by a much longer and, as it would turn out, more revelatory spell in India.

We toured England. It was fine. No complaints there. Then we arrived in Bombay (as it then was) just in time for the New Year's celebrations, and my God, it was an eye-opening experience. Living the life I had, I knew poverty, but nothing like on this scale. Wherever we went, hands reached out to us. Any car journey would be interrupted by the amputated stumps of young children thrust through car windows. It was utterly depressing.

Rather foolishly, we arranged to try to see in the new year at the Gate of India, near to Bombay's famous Taj Mahal Hotel, a time when over 2,000 Hindus, Muslims and Sikhs were due to gather there. Our cab pulled up and within seconds we were surrounded by a mob. Our clothes were pawed at and torn. Hands reached into our pockets. The women were groped. Thanks to a group of nearby policemen we were able to make our escape knowing that we were guilty of the sin of presumption. We had taken our welcome for granted.

Macbeth was good, though, at least. The Indian audiences were much more participatory than we were used to, but that was fine. Preferable, even. I'm quite sure that Shakespeare himself would have approved.

Something happened to me while I was there. A very important lesson. My dresser was a young Indian dancer and during the performances she would watch from the wings. One night in the interval I asked her, 'Are you enjoying it?'

'Yes, I think it's wonderful.'

'That's good,' I said.

'I think you're marvellous.'

I tried not to preen. Difficult. Compliments are to an actor as nectar is to a bee. How pleasing that I, a British Shakespearean actor of some repute, had made such an impression on this young—

'There's just one thing, though,' she said.

That brought me up short. Have you ever heard the expression 'shit sandwich' used when giving criticism? You hide a negative comment between two good ones. In this case, it was a less carby version. An open shit sandwich, if you like. It was compliment followed by a . . . well, let's not call it a criticism because it wasn't quite that. It was more of an observation. A spot of feedback.

It was, in fact, a note.

And the note was this: 'I think you want to move.'

'What do you mean, move?'

'Well, you know your speech, the one about the dagger? You speak it beautifully, but it's just that looking at you I know I can feel that you want to move.'

God. She was right. Perhaps it went all the way back to Lindsay and his advice to 'don't just do something, stand there'. Certainly, I had gone down that route as an actor. But perhaps I'd taken it so much to heart that I had inhibited myself physically.

'Well, I'll try something new,' I told her. 'Can you stay in the wings and watch me?'

She agreed, and so every night I would go on and I would begin to physicalize more. Be more open. More expressive.

'Enough?' I would say to her.

'More,' she would reply.

I'd go on, do my thing, come off. 'Well?'

'Yes, it's fantastic,' she would tell me, and then hesitate. 'But do more.'

Again.

'Enough?'

'More.'

Until, by the end of the run, I was literally crawling all over the stage, throwing myself about, and I found it exhilarating – absolutely, totally and utterly liberating. The thing was that Jonathan, the director, had not joined us on tour. Had he been there, who knows what he might have said, and the last thing I want to do is second-guess his reaction. The point is that perhaps I was subconsciously inhibiting myself partly to win his approval. After all, we actors are whores for praise, locked into approbation, capable of killing our offspring in return for validation and living only for applause, both literally and figuratively. I probably only ever met one actor who didn't give a shit and that was Nicol Williamson, but do you know what? I bet he did, deep down. I bet that his pretending not to care was in itself another exercise in the building of self-esteem.

But Jonathan wasn't there. I didn't need his approval or absence thereof. In fact, it was the approval of my sixteen-year-old dresser that I sought and it had opened up a whole new vista for me, because prior to that, I had all the theory I needed in order to bring that physicality to my acting, but for one reason or another I had not been able to put it into practice. That was what she gave me. She gave me the freedom to bring it out.

It wasn't that from then on I did everything in a particularly physical fashion. Just that I now had an access to my physical self.

It was a lesson I never forget. One of the most valuable I have ever been given (and it perhaps goes some way towards explaining my antipathy for directors and their notes, when the best note I've ever had came from a sixteen-year-old).

Later, all of these elements, by which I mean the lessons taught to me by the Indian dancer, by Fulton, Duncan, Lindsay and Michael Elliott, came together in what I consider to be my best – and it's certainly my favourite – performance: *Titus Andronicus*. But that's another story. Titus was some way off yet. Before all that, I had to be the guy who booked you in for a bikini wax.

CHAPTER 29

If you remember the 1980s then you may remember that there was only one gym name to drop and it was Holmes Place. That's where you'd go if you wanted to get toned up and waxed, and that's where I wound up for a short time, wondering what had gone wrong.

What happened was this: the experience of *Macbeth* in India had been superb, but on my return things were not quite gelling. I drifted a little, doing bits of theatre and TV, as well as teaching. I had joined a group of actors for a project that took us to the States where the idea was that we would do five-man Shakespeares. There were five of us in a little van and we drove up the Californian coast. The organiser, a guy called Homer Swander, had been Michael Douglas's professor so we ended up doing a recital at Michael Douglas's home, a huge place in Santa Barbara, the idea being that we would do the show and raise a bit of money for charity.

Douglas was there and clearly slightly embarrassed. He was the same age as us, maybe just a touch older, and I think he felt the pressure of being the host and doing it for his old professor. Nice guy though. At that stage he was quite a big TV star from the *Streets of San Francisco* and had made a name producing movies.

It was also during this period that I was teaching an English class at UCLA on *Othello*. I have a whole thing about Iago infecting Othello that goes right back to my days with Peter Dews, how he would break down the text and how that made me begin to understand the play and its ramifications.

So anyway, I was teaching this class when I looked to my left and sitting there was Eva Marie Saint.

Eva *On the Waterfront* Marie Saint. Eva *North by Northwest* Marie Saint.

Now, this was – well, talk about star-struck. This was me in the presence of a total, total legend – if I had a personal Brian Cox Mount Rushmore, she would be on it.

I couldn't help myself. I stopped. 'I'm terribly sorry, everybody, but I've just recognized one of your classmates, and I'm completely blown away by the fact that here I am giving a lecture and there is Eva Marie Saint sitting there.'

What's more, we actually became friends after that and stayed in touch for a while. We would lose touch, which was sad, but still. Still. Eva Marie Saint.

As well as teaching I dabbled in directing. I had in fact already directed the odd bit, including *The Man with a Flower in His Mouth* by Luigi Pirandello at the Orange Tree Theatre in Richmond and the Edinburgh Festival all the way back in 1973, while in 1982 I found myself directing a production of *I Love My Love* by Fay Weldon at the Orange Tree Theatre.

I Love My Love was an interesting play. It was based on a slot on the topical news show *Nationwide* about husbands and wives doing a swap. Fay Weldon wrote the play, and my friend, Sam Walters, who ran the Orange Tree Theatre in Richmond for many years, asked me to direct it.

Now, you remember the workshop at the National Theatre? The one where Princess Margaret came, didn't like our work and conspicuously failed to remember touching me up many years previously? Well, that workshop featured a lovely actress called Morag Hood who became a friend, and I cast her in *I Love My Love*. I knew Morag and had had a crush on her for many years because when I was a kid she presented youth programmes on Scottish TV, where one of her jobs was to interview the Beatles. After that, she turned her hand to acting and had appeared with Anthony Hopkins in BBC's 1972 version of *War and Peace*. Morag was great in *I Love My Love*, so in 1993, when directing *The Master Builder*, I cast her again – as my wife – and she was great again.

She was a bit of a rehearsal hogger, was Morag. She tended to demand a lot of attention, which would normally have been fine, but on *The Master Builder* I was getting a bit weary. Not only was I trying to direct but I was also playing the lead. Oblivious to my great suffering, Morag would buttonhole me. 'Brian, do you think . . . blah-blah? Brian, what if . . . blah-blah? Brian, I feel . . .'

But I'm nitpicking, because she was a fine, fine actress and a very, very dear friend, and I adored her, right up until the end when uterine cancer got her, way too early at just fifty-nine. She was in a hospice in Hackney when it happened, not long after we had made a film together, *A Shot at Glory* in 2000, a footballing film with Robert Duvall and Michael Keaton. I think it was the last thing she did aside from an episode of *Heartbeat*. Another one gone.

Incidentally, I should mention here that we took *The Master Builder* to London, and to pay for that I did a fish commercial. This is the thing about theatre. You're always borrowing from Peter to pay Paul. Or, in that particular instance, getting paid twenty-five grand for pretending to cook fish and serve it to a beautiful blonde woman in order to transfer an Ibsen play to the West End. Same thing.

Anyway, back to *I Love My Love*, and at the same time as I was doing that, I made a return to the National Theatre, where I was being directed by old friend Peter Gill in Georg Büchner's *Danton's Death*. I'd be rehearsing in Richmond during the day and then clambering aboard my Yamaha 250 and putt-putting across town to the National Theatre for the evening.

One evening I was going through Putney, where it turned out there was some kind of police incident. The cops had stopped traffic, and I was craning my neck to see what they were up to when the guy in front of me, a Morris Minor, stopped suddenly.

Too late I saw him. Too late to do anything but slam right into him, and I somersaulted forward off the bike, a move that any stuntman would have been proud of, flipping gracefully through the air and thinking – I kid you not – that at least Caroline, Alan and Margaret were going to be looked after, because Caroline, ever canny with money, had me insured to the hilt.

And then I landed. I landed in front of the Moggy in a tangle of limbs, none of them broken, thank God, and my head saved from serious trauma by my helmet. Underneath my visor my glasses were skew-whiff, and I could feel something warm and wet running down my face.

'What happened?' I heard myself say.

Hovering above me was a man I recognized, and it took my accident-fogged brain a second or so to work out how I knew him. And then it hit me. It was Mr Snelling, my dentist.

Of course. I was in Putney. I lived nearby. Of all the places to have an accident, it had happened right outside my dentist's practice.

Except there was something wrong with Mr Snelling, I realized. Around his neck was some sort of collar, as though he, too, had suffered a mishap.

'Mr Snelling, what happened to you?' I said.

'What?' he said.

'What happened? What happened to your neck?'

Mr Snelling, of course, didn't recognize me. For a start I was an out-of-context patient; secondly, I was wearing a helmet, plus my face was covered in blood. It turned out that my glasses had broken and cut into my face. That being the worst of my injuries, I could count myself very, very lucky indeed.

'I threw my neck out, doing my job,' replied a clearly perplexed Mr Snelling.

'You've thrown your neck out being a dentist?' I said, muffled behind my visor.

'I'm sorry, do I know you?' he said. Other faces had appeared, peering down at me. One of the policemen. The driver of the Morris Minor. Their mouths were moving and no doubt they were talking but I wasn't listening. I was having my little moment with Mr Snelling.

'Yes, it's me. Brian. Brian Cox.'

And at last I pulled myself into a seating position and took off my helmet – ta-da! – to reveal myself as Mr Snelling's patient, alive and well and his teeth very much intact.

Luckily the bike was fine, too, and I was able to make my way to the theatre. They held curtain-up for me, but in the event I wasn't too late. A nurse saw me in the interval. 'Your blood pressure's through the roof,' she told me.

I said, 'Well, you know, I've just had this accident. That's probably why.'

She said, 'Yes, but I think you should stop.'

'No, I can't stop,' I told her, 'I've only got one more act to do. I tell you what. Come back tomorrow night when I'm feeling better and take the blood pressure again and you'll see that my blood pressure is usually high after one act of *Danton's Death*.'

So she did. She came back and took my blood pressure. 'It's a little down, but it's still high,' she told me.

'Oh, that's the theatre for you,' I said, 'that's the adrenaline. That's what it does.'

I was pleased with *Danton* and Peter had gathered a tremendous company. We were supposed to do another production, but they cancelled that from beneath us. Peter Gill went on to do *Major Barbara* by George Bernard Shaw, and I could have done something in that, but no. I was out. The whole thing just confirmed what I felt about the National Theatre. Which was that it could go fuck itself.

I did a film with Albert Finney, *Pope John Paul II*. I was supposed to play both the younger and the older version of my character and we were filming in Zagreb, only somebody tried to assassinate the real Pope and we weren't allowed to go to Zagreb so everything ground to a halt. I was literally on the plane ready to go when it all stopped. Instead, we went to Gratz and I filmed a bit, but then it transpired that while I'd still play the older version of my character, they were casting somebody else as the younger me, and that was another blow.

Things in my marriage weren't exactly rosy, either. Now, you might say that those trying to maintain a happy marriage should probably not embark upon affairs. Point taken. I'm prepared to admit to another dalliance during *The Changeling*. It didn't help that Caroline and I were doing up a house in Fulham at the time, and as anybody who's ever done up a house will tell you, it registers a ten on the stress-and-marriage-busting scale. I'm not sure if this project was more or less taxing than any other undertaking of the same type, but to give you an idea, we had taken to calling it 'Brian's Folly'.

My absence was a problem. That literal and metaphorical void. Eventually I'd go to therapy to try and understand that side of me, but for the time being, it merely manifested itself as a desire to be alone.

All of which led up to me taking that job at Holmes Place.

It was my first-ever proper job, unless you consider acting a proper job, which, let's face it, nobody does. It was the first time I realized that there were far more actors out of work than there were in work. I had been lucky up till then. Never really unemployed. Yet here, at thirty-seven, I was suddenly out of acting work and booking bikini waxes instead. There was a strange Swedish woman who kept saying to me, 'Have you ever been to one of my parties?'

'No, I don't think so, ma'am. What do you want? A full wax or half a wax?'

It was so weird, but in one sense an instructive experience because I saw more actors on the other side of the counter than I'd ever seen in the theatre. Everybody comes in with a performance. They're all doing their thing. And what I realized sitting behind that desk was that human beings are natural actors, just that they don't realize it. They're acting situations all the time. Put them into an unfamiliar scenario and they go into performance mode; they act out the part of the person they want to be.

Perhaps I might have stayed on reception at Holmes Place (and then Virgin, as it later became), were it not for Patrick McGoohan. You'll recall that *Danger Man* didn't fancy strapping up his leg to play Captain Ahab and so Michael Elliott got on the blower to me, I did

Moby-Dick and put the hiccup of Holmes Place behind me. Not once since then have I ever booked someone in for a bikini wax. Not once.

The funny thing was that my period of relative inactivity coincided with a feeling that I had become a much more rounded actor. I put my lessons into practice for *Moby-Dick* and thus came out of the experience with a renewed vigour, determined to be more 'in the moment' both professionally and privately. The former worked out fine; the latter, not so much. On stage I was more open, less inhibited, not so much the Presbyterian Scot, more so the Roman Catholic Mick. Perhaps it was no coincidence that the work followed, capped by that revival of Eugene O'Neill's *Strange Interlude* at the Duke of York's Theatre, the one with Glenda Jackson.

We've touched on it before, but *Strange Interlude* was O'Neill's attempt to bring together the mediums of the novel and of the theatre. In fact, you could have read a novel in the time it took to perform the play. Five hours, nine acts.

Then again, it does have a lot of ground to cover, detailing the twenty-five-year relationship of Nina Leeds – that was Glenda Jackson – with the three men in her life, me being one of them, Edmund Darrell. The novelistic flourishes of the piece included spoken thoughts or asides throughout, and because of the unusual nature of the performance there was a great deal of discussion as to how we should achieve the various effects. Should the asides be addressed directly to the audience, for example, or merely overheard by them? We chose to make the asides indirect, but this, in turn, produced a comic effect. Further discussion followed as to whether audience laughter would undermine or enhance the effect.

What we discovered, also, was that at the Duke of York's we had to almost encourage British audiences to appreciate the irony. When we transferred to Broadway the following year, 1985, we found that things were the other way around. There, the audiences would be much more given to laughter and we had to exert a far greater control over any comic potential.

However, before travelling to America with *Strange Interlude*, there came another production in the UK, this one at the Royal Court, where Max Stafford-Clark was artistic director (and indeed would stay there until 1996, still the longest-serving artistic director at the Court).

Max had sent me Ron Hutchinson's *Rat in the Skull*, a drama set during the Northern Irish Troubles, suggesting me for the part of Nelson. The play was superb. It was urgent and gritty and bristling with interesting themes, but I was put off by the fact that Nelson had a thirty-five-minute monologue slap-bang in the middle of it.

Thirty-five minutes. A thirty-five-minute monologue.

'This is what you should be doing,' insisted Max, who was to direct. 'This is where you should be at.'

Moby-Dick was a big part. So was *Strange Interlude*. But this – this was a half-hour monologue and it wasn't like I was frightened or anything (well, maybe a bit), just that I needed to give the matter a little thought.

'Well, Max,' I prevaricated, 'I'm not sure, let me think about it.'

In the meantime, he sounded out Bill Paterson, who refused it point-blank on the grounds that he couldn't do the accent. The play is about an RUC detective sergeant's interrogation of a young IRA suspect, hoping to turn him into an informer, so there was rather a lot of Northern Irish accenting involved.

I was furious with Bill about that. I thought, *We're actors, for fuck's sake*. I called up Max and accepted it. Glad I did, too. *Rat in the Skull*, which, like *Strange Interlude*, also transferred to Broadway, ended up being something of a calling card.

Not that it was without its problems. I remember that during a run-through at the Court we assembled downstairs in the stalls where Max was giving us notes. I say 'us'. He gave notes to every member of the cast apart from me.

What's going on? I thought.

In the end the rest of the cast left and I was about to join them when he asked me to stay behind. And then he let me have it. 'Brian,' he said, 'You really find it difficult to be boring. You just have to be constantly interesting.'

'What do you mean?' I said.

'Your performance tonight was indulgent, unspecific, audience-pleasing, generalized crap.'

I knew what he was talking about. I had taken the role and done a schtick.

CHAPTER 30

To explain what I mean about 'doing a schtick' it's worth looking at the example of Sir Ian McKellen.

Now, before I go on to talk about Ian McKellen again, I want to make it absolutely clear that I do not in any way, shape or form *dislike* Ian McKellen. I've worked with him closely, not only on an *X-Men* film we did together, *X2* in 2003, but also on a year-long tour of a double-headed production of *King Lear* and *Richard III* in 1990/1991, as well as various other bits and pieces. And we get along fine. He's a knight of the realm, a very successful, beloved actor. You'd have to say, in fact, that he is arguably the British theatre's greatest ambassador. His commitment to the English stage is far and away superior to mine, and he's always innovative in his ideas about a progressive theatre, a perfect example being his recent commitment to an anti-ageist production of *Hamlet* performed at one of the country's oldest theatres, Windsor Rep. As well as that, he's a sweet man whose politics are beyond reproach, and someone who puts his money where his mouth is.

In short, there are many, many great things about Sir Ian McKellen. It's just that when it comes to acting he and I are of different worlds, different tastes, different traditions. He is a master at what I'd call 'front-foot' acting. It's very effective and offers great clarity for the audience, gives them lots of bang for their buck. But, for me at least, it doesn't quite fulfil what I believe is one of the key functions of acting. It offers no expiation.

What do I mean? I mean that when you see a great performance by, say, Judi Dench, you witness a process of *expiation*, in which actor and audience go on a journey together, working out their hidden issues. It's almost spiritual. Almost religious. And we immediately feel expiated because we see the truth in the situation and in the performance. We see how our life resonates with that of the character. Not the performer. *The character.* And that to me is what is vital about the theatre. That's what makes it one of the great arts. It's that sense of wonderment of being human. The complex nature of it. It's why the people in the vanguard, those like Judi who push the envelope, are so admirable. They're the people who don't let personalities or politics get in the way of deeper thinking; they're all about that process of expiation rather than simply emoting.

Me, I was very good at emoting. But that's not the key thing. The key thing is the finessing of that. Personally, I vacillate. I can be quite emotional in my acting. But equally I need to occasionally pull back from that. I can be physical. At the same time I need to remember the value of stillness.

Now, say what you like about McKellen – and I suppose that I just have – but while his acting is not to my taste, he is, without doubt, incredible at doing what he does. On stage, and especially as a leading actor, you have to rally the troops, you have to keep up the impetus, and he is an absolute master at that. He does it brilliantly. I wouldn't call it a technique, it's more an instinct with him.

While we were maybe a little guarded on the *Richard/Lear* tour, we got on much better in 2003 when we did *X2*. The problem with that show was the demands that it made on the director, Bryan Singer. Bryan had been a fan of mine, having loved my performance in *Manhunter*. I'd met him socially in London a couple of times, and then I did this film, *L.I.E*, which he saw and loved and as a result of that was determined to get me into *X2*.

So I flew to Vancouver, met him again, but this time on a business footing, and he said, 'Brian, are you okay to just hang on, because I've got to deal with the front office and they keep throwing people at me. Geoffrey Rush, people like that.'

Two weeks before shooting started. I still didn't know whether I had the part, but then suddenly it was mine, and I signed on.

The problem with that movie set was that there were a huge number of 'forced calls'. Normally if they've worked you until 1 a.m. you don't have to come in until later the next day. A forced call is when you've worked until the wee small hours but they insist on you turning up early the following day.

They have to pay for the privilege; it costs them dear. Actors, if they're hard-up, might quite like a forced call because they're well compensated. But for the principals of *X2* – Sir Ian McKellen, Patrick Stewart, Hugh Jackman, Halle Berry – money was less important than sleep. They were just pissed off at having to work such crazy hours.

Bryan was working crazy hours, too. I mean, crazy, crazy hours. But it was his show, his gig, all the responsibility lay with him and, as it turned out, one of his responsibilities was to quell a near-rebellion among his leads. I wasn't there and thus it would be improper of me to report what went on, so I can't possibly reveal which of the cast angrily told Bryan, 'You can kiss my black ass.'

Tempers flared, let's put it that way, and for Bryan, things didn't really improve. At one point I went away for a break and told them I was going to Venice. Being Americans they assumed I was going to Venice in LA and waved me off without complaint. But of course it was actually Venice, Italy, where my wife Nicole was performing in a site-specific play about Alma Mahler, *Alma*, that she was doing in an old Armenian refectory in Venice.

Needless to say, they had to recall me. I came back quickly to find that there was a new set. Bryan had a thing about new sets. They always threw him. He needed a day to get a sense of what the set was like.

So anyway I arrived back, appeared on the set – the new set – and Bryan looked at me in my suit and said, 'Oh, I don't like your costume. We need to change the costume.'

The production ground to a halt while they found me a new costume.

I stood there in my new costume, ready at last.

'Where's your assistant?'

My character had an assistant.

'I don't know,' I said.

'Well, your assistant should be here.' The assistant was one of those small, silent roles played by a British actor who lived in Vancouver. They're not all played by British actors who live in Vancouver, but this one was. They spent the early afternoon looking for him and eventually tracked him down to the gym. By this time I'd been there since 9 a.m., having journeyed back from Venice – Venice in Italy.

The guy playing the assistant arrived at 3 p.m. About 5 p.m. we were ready to start filming.

'Are you okay?' said Bryan to me.

'I'm fine, Bryan.'

He looked doubtful. 'You seem tired.'

'No, no, I'm not tired. I'm okay. I really am fine.'

'No, I think you're tired. Right, everybody, it's a wrap. We going to wrap.'

'What?'

Lauren Shuler Donner, who was the producer and – together with her husband Richard, who directed *The Omen* and *Superman* among others – one of the most powerful people in the industry, came hurrying over. 'What's going on?'

'I don't know what happened,' I replied, 'he just decided to wrap. We wrap.'

She threw up her hands and stalked off, but whatever was subsequently said, it wasn't enough. We did indeed wrap for the day.

Bryan actually came to me later with a bottle of gold tequila by way of apology. I realized then that he hadn't had a day off for a hundred days. I mean, a film like that is a huge proposition. In the old days these epics would take forever to make. David Lean would shoot his over a period of eighteen months or so. Nowadays they have to do it in eight to ten weeks. The pressure is absolutely phenomenal.

I was completely sympathetic. I said to him, 'You need to have a break,' and of course he went and told Lauren what I'd said, and in short order she was coming up to me. 'What are you doing telling Bryan that he should have a couple of days off? We've got to get on with the shoot.'

'Well, the poor guy is exhausted,' I told her, 'I was just trying to be kind.'

'Well, don't,' she said, and stalked off (again).

All of which lengthy digressions brings us back to the schtick. As

Playing Macbeth with
Gemma Jones (1980)

With Ian Charleson in
Scotland's Story (1984)

As the first Hannibal Lecktor in *Manhunter* (1986)

As Titus in *Titus Andronicus* (1987)

With Fiona Shaw in *The Taming of the Shrew* (1987)

In *Fashion* with Alun Armstrong (1987)

With my Russian students of the Moscow Art Theatre (1988)

With Harriet Walter in *The Three Sisters* (1988)

With Julie Walters in *Frankie & Johnny in the Clair de Lune* (1989)

With David Bradley and Ian McKellen in *King Lear* (1990)

Deborah Warner and Ian McKellen durin *King Lear* (1990)

With Frances
McDormand and Ken
Loach at the Cannes
Film Festival (1990)

As Solness in Ibsen's *The
Master Builder* (1993)

As William Stryker in *X2: X-Men United* (2003)

Playing Agamemnon in *Troy* (2004)

Nicole and I on our wedding day in Las Vegas (2001)

My brother Charlie (2006)

With Nicole, Billy Connolly and Pamela Stephenson at our vows renewal (2006)

Nicole (2006)

Orson, Nicole and Torin (2009)

My sisters, Bette and May (2014)

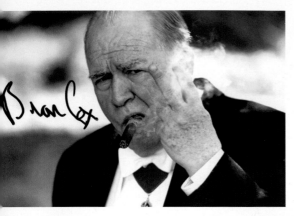

Playing Winston Churchill
(2017)

With Jesse Armstrong, the
writer/creator of *Succession*
(2019)

As Logan Roy in *Succession* (2019)

in doing something that looks very wow but is in fact about as deep as a blackhead. And that was me during the run-through for *Rat in the Skull*. I was doing the schtick. Smoke and mirrors. Front-foot acting. Using volume in place of depth. Power for understanding.

And Max had exposed me. He had called me on it, and he was absolutely right, totally spot on. I was the engine of the play and it's an awfully big job for one young lad on his own, so I had overcompensated. I thought, rather successfully. But no, it was terrible.

I felt panicked, exposed. I went home that night and had a bit of a word with myself. It's at times like that that you have to go back to basics. I realized that I was trying to be dazzling when in fact I should have been rooted. I needed to drill into the material, really hone things.

And I did it simply by reading and thinking and working on the piece until I got it right. I realized that it went back to that moment when Albert Finney told us that we needed to get the rabbit out of the hat and Oliver Cotton had said, 'But how'd we get the rabbit into the hat?' That's what I had done. I had been so busy getting the rabbit out of the hat that I'd forgotten to put it in in the first place.

So where did all of this leave me? It's all very well talking about 'Ian McKellen this' and 'Judi Dench that', but where did I personally stand? On reflection, I think that I spent a long time caught between two traditions of the craft: the classical on the one hand, and the 'kitchen sink' on the other, that style of acting which had been liberating for a generation of working-class actors, Albert Finney and Tom Courtenay among them. In my heart and soul, I knew that if I were to develop as an actor I had to synthesize all its contradictory factors. I needed to take all of this advice and feedback, some of it which seemed on the face of things so conflicting, and bring it all together.

You may remember that during my time at Dundee Rep, the artistic director, John Henderson, would invite us actors to listen to his recordings of classical actors from the past. This was my very first experience of a form of theatrical history.

On one occasion he played us a series of recordings of actors doing Hamlet's 'rogue and peasant slave' speech. John Barrymore's rendition was awful. Self-indulgent, pyrotechnical and ridiculously ponderous. His was the longest version. Second was the young Gielgud, wallowing in poetic profligacy (although in fairness, Gielgud himself would admit in later life that as a young actor he did on occasion allow the verbiage to carry him away). Third was Ernest Milton, very much treading a sub-Gielgudian path. Fourth and by far and away the quickest and to my mind most true, almost three minutes faster than the others, was the absolutely compelling Johnston Forbes-Robertson. In that moment, I had a vision of what classical acting truly was. It was clarity of purpose. It was a case of not getting in the way of the linguistic imperative.

I worked with Vanessa Redgrave, who was playing Volumnia in Ralph Fiennes's film version of *Coriolanus* (I was Menenius on that show – a tremendous film) and her rendering of the text had this gift of allowing the text to do its job without her getting in the way, while at the same time illuminating it in the most true and profound way. She's a bit good is our Vanessa.

For me, it was with Lindsay at the Court that I rooted myself as a 'modern' actor, learning how to harness an inner power, which after my years as a rough diamond needed to be filed down and polished to a degree of refinement. And that's it, really; the story of my career in a nutshell is a story of learning and continuing to learn, of wrestling with a conundrum, of sifting through the available evidence and deciding which offered wisdom to take on board and which to discard.

Ultimately, the answer to the question wrapped up in acting is that there is no answer. But if I were to impart any lesson from within the pages of this book, just one essential nugget of wisdom, then it would be a borrowed one, and it would come, of course, from Shakespeare. *Hamlet*, in fact. 'Speak the speech, I pray you, as I pronounced it to you, trippingly on the tongue. But if you mouth it, as many of your players do, I had as lief the town crier spoke my lines. Nor do not saw the air too much with your hand thus, but use all gently . . .

'Be not too tame neither, but let your own discretion be your tutor. Suit the action to the word, the word to the action, with this special observance that you o'erstep not the modesty of nature. For anything so overdone is from the purpose of playing, whose end, both at the first and now, was and is to hold, as 'twere, the mirror up to nature, to show virtue her own feature, scorn her own image, and the very age and body of the time his form and pressure.'

And that's always meant a lot to me in terms of how I approach my work. How the work is about holding a mirror up to nature, about reflecting the truth, and that's what makes it interesting. That's what makes it an almost spiritual experience, a process, as I say, of expiation. It really is about reflecting back to people how we are. The great writers do that, and the actors who serve it don't get in the way of it, which is what Hamlet is saying: don't get in the way, just allow that transfer of energy from the page to performance. This is the responsibility we have, and we have to do it with great care and attention. And this is why, when I see actors who are self-serving, I think, *No, you're not doing the job.* That, at the end of the day, is the problem I have with a certain type of actor. I don't believe it. I don't believe a word they say. I just want them to get real.

CHAPTER 31

A word here on monologues, for my thirty-five-minute marathon during *Rat in the Skull* was the exact moment that a long-held and deep-seated dislike of monologues began to wane. When, thanks to Max's note, I eventually got into the guts of the piece, I realized that the format allowed for a very precise discipline: storytelling through character revelation.

Of course, there's an awful lot of drama that uses the monologue in some way, shape or form. As we've been talking *Hamlet*, well, there you go: Shakespeare was well aware that the key to pulling it off was the depth of the relationship between player and audience.

However, in most dialogue-based drama, the audience exists in a much more indirect way. As observers of the event they pick up on almost unconscious cues, the different sorts of interplay between the characters. Safe in the darkness, and protected behind the fourth wall of the stage, they are offered a choice of whether to be involved or detached. They can, if they want, perhaps because they've had a hard day at work, or are having relationship problems, or would rather be at home watching Robert Baratheon be gored to death by a boar, completely switch off, glaze over and spend the next couple of hours in a happy daydream.

But can they do that during a monologue? Not so much. Here the role of the audience changes because that fourth wall is broken. It strips them of that layer of security for the simple reason that they, the audience, have become a hidden character in the drama, the people to whom the story is told.

Years after *Rat in the Skull*, I performed the part of the Critic in Conor McPherson's *St. Nicholas*.

Very different to *Rat in the Skull*, *St. Nicholas* concerns a weathered and cynical Irish theatre critic who goes after a beautiful young actress and in so doing strikes a bargain with a band of modern-day vampires. I thought that it was one of the weirdest and coolest things I'd ever read. Indeed, Conor McPherson is an absolutely superb writer, and he and I have worked together several times: *St. Nicholas* in 1997, *Saltwater* in 2000, which was the film version of his play *This Lime Tree Bower*; *Dublin Carol*, also in 2000, a play that we performed first at the Old Vic and then at the newly refurbished Royal Court, and *The Weir* in 2014 at Wyndham's Theatre, London.

As for *St. Nicholas*, it poses the questions, what is truth? What is fantasy and lies? It's a one-man and therefore monologued piece so we only have the critic's word for what goes on. In 1997, when I first performed it, I was at the time becoming increasingly near-sighted, which meant I had to use contact lenses. It's fairly common for actors to use contact lenses in order to see their fellow players, but actually the last thing in the world we want to see is the audience – very distracting. For *St. Nicholas*, however, indeed any one-person play, clarity of vision was required. The audience, remember, is the character.

This obviously can have its downsides. During the run in London (I subsequently did *St. Nicholas* in New York, Los Angeles and then in Dundee, would you believe?) at the Bush Theatre, the audience was on three sides of me. Everything was going okay until I turned to one side and saw somebody I recognized. It was my ex ex-girlfriend, Irina. As if that wasn't off-putting enough, when I turned to the other side I saw somebody else I recognized, another ex, Siri. Because of the arrangement, they were literally sitting opposite one another.

I couldn't believe it. I was thinking, *What on earth are they doing in the same theatre on the same night?* And, as soon as I had that thought, I was scuppered. I lost the piece. I lost my place. My concentration was shot.

And I'm monologuing, remember. There's no space in which to gather your thoughts. No handy pause you can use to pull yourself together.

So I had to stop. 'Ladies and gentlemen, I'm afraid that I shall have to begin again. Due to unforeseen circumstances, I have completely lost my way. Thank you.'

I was about ten minutes into it at the time, so the best thing to do was rewind and take it from the top again, which I did. Approaching the moment when I had dried up was like Becher's Brook at the Grand National. I was thinking, *Am I going to get over this?*

Whoosh. I did.

In 1999 I saw my wife, Nicole, in Vienna in a monologue about the life of the film star Romy Schneider. (I actually had a small part in it, a recorded voice playing the film director Luchino Visconti. Visconti in this recording needed to speak German with a strong Italian accent, so of course some bloke from Dundee was perfect. Nicole, who is German, instructed me in phonetically reciting the lines and we got through it.) At one performance, Nicole was told there was a full house, only to arrive in the wings and find that there were only five people in the auditorium. The loneliness and desolation of that moment collided with her anger, and in a flash the question arose, *Why do I feel so worthless? Should I stop or should I go on? Are these five people worth playing to? Am I being a diva if I even debate this?*

But on she went and within about ten minutes there was a real connection with the audience. Nicole had a revelation: at the beginning of a performance the actor is in a heightened state of being, which creates a high frequency of energy. When there are very few members of the audience the frequency becomes lowered and the actor's alienation becomes acute. At the same time, the audience has a similar experience.

What we both know, what any actor familiar with the form knows, is that it's all about a direct relationship with the audience. You're telling that particular story of those particular individuals, and that's the journey that you embark upon together. It's not a case of 'I'll show you this,' rather it's a case of 'I'll share this with you.'

Not long ago I did a thing with Ian Rankin. A series of soliloquies for the National Theatre of Scotland in which I played Rebus in lockdown, which was streamed. It was great. Really successful. Ian said to me, 'You know, I'd never written direct address before, because it's always frightened me. But it's actually really liberating.'

'It's *absolutely* liberating, Ian,' I told him, 'because once you've done direct address you can go anywhere with it. You can ask the reader to hold on. You can ask the reader to bear with you. You can tell the reader to fuck off. You can do anything in writing terms and do it in theatre terms as well.'

And if the audience is misbehaving? Something I remember seeing was Alec Guinness playing Macbeth way back in the 1960s. Simone Signoret was playing Lady Macbeth. An old lady in the front row was looking at her programme when Guinness was making his entrance. He literally walked over and kicked the programme out of her hand.

Later, I saw him in *The Cocktail Party*. This was when I was at LAMDA and spending time with his son, Matthew. In the opening scene of the second half there were so many people coughing in the auditorium that Alec joined them. There, on stage, he began coughing.

He continued coughing.

He coughed for, God, it must have been up to three minutes until the auditorium was silent, gobsmacked with amazement, thinking, *What's going on here? Are we being reprimanded? Are we witnessing a medical episode? Is this part of the play? What?*

And then he stopped. He stopped, and he looked at his co-star Eileen Atkins and said, 'Now, shall we start?'

Perhaps it was the spirit of Guinness within me when, one night performing *St. Nicholas*, I was beginning the piece by walking along the aisle when I passed a guy on an end seat. I noticed that instead of paying attention he was looking at his programme so I plucked the bloody thing out of his hand and walked on.

Later he made noises about wanting to sue me because I'd embarrassed him needlessly. Knowing that, you can guess where we were at the time. Exactly. New York, where I went on to win the Lucille Lortel off-Broadway award for my work on *St. Nicholas*.

Alec, I'm sure, would have approved.

CHAPTER 32

So, *Rat in the Skull* proved to be an important experience. Something of a learning curve – but then again, every day is a school day – and also a great stepping stone in my career. I won an Olivier award for it, plus we went on to make a film, which was only a TV film, but was okay. Gary Oldman, who had played the policeman on stage, came back for it, but this was in 1987, by which time he'd played Joe Orton in *Prick Up Your Ears* and Sid Vicious in *Sid and Nancy*, enjoying considerable acclaim for both. When it came to revisiting *Rat in the Skull*, he was, how to put it politely? Slightly sniffy about the whole thing. Years later we were in competing Churchill movies, but that's another story.

The thing for me was that *Rat* opened doors, especially in America, where I was this guy who had done *Strange Interlude* and *Rat in the Skull*, a guy who could be commanding and powerful one minute, reticent and mysterious the next, who could go from roar to whisper within the space of a single line of dialogue.

Who better, then, to play cinema's first incarnation of Hannibal Lecktor, a serial killer featured in a bestselling novel by Thomas Harris?

The film was *Manhunter* and would be my US movie debut. It came about because my late friend Brian Dennehy had been due to star in the first American production of *Rat in the Skull*, and so while the show was in New York, he was turning up on a regular basis to get some pointers on the role. He once said to me, 'You were mesmerizing, mesmerizing.' And I replied, 'Yes, and you were memorizing, memorizing.'

Brian had worked with the director Michael Mann on a 1979 film called *The Jericho Mile*, and Michael was tapping him up to play Lecktor in his upcoming *Manhunter*. Brian didn't think he was right for the role but recommended me, bless him.

At this point, Brian wasn't the only person in line for the role. John Lithgow was being considered. Mandy Patinkin was up for it, too. However, the next thing I knew, the legendary casting director Bonnie Timmerman had her name down to see *Rat in the Skull* and she must have liked it, because shortly after that, I was sent some pages of the script and invited to her office to do a tape.

My friend Philip Jackson was playing opposite me in *Rat*. He's great. A lovely man. Still my friend. He agreed to do my off-lines for the audition, and together we went to Bonnie's office where she said to me, 'I don't actually want to see you.'

I looked at Philip, who pulled a face.

'What?' I said.

She said, 'No, I want to see you. I just don't want to *see* you. Can you turn away from the camera? Can I just hear you?'

'You want me to do an audition not looking at the camera . . .?'

'Yes.'

I did the audition. It was the scene where Will Graham, who was eventually played by Bill Petersen, goes to see Lecktor in his prison cell. As Lecktor, I said, 'That's the same atrocious aftershave you wore in court three years ago.'

'Yeah,' said Phil, doing my off-lines, 'I keep getting it for Christmas.'

'Did you get my card?'

'I got it, thank you.'

'And how is Officer Stuart, the one who was first to see my basement?'

'Stuart's fine.'

'Emotional problems, I hear . . . Do you have any problems, Will?'

And so on, and so on, like that. The dialogue was the same as it was in the movie (and, indeed, virtually the same as they used in the remake, *Red Dragon*, with Anthony Hopkins as 'Lecter' – different spelling because of a rights issue, I gather – years later) and I played it just as I played it in the film.

The audition went well.

'So why did you ask me to do it that way, without seeing me?' I asked Bonnie.

'Well,' she said, 'I came to see you in *Rat in the Skull*, but I arrived late and couldn't get my seat, and so I was sitting where I couldn't see you. But I could hear you, and it was your voice that really made me think, *Wow, this is the voice. This is the voice of Hannibal Lecktor*.'

She loved me. She loved the audition. She recommended me to Michael, who saw the tape and that was it, boom, I got the role.

I didn't use an American accent. Tony Hopkins, when he went on to play him in *The Silence of the Lambs*, then *Hannibal*, then *Red Dragon*, always played him with an American accent. The trouble was that while not knowing exactly where Lecktor was supposed to be from, I never really thought of him as American, so I just played him more or less with received pronunciation. Maybe a little hint of Scottish crept in every now and then, but that was about it.

The film opened and had incredible reviews. The *Los Angeles*

Times, in particular, went nuts for it, but then the producer, Dino De Laurentiis, went bust so the film went into escrow, which meant he couldn't get it shown. As a result it became this film that everybody talked about but nobody had seen, until in the end, the British producer Jeremy Thomas got hold of it and released it in the UK, where it finally came out in 1988, perhaps three years after we'd made it, at which point it was already a bit of a cult hit.

Personally, I loved the film. I thought it was great and still think so. The only thing I don't love about it is the synthesiser score. And I'd loved working with Michael. I've never worked with him since, which is a shame, but for me a very common happenstance. There are actors who work with the same director time and again. But, with the notable exception of Michael Elliott, with whom I worked consistently over a period of about fifteen years, I'm not one of them. I've worked with a few writer-directors recurrently. Conor McPherson and David Storey spring to mind. But other than that, I very rarely get asked for a return match. I think I probably piss a lot of them off.

People often ask me about my performance of Hannibal, which differs quite considerably from those that came afterwards. As for other actors' interpretations, I can't say. It's the kind of part that everybody will come at from a different angle. I do it one way, Tony Hopkins approaches it another, Mads Mikkelsen and Gaspard Ulliel choose a third way. The nature of the role lends itself to myriad interpretations, like the great classical roles of Macbeth or Iago.

Where I came from was Peter Manuel, a serial killer who had terrified us all in Scotland when I was a kid. Manuel was born in New York of Portuguese extraction but brought up in Glasgow, and he was very ordinary, almost like Peter Sutcliffe in that way. The other person who influenced me was Ted Bundy, who was the exact opposite: very charismatic but with that sort of politician's charisma. I saw Lecktor as a kind of a cross between those two personalities.

I also played down the psychosis. A chief difference between my portrayal and Tony's was that Tony played him crazy whereas I played him insane, and there's a difference between madness and insanity. Tony was scary and very Grand Guignol, but that wasn't my and Michael Mann's take. Our take was, this guy is an intellectual. He's very, very clever. But if you saw him in the street you wouldn't look twice at him. He wouldn't stand out for his manners or his clothes or some kind of exaggerated charisma. He's just an ordinary-looking, sounding and acting guy who happens to have an absolutely razor-sharp brain.

A few years after I'd done the movie, my agent, Jeremy, called me. He was also Tony Hopkins's agent. He said, 'This script has come in for Tony, but the character is very much like that character you played in that film.'

That was it. That was what he said. 'That character in that film'. He couldn't remember the name.

'Quigley?' tried Jeremy. 'Was he called Quigley?'

This, it turned out – and I'm sure you're way ahead of me here – was *The Silence of the Lambs* directed by Jonathan Demme, with Tony as Lecter.

Anyway, eventually we worked out exactly what he meant, and I must confess to being a bit disappointed, because Thomas Harris had in fact sent me a proof copy of *The Silence of the Lambs* with a note enclosed, saying, 'I hope that one day you'll do this,' and of course I'd loved the book, I'd loved playing Lecter and would have jumped at the chance to be in *The Silence of the Lambs*. When I eventually saw it, I confess to being surprised at just how similar it was to *Manhunter*.

The killer guy is different. As is the agent, of course. But the set-up and structure are almost exactly the same.

Why wasn't I asked back? Well, firstly because Michael had let go of the property and it had all got very complicated, as these things do. Gene Hackman had been approached to direct it, but he jumped ship. Then Jonathan Demme came on board and of course he wanted to be a new broom. He wanted to do everything in a fresh and original way, and he wasn't interested in who had played Hannibal first. Directors are like that. They want their own creations. They want their own people on it.

I wasn't bothered. I mean, I would have liked to do it, but I didn't lose any sleep over not getting it.

Okay, I tell a lie. One thing that did bother me was the money, because of course Tony went on to win the best actor Oscar for it and when you win an Oscar your salary goes whoosh.

After all, I'd been paid $10,000 to do *Manhunter* and he made at least a million from *The Silence of the Lambs*. That kind of disparity is somewhat bewildering. We met during his rehearsals for *King Lear*, before I had done my Lear and around the same time as I had been playing Lektor. 'So, how's it going?' I asked him.

'Oh, it's all right,' he told me, 'it's okay. It's a hard part. Gambon's given me some advice.'

'Oh yes?'

'He says all you have to do is stand in the middle of the stage and do a bit of shaking and shouting.'

'Well,' I said, 'that's a viewpoint.'

And then Tony said a very revealing thing. He told me that the other day he had been talking to the director, David Hare, and mentioned that he'd had an idea. Something he'd like to do in rehearsal.

He'd said, 'I think I'd like to . . .' and David had looked at him and said, 'Oh, you think *that*, do you, Tony?'

The response brought Tony to a sharp stop. It was the most withering put-down. The school prefect telling the first-year kid off, and it was just . . . horrible. There's no other word for it. Hare was being an absolute 'see you next Tuesday' of the highest order. And I thought at the time, and still think, *that* is the state of English theatre. That kind of patrician attitude. A terrible way to behave.

And still, although Tony and I have had some wonderful conversations over the years, the one thing we've never talked about, and no doubt never will, is *The Silence of the Lambs*.

CHAPTER 33

With *Manhunter* I had a calling card, and Hollywood was beckoning. My agent in the States kept saying, 'You've got to come, you've got to come.'

The trouble was that although Lecktor is only on screen for about ten minutes, it's a really significant role, and the couple of bits offered to me afterwards just weren't on that level.

More significant, though, were events on the domestic front. At this point, my son, Alan, was in his mid-teens and had already secured some work as an actor, particularly playing the teenage Dr Watson in *Young Sherlock Holmes*. Margaret, though, was still very young. We'd got her into Cheltenham Ladies' College and I remember being in the car, driving down the A1 and Caroline saying to me, 'I think that when Margaret starts school, we should part.'

'Oh,' I said. And that was it. Our marriage was effectively over.

At that point we were still in the process of doing up the bloody house. Brian's folly. That it was, that it surely was. I didn't particularly want to get a divorce, but Caroline . . . I don't know, I still don't know, and there's been so much water under the bridge, but I think Caroline was very broken down by everything. She didn't want to go to America; she had found out about certain of my 'relationships' in New York, where I must admit I'd gone a little mad for a while, and at the same time her career had not flourished. For a while she'd poured herself into the family finances; indeed, her wheeler-dealing was how we were able to afford to get Margaret into Cheltenham. But once such milestones are achieved, one's attention goes elsewhere. She was disappointed with the way things had turned out, and she was disappointed with me. And I could fully understand that. I'd been so consumed with my career. I'd been unfaithful. Who wants half a husband? Better to have none at all.

Of course, the whole thing put a hole in my bows. Suddenly the idea of going to America to pursue a film career just didn't seem feasible. 'Oh, you should come and strike while the iron's hot,' was the constant refrain, but it's not like any of my ducks would form a nice orderly row. Projects didn't quite pan out. A promising audition turned to shit. All this against a background of my family breaking up.

I moved in with Nigel Terry. I went into therapy to try and find the root of my inclination for absence, and I discovered it was some kind of defence mechanism that I was using to prevent myself from being hurt, something that stemmed from childhood. I seemingly had this feeling of not being loved, and indeed not deserving love.

In the sessions I soon understood that I was indeed loved, but by my sisters, who very much carried me in their hearts. Believe it or not, this all came as a huge surprise, not to mention an enormous relief. As a means of immediate help, though: not so great. After all, they lived where they lived, and I lived where I lived, which, then, in the wake of the divorce, was in a bachelor house with Nigel Terry, whose well-meaning parents caused him such distress. It was nice to know that the love was there. A different matter to experience it up close.

In the meantime, and with thoughts of Hollywood domination seemingly disappearing over the horizon, I went to the RSC.

As you can imagine, I went with a somewhat heavy heart. I had auditioned for the company in the late 1960s, at which point I was politely shown the exit door, regarded as being a touch too pyrotechnic. Ironically, Caroline became a member when we were first married, and so I had to join 'the Stratford widows and widowers', that group of actors, male and female, who were married to members of the company. Caroline at that point chose to start a family rather than go on an American tour with the company, which resulted in the birth of Alan, so of course I was, and always will be, grateful to her for that sacrifice.

Funny, then, that my divorce from her should find me at the door of the RSC. I joined them at their London home in the Barbican where I had initially committed just to playing Danton in *The Danton Affair*, but other offers started to come in from the company: George Bernard Shaw's *Misalliance* to be directed by John Caird. *A Penny for a Song* directed by Howard Davies. Both unique comedies. I was not considered a comic actor at all, but both of those roles – especially *Misalliance*, for which I was nominated for an Olivier – went some way to altering that perception.

To my surprise, the RSC was much more of an ensemble-orientated company than the National Theatre in the late 1970s. Where Peter Hall at the NT had seemed bogged down in politics and as a result wore a somewhat cynical air, Terry Hands, artistic director of the RSC, was a genuine enthusiast. Guiltily, I mused upon the fact that for years I had been rather scathing about the whole Stratford set-up, not to mention their work, but now I sensed that there was a genuine ethos that I was more than happy to embrace.

With *Danton* and the comedies my dance card was well and truly filled until the end of 1986, while as the end of that year approached, I had a meeting with Terry, who invited me to move from the Barbican to Stratford for the 1987 season. To do what? How about the male leads in *Fashion*, *Titus Andronicus* and *The Taming of the Shrew*?

All three sounded brilliant, but typically it was *Titus Andronicus*, a notoriously difficult play, a play that many directors and actors avoid like the plague because of its demands, that was the one for which I felt the most enthusiasm.

We began to think about directors, and my mind went to an impressive review I'd read of a production of *Coriolanus* by a group called the Kick Theatre Company. The founder and director was a young woman, but I couldn't for the life of me remember her name. Thankfully, Terry knew who I meant: Deborah Warner. It turned out that her subsidy for Kick having been cut, she was on the verge of leaving the country to look for work elsewhere. We had a meeting with her the day she was supposed to fly out, and within minutes I knew that she was the right director for *Titus*. She had a direct approach, a tremendous wry wit and none of the theatrical jaundice you tended to encounter elsewhere.

She came on board and right away she saw in me something that I had identified in myself: the fact that I often felt like a fish out of water, knowing that deep down I wasn't conventional in terms of my playing. I wasn't your effete young Englishman or poetic

Welshman, and while at heart I was a pretty uncouth, rough-hewn Scot, it wasn't necessarily a pigeonhole in which I wanted to remain. Perhaps playing Titus would lead to some kind of release, maybe even a harmony of spirit.

As a young man I had always been encouraged to be decorous in my approach, to avoid what is considered bad taste, but as preparations for the production commenced, I found that what Deborah wanted from me was the exact opposite. Slightly reminiscent of my young dresser in India, she encouraged me to go further, further, talking up my clowning, the roots of which lay not only in comedians such as Danny Kaye and Jerry Lewis, but also the Scottish vaudeville tradition, a tradition my late da exposed to me when he would take me, knee-high to a grasshopper, to the Palace Variety Theatre back home, a tradition so brilliantly embodied by Fulton, of course, as well as Duncan Macrae, Stanley Baxter, Alastair Sim, and also the great John Laurie, probably best remembered as Fraser in *Dad's Army,* but who had been one of the leading actors of the post-First World War Shakespeare revival at the Old Vic, playing a myriad of the great roles including Hamlet.

Meanwhile, Terry and I were not done finding directors for the 1987 Stratford season. Next there was *The Taming of the Shrew,* for which the name Jonathan Miller came to mind. I'd seen his 1980 BBC production of *Shrew* starring the formidable John Cleese and the deeply underrated Sarah Badel, so he'd already made an impression on me. Jonathan had never been asked to direct at the RSC. This would be his debut. What's more, the inimitable Fiona Shaw was to be Kate, who I greatly looked forward to working with.

I suddenly became tremendously excited by the prospect of

appearing in these three productions. The balance and contrast of the roles filled me with a great sense of purpose.

But, of course, as my ma would say, 'Brian, it's just a play! It's no real.'

'Yeah, Ma, you're right. They're no real.'

CHAPTER 34

At the RSC, you're doing more than one play at a time, keeping those plates spinning and staying busy, which, as you can well imagine, suited me down to the ground at the time. If anything could keep my mind off my financial woes, the divorce, the all-pervading sense of guilt I felt over Caroline, then it was work. And in 1987, work was *Fashion*, *Titus Andronicus* and *The Taming of the Shrew*.

Fashion was a play by Doug Lucie, who was a tremendously good writer and very popular in the mid-eighties, ushering in a new school of English theatre. The play was a scabrous satire on PR, and I played a character called Paul Cash, who starts the play stark naked, although eventually I switched to wearing underpants.

Why, you ask, did you wear underpants when the script called for full nudity? What happened was that the play began with my character doing a yoga routine. I was doing these workouts in the nude and during one particular performance one of my testicles slipped up inside my body. The floor was constructed of a kind of knobbly rubber, which when I lay on it created a form of suction cup. Which literally sucked at my privates, causing a retreat.

I struggled manfully on, managing to hide the mishap, and back in my dressing room I was able to sort things out with a bit of, let's just say, 'manual manipulation'. The trouble was that it kept happening: during my carefully worked-out yoga routine in the first scene, up it popped, leaving me in agony for most of the rest of the act until I could get into my dressing room and sort myself out.

After that I insisted on wearing underpants, on the basis that doing the performance naked was injurious, but couldn't bring myself to tell anybody why. The writer, Doug, was furious. 'He's supposed to be naked.'

He thought I was being a prude, of course. So if he reads this, then sorry, Doug, but I had my reasons. Well, I had one reason, and on occasion two reasons, when they were inside and they should have been outside.

January 1987 found me rehearsing that and *Titus* simultaneously, which is a very demanding workload because you're being asked to hold two roles in your head at the same time. Like the piano player whose two hands perform different actions so that one tune should play, you have to try and make the one complement the other. Of the two, *Fashion* was great. A modern-day story of odious yuppies dragging society to the right, it proved to be a hit, not just commercially but with critics, too. But *Titus* was the one. *Titus* saved me. After all, this was a year that I got my decree nisi and my best friend, Fulton Mackay, passed away. *Titus* was a silver lining to which I clung tight.

Deborah, my director, was a marvel as I knew she would be, bringing a freshness to the rehearsals. She had a remarkable confidence and yet would never pretend to know more than she did at any given time. She conducted rehearsals in an egalitarian manner, encouraging every cast member to contribute equally. She herself was a constant fountain of ideas and she brought that out in her colleagues, too. I thought of her technique as that of a gardener who treats each scene as if it is its own little allotment, fitting each one together to make a magnificent whole. Her great gift was to allow the play to develop organically. An actor would do something and she'd go with it, forever encouraging a flexibility in the performance that I personally found enormously liberating, not least because it meant that every performance was a new performance, a new experience. It's a philosophy that I have carried forward in all of my stage work. The script may remain the same; the performance doesn't. Deborah attended almost every one and she absolutely encouraged that spontaneity, perhaps to keep herself interested. Who knows? But it worked.

Titus is thought by some to be Shakespeare's first play, and it contains elements of what came later. There's bits of *Richard III* in there. Elements of *Lear* and of *Hamlet*. It became a sampler, almost a template for other plays. It was Shakespeare getting his gun off, trying out all his ideas.

It's also his bloodiest play. Lavinia's raped. She has her hands cut off and then her tongue cut out. It wasn't exactly torture porn, but it was pretty shocking for the stage.

We brought out the violence of the piece in the most audacious of ways, riffing on the comedy inherent in the piece and teetering on ludicrousness but never quite crossing into farce. At one point I had to bring on the heads of my sons encased in crimson-soaked cheesecloth and then throw one of these bloody heads at my brother. The audience was so wrapped up in the moment that at the first matinee we had about seven people carried out by St John Ambulance. At the Barbican, a female audience member walked on stage, saying, 'Help me . . .' and I had to usher her off into the wings. This was not a woman who was deranged or had got lost on her way to Moorgate tube station. It was just the effect that the play was having upon her. This was the power of the theatre. And, yes, you see gore and terror on your TV screen all the time, but this was not a film, not television. It was live and in your face; it was the power of, firstly, the production itself, which is over the top and intense enough anyway, but, secondly, our staging of it, which was deliberately bloody and visceral, combining the comedic elements with the tragedy to create something that was almost on the edge of hysteria.

Theatre pitched at that level can have a strange effect on the audience. You reach a stage where the audience is working out all the stuff that's going on with them individually. Their hopes, their fears. A play like *Titus* touches on all of that, and it can – well, it *did* – have an amazing effect. Audiences were bowled over. Taken to the limit by a process in which we were conduits for Shakespeare testing himself. Instruments for his emerging genius.

That's why it's my favourite performance. I hesitate to say I nailed it, not only because it's a hideous expression but because it's a vainglorious way to think, and yet I think I probably *did* nail it. And the reason I was able to nail it was because I was going through so much stuff myself: the failure of my marriage, my worry for my kids, my financial concerns. I think I was able to bring that out in my Titus. I pushed myself because I felt that I no longer had anything to lose. I was expiating myself up there on the stage.

I was performing *Titus* when I went into rehearsals for *The Taming of the Shrew*. For that, I played opposite Fiona Shaw – a very gifted actress, extremely complicated and thoughtful – as Katherina. It was here at the RSC that her path crossed that of Deborah Warner and the two of them began a creative partnership that included too many productions to list here, the most famous of which was probably Deborah's version of *Richard II* with Fiona in the title role.

Unsurprisingly, Fiona found the part of Katherina problematic and she was quite right to do so. After all, *The Taming of the Shrew* involves Petruchio, my character, tricking Katherina into becoming compliant and obedient. It's about gender politics with female submissiveness played for laughs. And you can't get round that; the play was written in the 1590s, a time when women were little more than dowries, when marriage was about property. In this scenario, Katherina's quandary is about how to survive in such a patrician society, while Shakespeare's salve is to say, 'We know that it's all bullshit, but we have to serve it, so let's find a humorous way of dealing with it, a language that we can share.' True, his perspective is a million miles away from anything that a modern playwright would offer, but it's still the saving grace of the play, and why it should most definitely not be consigned to the history books.

None of which stops people discussing its misogyny. Not now and not even in 1988. One afternoon we were rehearsing a particular bit in which Fiona had a line, just one line. We started to rehearse this scene at about 2 p.m. when she raised a point. 'How has he got the right to talk to me like this?'

Petruchio, she meant, not me. It was the beginning of a discussion that went on, non-stop, for two hours. I mean, I can talk. Jonathan can talk. But Fiona? Wow. I was thinking, *Maybe you shouldn't do the play. Maybe it's not your part.* And that wasn't the first or the last time I had that very same thought. One night I was playing Titus and got a message during the interval asking if I could join Jonathan in the pub when the show was over. So, when Titus was finished and all the blood washed up, I joined Jonathan in the Dirty Duck, only to find that he was in a bit of a state. This by itself wasn't especially surprising. Jonathan's default mode was 'a bit of a state'. He had a long face, figuratively and literally.

'I can't speak,' he told me over drinks, somewhat contradictorily.

'What do you mean?'

'I mean that it's impossible to get through to her. I'm trying to have a rational conversation with her but she has so many ideas. I mean, they're good ideas, but there are so many of them. I can't act them all out.' He looked at me. 'I think I'm going to have to resign.'

'No, Jonathan, you don't have to resign,' I urged. 'We'll get through this. Fiona is going to be great.'

'Oh, I know she's going to be great. It's just that it's so *hard*.'

'Come on, let's try and persevere.'

Jonathan, a confirmed atheist, would sit by Shakespeare's supposed grave in Stratford church, apparently hoping for inspiration, and he must have found some, because we got there in the end, and I know that he loved working with Fiona. He loved her brain, and besides which, Fiona was right. I don't want you to come away with the impression that she was being a pain in the arse. She was right to question. So she should. That, after all, is the point of rehearsal: it's to interrogate the text. Just that it can make things difficult for other members of the cast – members of the cast who, perhaps, don't have such a great problem with the text. For me, doing *Titus* at night and then coming in to rehearse *The Taming of the Shrew* during the day, only to find that so much of rehearsals was being taken up by these issues, was hard work.

But, you know, first-world problems and all that. One way or another, and despite the personal trauma in the background, my time at the RSC was shaping up to be the most professionally contented of my career. I learned so much there that I found myself wanting to pass on my newfound knowledge.

CHAPTER 35

Immediately prior to moving from the Barbican to Stratford with the RSC, I had worked at Balliol College, Oxford, on a summer drama course run by the British American Drama Academy (BADA). There I rekindled a passion for teaching, and although work kept me away from the BADA over the following year, I kept in touch, until one afternoon, BADA's managing director, Tony Branch, called to say that a group from the Moscow Art Theatre, headed by Oleg Efremov, was coming to give a series of masterclasses.

I ended up having lunch with Efremov and we became friends. Through him I became impressed with the Russian attitude towards the craft and began thinking about going to Moscow myself. To cut a long story short, a trip was planned and my first visit to Moscow found me joined by the sports journalist Hugh McIlvanney, who was writing it up for the *Observer* colour supplement, as well as a photographer, Richard Mildenhall.

At Sheremetyevo airport, myself and the two *Observer* blokes were met by a woman who wore an air of weariness that, I would soon discover, was permanent. Her name was Nadia and she would be my interpreter for the next two weeks. The *Observer* blokes were dropped off at the National Hotel. Very nice. I, meanwhile, was ferried to a hotel so grim that Nadia immediately promised to get me moved – the next day.

One quick sleep later, I met the students of the Moscow Art Theatre who would turn out to be a great bunch. For the next two weeks, and with Nadia's help, I taught them Shakespeare, a period at the end of which I took a slightly heavy heart back to the UK where I continued my work at the RSC.

'You must come back soon,' I was told by one of my students, Tania, who knew a little English. I hoped so. Tania was the one who had told me the problem about British actors. How they don't go down to the bottom of their souls. And being in the land of Stanislavski, while not exactly converting me to the ways of 'the method', had certainly reminded me what was valid as an actor, taking me right back to the kind of emotional commitment that had impressed me from the likes of James Dean.

I had just opened *Fashion* when I got the call to come back. I had already declared an interest in directing a full production with the kids and needed no persuasion. I would direct them, language barrier be damned.

But direct them in what?

I hit on the idea of Arthur Miller's *The Crucible*. The play deals with the witch trials in Salem, Massachusetts in 1692, when a group of girls accused community members of witchcraft. Miller had written it as a scathing indictment of the McCarthy witch-hunts of the late 1940s and early 1950s, but I hit upon the idea of treating it as an allegory of Russia's Stalinist past. It was the era of perestroika and glasnost. The time was ripe.

I flew back to Moscow, there to be met by Nadia. The first problem was getting scripts to the group. It turned out that there were no privately owned photocopying machines in Moscow. They were available to non-Russians, but not for the Soviets themselves.

For a time it looked as though we would not be able to begin rehearsals at all, until a miracle took place. One of our group, Masha, had rustled up some typists and, using the old-fashioned carbon-ribbon method, successfully produced ten copies of act one. Rehearsals were on.

Over the next ten days, rehearsals moved forward brilliantly, and at some point it was decided by me in conjunction with Tabakov, the principal, that the students should come to London. When I returned to the UK myself, I went into prep for Chekhov's *Three Sisters*, which was very apt, and the time flew until five months later, when we found ourselves hosting the Russian students. The idea was that they would rehearse *The Crucible* in the mornings, while in the afternoons they would divide into groups and work on Shakespeare scenes. The fact that Shakespeare took them away from rehearsing *The Crucible* was a matter of some concern to them. After all, they were students and studying towards a diploma for which *The Crucible* was key. I reassured them – or at least tried to – that the purpose of the trip was to gain access to other theatrical influences. Besides which, their visit to London would give them something that no diploma ever would: an experience that they would value for the rest of their lives.

And they really were a great group. Jonathan Miller wouldn't believe that the language barrier wasn't a problem. Well, of course it was a 'problem', but it wasn't a 'barrier', and that was the important thing.

'Oh no, we have to understand each other,' he said, 'otherwise we lose the sense.'

But I don't agree. Or at least I didn't agree in that case. I had

formed a bond with my students and there was a deeper understanding, an understanding that went beyond words.

We found ourselves the subject of a great deal of press interest.
Newspaper and radio interviews were being held daily. We worked
towards a grand gala, a special performance called *Raising the Curtain*
which included sections of a musical Brecht piece the students had
devised themselves, called *The Poker Players*, as well as extracts from
Uncle Vanya. British actors rallied and we had onstage support that
night from Ian McKellen, Alan Bates, Prunella Scales, Timothy West,
Jonathan Pryce and Imelda Staunton, among others. Audiences
were treated to sections of Chekhov in both languages, as well as
Shakespeare performed in Russian and the music of Tchaikovsky's
Romeo and Juliet. There were hiccups, but even so, the evening was
perfect, and I'm happy to report that my students were the stars,
particularly in a rousing group finale that I daresay touched the heart
of every member of that audience. Peggy Ashcroft, when she arrived
on stage to give the farewell, was still overcome by it.

At the end of the performance I was grabbed by the kids and
tossed into the air, each throw taking me higher, until after about
the fourth one I gave up hope of ever setting foot on land again. If
it sounds like the ending of a heart-lifting musical, then that's how
it felt.

A week later I was returning to Moscow. Arriving at the airport,
I was struck by how the onset of glasnost had changed things, even
in the relatively short space of time since my first visit. There were
more and more people arriving into the country; I noticed a greater
variety of languages being spoken on the tannoy and a more formal,
and yet conversely less intimidating, process of passing through the
various channels, customs and the like.

Not that I had much time to muse upon such things. We had *The Crucible* to perform. At last. It seemed like a long time since I had first proposed the idea. For someone like me, as in somebody from the UK, the lengthy rehearsal process for *The Crucible* was anathema. I was used to doing things in about six weeks. For the Russians, though, this was all par for the course. They don't rehearse every day; instead they let things percolate over a longer period of time.

And yet, for all our percolation, moving towards the opening night, we had a problem; a major problem. Our sets didn't turn up. As a result the opening was postponed by a month.

However, the delay gave me the opportunity to solve another one of my problems. There is a black character in *The Crucible*, Tituba. The woman we had playing her, Leila, was inexperienced and asked to be removed. I vetoed a somewhat naïve suggestion that another member of the group should black up to play Tituba, but in doing so left myself with a huge problem. Moscow back then was hardly a multiracial melting pot in which to go looking for a black woman – a black woman who also had designs on performing.

It was an American friend of mine, Craig, who came up with the solution. He had seen a girl singing Cole Porter songs at a restaurant. 'This is your Tituba,' he told me. One trip later and we had indeed found our replacement.

With that done, I returned to London. Without going into too many details – I have, after all, gone into the minutiae of the entire *Crucible* adventure in a previous book – there were problems regarding the opening and my availability for it. Deborah Warner had won the 1988 *Evening Standard* drama award for best director for *Titus*, and I was being asked to record an excerpt for the televised award presentation. Then there was the fact that I was playing in

Three Sisters on the very same night that *The Crucible* was due to open in Moscow, a scheduling disaster not of my making but one for which I suffered nonetheless.

In the end, the opening of *The Crucible* was delayed yet again. This time, however, for much longer. Initially due to open in November 1988, curtain-up would now take place in January 1989. This, I worked out, was a full ten months after my first visit to Moscow.

And at last the day came. The feeling on the first night, common to all directors, is one of impotence. Well, that may be true when working to the six-to-eight week schedule, but not when the piece has been gestating for a full eight months. I felt only relief. This was a journey I had embarked upon in a spirit of adventure. I've never been one who enjoyed taking the path of least resistance. I had found myself falling in love with the Russian people and nurturing a deep regard for the country's more egalitarian society. I found myself falling for the students and their irrepressible enthusiasm, their dramatic ethos. But, by God, it had been hard.

The opening was a major event for the city. The wife of the British ambassador was there as well as representatives from other embassies. The place was full of VIPs. At some point during the performance I found myself alone in an office in order to take a phone call, and when the call was over, I sat and had a little cry, a mixture of relief and happiness. I made my way back to the auditorium, entering to find the audience rapt, held firm in a state of tension. At one point, one spectator, one of the many elder stateswomen of Moscow Art Theatre, fully immersed in the action, leapt to her feet and shouted at the stage, a cry of frustration at the injustice of the witch trials. Another followed suit. And another.

Oleg, who was sitting beside me, who had been a constant presence and support throughout the entire process, gripped my arm. 'Look, Brian,' he whispered urgently, 'the play. It's working.'

It was, and when the curtain went down at the close of the drama, the audience erupted. Amid cheers and whistles I was grabbed by the actors and pulled onto the stage. 'This is an historic night for our theatre in Moscow,' said Oleg, 'Now we begin to work with our friends in the West.'

What a hangover I had after the farewell party. But it was worth it. By God it was worth it.

Subsequently, *The Crucible* was admitted into the Moscow Art repertoire, which is an amazing, incredible honour. The fact that I had directed a play that was in the Moscow Art repertoire. Well, they can't take that away from me, as they say.

There were, of course, thoughts of going back and doing it again, but in the end I think I prefer the fact that it lives on in my life and career as a true one-off. I did eventually return to Russia many years later, in 2017, when my daughter Margaret and I made a programme, *Brian Cox's Russia*. It was interesting to see how much Moscow had changed in the intervening period. The cleanliness was something I had noticed. During that period of the late 1980s it had been a much cleaner city. At midnight, workers would appear and tidy up litter left during the day. Not so much any more, it seemed, from the state of the place. I don't suppose you can stop the march of time.

Ostensibly, Margaret and I were there to uncover stories of Scots who had made their home in the Soviet Union, but of course the series also touched on my time at the Moscow Art Theatre, the staging of the gala performance and the production of *The Crucible*.

Wonderfully, I was able to reunite with some of my students from that time, none of whom I had seen for thirty years, which was very touching. Of course, there had been some casualties along the way. Deaths, alcoholism. But it was great to see them, and meeting them again I knew one thing, and that was that I had been right all the way back in 1987. Even though some of them had gone on to get their diploma, and some hadn't, the experience of creating *The Crucible* and their trip to London was something they had treasured ever since – and something they would continue to treasure, always.

CHAPTER 36

To return to the business of acting for a moment. This expiation I'm talking about. For me, a perfect example of this in action occurred in 1990 during that worldwide double-header tour of *Richard III* and *King Lear*. But not at one of the many theatres we visited during that tour. No, this happened somewhere else.

We're getting ahead of ourselves. First, and as backdrop to much of what later took place, there were further developments in my private life. My Russian jaunt had been a tonic in more ways than one. During my time there I'd had a wonderful love affair, which only ended by dint of the fact that you can't realistically conduct a relationship at a distance of 8,000 miles.

There was, however, more romance on the horizon, and it dated back to the night of the gala, *Raising the Curtain*. Unbeknownst to me, in the audience that evening was Irina Brook, the daughter of Peter Brook, the legendary director, as well as being a director in her own right.

I didn't know that then, of course, being far too preoccupied with staging the events of the gala and then subsequently being repeatedly hurled into the air by the students. I was even less aware that Irina, that night . . . what's the expression? . . . 'set her cap at me'.

Next thing, I was being given a magazine award, and she was at the ceremony, picking up an award on behalf of her father; we got talking, things developed, and we fell in love.

I would eventually move in with her; we'd renovate a house together (sucker for punishment, me), and there was even an engagement. But the problem was that Irina was never really happy. She wanted to be an actress, but it wasn't working out for her. She would eventually settle into becoming a rather fine director, but that was to be some years off. In the meantime I would direct something, together with her and her mum, Natasha Parry, *Mrs Warren's Profession*, a George Bernard Shaw piece, at the Orange Tree. Even so, there was – during our relationship at least – a somewhat thwarted aspect to her. A restlessness.

Meanwhile, there were preparations afoot for a new Shakespearean production, again directed by Deborah and with me in the lead. Ambitious plans were formed for a double-header tour, the wheeze being that Richard Eyre would direct *Richard III* starring Ian McKellen as Richard and me as Buckingham, alongside my and Deborah's version of *King Lear*, with me as Lear and McKellen as the Earl of Kent. It was quite a commitment. Twelve months of touring, all told.

As talks for that progressed, I worked on a production of *Frankie and Johnny in the Clair de Lune* by Terence McNally at the Comedy Theatre in London, with Julie Walters the Frankie to my Johnny. This was directed by a great friend of mine, Paul Benedict, who was perhaps best known as an actor. He'd played Guffman in *Waiting for Guffman*, as well as a receptionist in *This Is Spinal Tap*, the fellow who gets called 'a twisted old fruit' by the band's manager, replying, 'I'm just as God made me, sir.'

The way God made Paul was with acromegaly, a disorder that results from excess growth hormone, giving him an oversized jaw and nose. Treatment for it included bolts of radium into his back, which I think ultimately hastened his demise in 2008 of cancer, aged seventy.

Around then I was doing *Hidden Agenda* for Ken Loach. *Hidden Agenda* was set in Northern Ireland and had a great script. Gambon was going to do it, but it all fell apart and so they came to me. The trouble was that at the time I was involved with *Frankie and Johnny* in London, and they needed me in Belfast for *Hidden Agenda*, so what the *Hidden Agenda* people did was to buy the theatre out for a couple of performances so that I could go and film in Northern Ireland. Hopefully I made it worth their while. I certainly enjoyed the experience. Loach was fantastic. An incredible guy, amazingly true to his principles. He's been through hard times financially and always refused to support himself by doing commercials, even though he could easily have done that.

The whole time all this was going on, *Lear* was in the background, until mid-March 1990, when I at last found myself in first rehearsal. I arrived in a somewhat conflicted state of mind, because for the first time in ages I was settled domestically, living with Irina. Why would I want to embark on a year-long tour when that was the case? My nerves weren't exactly settled when I arrived at the National to find that Ian McKellen had laid on champagne and orange juice and Richard Eyre was reassuring us that we had nothing to be scared of, since this was only the biggest venture that the National Theatre had ever been involved with.

Still, we had assembled an incredible cast that included Susan Engel, Clare Higgins, Mark Strong, Eve Matheson, Stephen Marchant, David Bradley, Peter Geoffrey and my old friend Sam Beazley.

Sam had only recently returned to acting after a near fifty-year gap. He had owned a very prosperous antique business in the interim, Portmerion Antiques. He and I walked to the first read-through of *Lear*. He told me the last Shakespeare read-through he'd attended was in 1935, *Romeo and Juliet*, where Olivier and Gielgud had alternated Romeo and Mercutio. Sam was playing Paris. He then went on to say that his reviews weren't kind. 'The young actor playing Paris was woefully inadequate.'

'I was only nineteen, for God's sake, and this was virtually my first grown-up professional role. I then had to go on tour around the UK. I became very close to Edith Evans, who was amazingly kind to me. All was well until we got to Glasgow, and Edith persuaded me to go ice skating. And blow me, she fell and broke her ankle. Well, she was a Christian Scientist, which meant she wouldn't accept conventional treatment. The company was in an uproar and I became the scapegoat. As an actor I stumbled about a bit for a few years. Then I pursued my love of decoration and antiques, became an antiques dealer. Eventually, after nearly fifty years, I decided to return to acting. Acting was never really my idea – it was my mother's. She started me off as a child actor. But you know something, it's a very hard thing to get out of your system. I think what I missed and what I yearned for during all that time was . . . community.'

Sam had indeed refound his community, and remained there till the end of his life.

He died in 2017, aged a hundred and one.

To help me prepare for Lear, I had watched a TV broadcast of the film *King Lear* directed by Irina's father and starring Paul Scofield. What struck me was the lack of humour in Peter's version (not that I told Irina, mind you), so, just as we had done with *Titus*, Deborah and I began teasing out some of the more comedic aspects of the piece, reasoning that Lear is something of a curmudgeon, and a curmudgeon can be funny. I had noticed that perfectly healthy older people, when checking in at airports, would be offered wheelchair assistance. As soon as they got into the wheelchair, they would immediately assume a more decrepit state. We decided to play him in a wheelchair to enhance the effect. An old man shaking his fist at clouds.

It was during the rehearsals for Lear that I attended the memorial service for Ian Charleson, the *Chariots of Fire* actor who died terribly early of AIDS complications. He and I went back to LAMDA where dear old Norman Ayrton, who was the principal, had told me, 'You know, Brian, you should come and teach here.'

On the one hand, I was only twenty-four at the time. But on the other, I had been working five years and built up quite a reputation within the repertory system. Why not have a crack? In my group of students was Harriet Walter, now Dame Harriet Walter. A brilliant actress – well she would be, she had a good teacher – who has done so much great work over the years, not least playing Logan's English ex-wife in *Succession*.

I also had Ian, who was such a gifted lad, so full of energy. I ended up directing him in an in-house production of *In Celebration*, in which he played the part that I had played all those years ago. He would be moving all of the time, and wouldn't rein it back, until eventually I tied him to a chair and said, 'Now try doing it without moving.'

He was a bit annoyed about that, but it worked, and years later, he admitted, 'You know that thing you did to me, when you tied me to a chair?'

'Aye, Ian, I do.'

'Well, it taught me so much about containment. About just being still.'

It's very possible that I went on to tell him my Lindsay Anderson story at that stage. Very possible indeed.

The last time I saw Ian properly was in 1984, when we did an episode of *Scotland's Story* together. This was some years before he was officially diagnosed with HIV, but I remember that he didn't look well and needed help with his lines. He passed in January 1990, just forty, but I think he made a good death. At the time, Daniel Day Lewis had crashed out of *Hamlet* at the National, having had some kind of breakdown literally mid-performance. In the aftermath, Dan claimed that he'd seen the ghost of his dead father on stage, although he later said it was more of a metaphorical sighting than a literal one. Either way, it left Richard Eyre without a Dane and so he went to Ian.

Initially, Ian was cross not to have been asked in the first place, but I'd seen his first Hamlet, just after he left LAMDA, and knew he'd be remarkable in the role; besides which, I myself have a history of being offered parts first shopped elsewhere. It's the nature of the beast. I was unable to see him do it in the end, but he was, by all accounts, superb. One of the best Hamlets ever, apparently. The fact that he performed in the knowledge of his own impending death must have had a considerable effect on Hamlet's constant meditations on death. It gives me the shivers just to think of it. Only days after the production ended, Ian was dead.

As well as attending Ian's memorial – as you can imagine, I have been to many of them over the years – I had two days off tour rehearsals in order to attend Cannes on *Hidden Agenda* business.

It was quite an extraordinary trip, marked by the fact that during a press conference, the Northern Irish *Evening Standard* film critic, Alexander Walker, launched an incredible attack on Ken, calling the film pro-IRA. Either way, the picture went on to win the festival's Jury Prize. I, meanwhile, celebrated my forty-fourth birthday with a cake, looking at wheelchairs. The wheelchair in *Lear* was swiftly becoming to us what the fake shark was to Spielberg in *Jaws*. It kept breaking, and it took a long time to get right. Why? It got a lot of punishment, did that wheelchair. In the eternal battle of Cox-as-Lear vs wheelchair there can be only one winner . . .

Of the two productions, *Richard* was the more sumptuous. Between them, Richard Eyre, McKellen and designer Bob Crowley had cooked up a grand visual spectacle, creating a kind of fascistic 1930s England on stage. People loved it, and they later used the same ruse for the film, also starring McKellen. *King Lear*, on the other hand, was a more bare-bones production. It was much more 'me' in other words, which possibly exemplifies the difference between McKellen and me. His work comes from a different source. He's one tradition, I'm another. Still, the marked difference between the two styles had us wondering which of the two the audiences would prefer.

The first night of *Richard III* was 26th July. We did *Lear* the following night. A short while ago, I would have said that the gala night with the Russian students, or perhaps the opening of *The Crucible*, were career highs never to be bettered. Yet here came another one, that opening night of *Lear*. Needless to say, I had taken note of the reception to *Richard* and was pleased to hear that our applause for *Lear* on the second night was just as tumultuous. Happy as Larry about that, I took myself, exhausted – as I would be every single night of *Lear*, utterly bloody wrecked – to my dressing room and received first Deborah, who bounded inside to hug me, and then my family. A Kodak moment if ever there was one.

The London end of things drew to a close and off we jetted to Tokyo, already feeling the first fingers of exhaustion. During a matinee I became distracted by a member of the audience who was obviously upset by the play and as a result sat flapping her hand, as though to somehow ward off the whole experience. It put me off my stride, to say the least, and my performance shifted slightly as a result. Coming off, I was shaken, upset and angry. My co-star, David Bradley, told me that he thought exhaustion was getting the better of me and suggested I should try to get out of Buckingham in *Richard*. After all, I didn't like the whole fascist concept (and when asked about it in an interview had made my feelings clear in a less than diplomatic manner); I didn't especially like the character, and I thought it was having a detrimental effect on my Lear.

Nevertheless, we soldiered on. Arriving back in the UK, I spent time with Irina, where the cracks were beginning to show. Meanwhile I told Richard and Ian that I wanted to be released from *Richard III* in the new year. Both were broadly sympathetic in that 'we want to be seen as being sympathetic, but . . .' kind of way. However, knowing this escape pod existed levelled me out somewhat. Plus I had a course of acupuncture which helped make me feel much calmer and more able to cope.

And then Irina and I decided on what I thought was a trial separation. Has there *ever* been a trial separation that's worked out well? I'm guessing not. But despite the writing being pretty much on the wall, for a brief moment we entered into it in the right spirit. But of course I was delusional.

A little later the tour arrived in Leeds, where Irina sent me a note calling time on the relationship – and that was pretty much that. Water under the bridge now, of course. Still, it was painful at the time.

We arrived in Belfast. Next, Hamburg, then Madrid, and then Paris, where we celebrated the resignation of Margaret Thatcher. Then Cork, then Cairo, where we visited the Pyramids.

Over the Christmas break it was announced that Ian had been knighted, although he had to weather a bit of controversy over that, with various people saying that he should have refused on principle. My talk of being released from *Richard III* came to nothing. Well, I made it come to nothing. I realized the real source of my discontent was the impending and final disintegration of my relationship with Irina. I made a public apology to the company for my state of discontent. I told them that I withdrew my request to be released from *Richard*. I would continue till the end of the run.

And then we reached Broadmoor. And here, really, is the point of this story. It was the middle of January, 1991, and I was in something of a state at the time. My private life was in tatters (again) and I was drained from playing both Lear and Buckingham. Just as the obsessive folly of Captain Ahab was gruelling. Just as the insanity of Titus was exhausting. So the madness of Lear was shattering.

They'd broached the subject thus. 'Brian, we're going to Broadway.'

'I haven't made any decision to go to Broadway,' I had replied tartly.

'But you did,' they said.

'No I didn't. I did nothing of the sort. I'm against the idea. I don't physically want to go and I never agreed.'

'Wait,' they said, 'did you say Broadway?'

'Well, didn't *you* say Broadway?'

'No, not Broadway. Broadmoor.'

And me being me, I liked that idea a lot.

It turned out that there was a wonderful man, Murray Cox, who had been the consultant psychotherapist at Broadmoor since 1970, and would be until his death in 2011. It was he who was responsible for inviting *King Lear* to Broadmoor, while he later worked with Mark Rylance to bring a series of RSC plays to the prison.

It wasn't the full bells-and-whistles performance of *Lear*. We did it in our own clothes, for instance. That didn't stop there being several momentous aspects to it. The fact that we were doing it in Broadmoor made it quite extraordinary, for a start. Also, I was taken aback by the fact that whenever a sword was drawn during the play, every member of the audience would look down, and then when the sword was away again they would look up.

There's a moment in the play where I had the line, 'Is there any cause in nature for these hard hearts?' and there was a young woman sitting in the front row who suddenly moaned in – what? Pain? Recognition? And let out the words, 'No cause, no cause . . .'

I later discovered that she rarely spoke, and she was inside for attacking her sister. There physically, actually in the flesh, was that process of guilt being worked out within her. Yes, that word again. Expiation.

She wasn't the only one who got something out of it. This was no group of bored schoolkids, forced to submit to a bit of culture or face the consequences. These guys, men and women, the inmates of a high-security psychiatric prison, came of their own free will; they came in a spirit of *why not*? And they allowed themselves to become totally involved. They loved Lear's bluntness, his directness. They especially got off on the interplay between Lear and the Fool.

Their response – total immersion, incredible, unexpected appreciation – reminded me that they, the audience, are why we do what we do. It's easy as an actor to get too wrapped up in yourself and your own problems, and certainly every production has its fair share of hurdles, *Lear* more than others, I daresay. But that experience forced me to confront the fact that such considerations were – or at least should be – secondary to the job of meeting and exceeding the expectations of the audience, of taking them on a journey whose primary purpose is entertainment, but entertainment with a broad remit: laughter, tears, escape. Where else but Broadmoor could that process be enacted so vividly?

When I later went back there with *The Master Builder* another extraordinary thing happened. The play features twin boys who die, and blow me down, but there were twins in the audience who had killed their mother. It's incredible moments like that that make the job worthwhile, they really do. They are the times you see yourself as an instrument. It's things just . . . happening. This is why I bang on about children being the best actors. Because it's all instinct with them. They're not overthinking it, preoccupied with some phoney idea of 'their process'. They just are. Theatre, eh? Fucking hell.

CHAPTER 37

In the mid-1990s, I made a decision. A decision that would open a new chapter of my life, the roots of which lay at the beginning of my career but really began to take shape in the early part of that decade, for it was while we were still on the *King Lear* jaunt that Ian McKellen gave me a script written by his then boyfriend, Sean Mathias. He literally threw it onto my lap while on the bus.

'Sean asked me to pass this to you,' he sniffed.

'Me?'

'Yes, you. He wants you to play this part. I don't know why he wants you to play the part, because I think I'd be very good in this part, but anyway, he'd like you for it.'

The piece was *The Lost Language of Cranes* and I played a university professor who comes out as gay. The BBC Two film, when it came out, turned out to be one of New York mayor Ed Koch's favourites. He was gay and it had struck a chord with him. It struck a chord with quite a few people, actually. For ages afterwards I would be upgraded on aeroplanes; it was critically well received here and abroad, and I was nominated for a BAFTA. (Didn't get it, though. John Thaw won for *Inspector Morse* that year.)

Then, in 1991, I did a TV thing, *The Cloning of Joanna May*, in which I played a mad millionaire who clones his ex-wife, played by Patricia Hodge, who I knew from LAMDA. It was another Fay Weldon piece, and very good it was too. Way ahead of its time. What's more it reunited me with the director, Philip Saville, who was a friend, and who was by then a big rave in British TV, having made yet another Fay Weldon project, *The Life and Loves of a She-Devil* a couple of years previously.

Philip, who passed on in 2016 at the grand old age of eighty-six, had begun his career with the first-ever television version of *Hamlet*, starring Christopher Plummer as Hamlet, Michael Caine as Horatio, Robert Shaw as Claudius and Donald Sutherland playing Fortinbras. He had an amazing visual sense, and we called him 'the Barber' (as in, 'the Barber of Saville').

Saville and I first met way back in 1975 when we made a TV show of Graham Greene short stories under the umbrella title *Shades of Greene*. The reason I mention this is because it represents what I suppose you might say is yet another of my many brushes with royalty.

Why? you ask. I'll tell you. The particular episode I was in, *The Blue Film*, involved the making of a porno movie. It was pretty risqué stuff, but what makes it even more noteworthy in retrospect – and here comes the royal connection – is the fact that the actress in the scene was a young Koo Stark.

(Those of a certain age will, of course, remember exactly who Koo Stark was and thus I have no need to ruin this pay-off by explaining it. If you haven't heard of Koo Stark, there's always Google.)

Going back to *The Cloning of Joanna May*, and it was on this set that I met Siri Neal, who at the time was eighteen, a full twenty-six years younger than I was. Siri had a strong female energy. She was quirky and unexpected, which made life interesting. We started seeing each other. But she was young, and there was no getting around that. It was a constant sticking point with me. A fact that kept me awake at nights until one evening, filming in Paris, I called her and during a long, tear-stained phone conversation, called it all off on the grounds of the huge age gap.

Then I went and had a lie down, thought about it, changed my mind, and would end up being with Siri for the next five years. She was twenty-four when we split, and I'm pleased to say it was amicable and that we're still friendly, and I have to say she taught me a lot. As did Caroline. As did Irina. I truly believe that these things happen for a reason, and that reason was Nicole.

Siri's legacy to me was her Uncle Jonnie. Jonnie had been living with his wife in Thailand. But they had broken up. One winter night he turned up at our door in Camden, totally bereft. Our house in Camden was a place I'd bought in 1990, and then, after a stay with my friend Brian Dennehy in Santa Fe, New Mexico, decided to convert into an adobe-style dwelling. Possibly I have the only adobe-style house in Camden, maybe the whole of London.

Anyway, when Siri left, I was left with Jonnie, who turned out to be an eccentric surprise. He had walked the walk and very much talked the talk. It could sometimes be an annoying talk and a mildly irritating walk, but he had a very good heart and great compassion. He came to be my assistant, taking care of my house in Camden, as I work-commuted between London and LA.

It was around this time that I also took up the late-night 'beverage' of cannabis.

In the 1960s and 1970s, really until I was fifty, I had very little respect for the beverage. From my chaotic childhood had come a need to keep body and soul together, and the hippy climate of the

1960s was too heady for me. I needed structure and continuity. I needed family. I had no time for such indulgences. I wasn't even a smoker. And I was ambitious. But approaching fifty, and with a few broken relationships behind me, I was open to finding a way to switch off and relax at the end of an incident-ridden day. The answer was spliffs. These days I now have a full New York State medical marijuana card so I am an official legal user.

While on the subject of assistants, in the last thirty or so years, I have been exceedingly lucky in the people I've worked with, managing my career. Of course, my long-time British agents Jeremy Conway and Nicki van Gelder, my manager Matthew Lesher. My US agent Sarah Fargo. My secretary Vanessa Green. But also my incredible and long-suffering assistants: the over-boisterous Jonnie, Miss Sensibility 'Ren' Knerr, my sweet Ozzie, whose organizational skills were paramount. Constant Cory, unwavering in his consistency and commitment, still in recovery from the surprising arrival of twin daughters. And finally the dearest Mickey Abbate, a hugely gifted writer with an equally huge caring heart. Mickey nursed me through the toughest theatrical experience ever, *The Great Society*. But more of that anon. I've had a helluva career. But for these latter years, I simply couldn't have achieved what I've achieved without the help of these magnificent enablers.

But back to our story, where after *The Cloning of Joanna May* came my TV Waterloo. The show that made me run for the hills. The one that hastened the decision. I was about to make the acquaintance of a protozoan parasite . . .

CHAPTER 38

Sharpe, as you may recall, was a series of TV films, usually three per season, based on the novels of Bernard Cornwell, in which Sean Bean starred as the titular Napoleonic soldier. I played Major Michael Hogan, one of Sharpe's spymasters, a role that, in theory, should have carried me almost all of the way through the series' entire run, right up to 2010.

We were to be filming in the Ukraine, and once there – a twenty-four-hour journey, if you please – the misery began almost immediately.

What were the problems? For a start, you had a bunch of film-makers from the UK, way out of their comfort zones in the former Soviet Union, working with Russian co-producers who cut corners by underpaying the local crew. On top of that, you had a horrible, run-down location, far too close to the fallout of Chernobyl for comfort and showing signs of having been severely affected; you had abysmal facilities, nothing like the standard we were used to at home; you had terrible, *terrible* food; you had a director who was either drunk or hung-over the whole time; and, worst of all, you had everybody struck down with illness.

Have you heard of a microbe called giardia? I hadn't. This is the

protozoan parasite I'm talking about. Sometimes called 'hiker's diar-
rhoea' or 'beaver fever'. Or, as I'm now prone to think of it, Sharpe's
Shits. You get it from water, either drinking it or swimming in it,
and we got it on that shoot; almost every member of the cast and
crew was at some point struck down with symptoms that included
stomach cramps and the dreaded squits. John Tams got so sick and
so thin that we joked of trying to fax him back to England. It was
ever-present throughout the three months we were there, a constant
queue for the toilets was its ongoing legacy. The Russians had been
suggesting that we had enemas to rid ourselves of it, but everybody
had been refusing, not really sure what they were trying to get at,
until it struck me what they meant: because the microbe was water-
based, you could flush it out. So I did. I had the enema, and they
flushed it out of me.

The local crew were terrible with the animals. They used tripwires
so the animals would fall, until we put a stop to it. I was lucky, I had
a wonderful horse, but I could see that none of the animals were
getting properly treated. At one point, the guy who was in charge
actually punched my horse and I went ballistic. I nearly went for
him. 'Don't you ever do that to horses.'

'I understand horses,' he told me, absolutely unrepentant, 'you
don't understand horses. I know—'

'I know that you have to treat horses with respect,' I bawled at
him, giving him the full Dundee, the fucker.

Meanwhile, our director, Jimmy Goddard, was downing vodka
slammers. Our producer, Muir Sutherland, tried to cheer us up by
bringing us bottles of wine, but it wasn't wine we needed, it was
decent food and medicine.

I felt like the elder statesman of the group, watching in wonderment as things spiralled out of control, occasionally doing my best to try and intervene and get things, well, if not back on track, then at least achieved with the minimum of casualties. Things were getting baggy on the safety front. In one fight scene – and you can actually see this in the first episode – Nolan Hemmings, who was David Hemmings's son, stabbed an extra with his sword and it went in, not shallow. Another member of the cast, Gavan O'Herlihy, came off his horse and fractured his arm.

At this stage, the part of Sharpe was played by Paul McGann. 'Wait a minute, Brian,' you say. 'You've just told us that Sean Bean played Sharpe. I distinctly remember Sean Bean on the cover of the *Radio Times*.' Exactly, and that's because we were in Odessa when some of the cast and crew began playing a game of football on a sort of tarmacadam pitch that was very new and as a result still sticky. At one stage our producer, Muir, challenged Paul; Paul tried to evade the tackle by going one way, but his legs stuck in the sticky tarmac and his cruciate ligament tore.

He was laid up for days but managed to pull himself out of bed and continued filming for a good few weeks, until a scene in which Jimmy Goddard made him clamber up a slope covered in stones and it finished him off. McGann was out.

As a result the production was thrown into even deeper turmoil. The idea was that we were there shooting three episodes, but right off the bat, one of them, *Sharpe's Gold*, had to be canned. They called a hiatus and we went home to regroup, all of us knowing that the pain was not yet over since we were contractually obliged to return. In the break, Jimmy Goddard was replaced. We also got a proper stuntman, Greg Powell, who shook his head in disbelief at the conditions that we'd been working under.

The part of Sharpe was recast for Sean Bean, at which point we all had to return and film the whole bloody thing again, only this time with Sean and a new director, the one saving grace being that, while it was still horrible, it was not quite as horrible as before because we were a little more prepared for the combat conditions in the Ukraine.

The two films were eventually made, and the series proved a success. They wanted me back for subsequent seasons, and while I didn't *literally* tell them to fuck off, in the same way that the shoot had *literally* been a shitfest, or that shit had *literally* hit the fan, I certainly did so metaphorically.

I actually liked the part. I just wasn't prepared to put up with the conditions. Those who were asking me for years afterwards, 'When is Major Hogan coming back?' were told, 'Never. He's fucking never coming back.'

By now, I had film projects on the horizon and I was on the verge of making my big decision, because I could see the way the wind was blowing with TV. Good projects like *The Cloning of Joanna May* were getting few and far between. I did a thing called *Grushko*, which we filmed in St Petersburg – then still called Leningrad – and where I was joined by Margaret for a while. She fell in love with St Petersburg and ultimately went to university there, so that was a pretty great experience. I did an episode of *Morse*. On stage I directed Ibsen's *The Master Builder*, which I did because I saw so much of Siri in the character of Hilda Wangel, the young woman who brings about the master builder's death.

Not long after that, I did the film which, perhaps more than any of them, proved the catalyst for the decision, and that was *Iron Will*, a Disney film about a kid who joins a cross-country dogsled race, which we filmed in Minnesota.

Of course, the only thing anybody wants to know about that job was the fact that it also starred Kevin Spacey who is, in my opinion, a great talent, but a stupid, stupid man. As an actor he was good. A little bit flashy at times. A little bit glib. But the trouble was that he was gay and would never own up to it. I mean, even in 1994 when we made *Iron Will*, this was known; it was an open secret. As was the fact that he could be somewhat predatory. You could see that it was just a habit with him. There was a party in my house, a couple of young guys there. I saw him home in on them. It was almost as though he felt like he had to hit on somebody, and that the evening was a washout if he didn't. As to why he hid his homosexuality from the public for so long, that's anyone's guess. Perhaps he wanted to retain his mystery; after all I have often felt that actors, when they come out, lose a certain mystique. The other big mistake he made was to come out at the same time as he was being accused of sexual misconduct, which was not the best thing to do and lost him a lot of support from the gay community.

Still, though, the film was okay and the experience of making it was great. I loved Minnesota, the people are the nicest; they have the best hearts. When they talk to you in that *Fargo* voice, they sound like friendly reindeer. 'So, do you like Minnesota? Oh, it's so great to have a film crew here, it's very good for the town.' Siri and I went cross-country skiing: she took to it like a duck to water; I was terrible.

Mainly, though, the film marked my reintroduction to American moviemaking after the stuttering false start of *Manhunter*. I moved off it and straight on to a brace of big pictures: *Rob Roy* and *Braveheart*.

Braveheart is the Mel Gibson film in which he plays William Wallace. Funnily enough, I had played Wallace all the way back in the 1970s in a thing called *Churchill's People*, which I thought was a pretty good adaptation. I read this new script and didn't think much of it.

Meanwhile, I was also considering *Rob Roy*. I loved the *Rob Roy* script. I have a connection to him, in fact. I think it's my great-great-grandmother, who was a Campbell. She ran off with an Irish groomsman called Jimmy McArdle, making her Rob Roy's aunt, or niece, or something. Either way, despite my familial connection, or probably because of it, Alan Sharp had come up with a great script. Of the two, that was the one I liked.

I went to meet Mel Gibson, who it turned out had been asked to play Rob Roy but declined in order to direct *Braveheart*.

Now, it seems that everybody in this book is either dead or cancelled, and Mel falls into the latter category. But when he got into his various bits of trouble, verbally abusing people and so on and so forth, I remember thinking that it wasn't the Mel that I knew from *Braveheart*, because the Mel I knew then was very compassionate, very kind and caring. On that particular set there was a gifted young actor who quite obviously had an alcohol problem. As a recovering alcoholic himself, Mel was extraordinarily gentle and compassionate to this young man and steered him wonderfully through his performance. Yes, clearly Mel had and has his demons. No one would deny that, least of all Mel. Like with Woody, I was only with him for a short while, but I loved working with him.

So. Terrible script, but I loved the director and star. That was a good start.

Michael Caton-Jones, on the other hand, the director of *Rob Roy*, I thought was a complete arsehole. Even so, the part was better, the script was better, and that's the role that I ended up pursuing, and despite what may have been a natural antipathy between myself and

Caton-Jones, I got the part. To Mel I said, 'Look, Mel, I'd love to do your movie, but I really like this role of Killearn in *Rob Roy*.'

Mel knew it was a good role in *Rob Roy*. He knew the part that he was offering me in *Braveheart* was a faceless, blink-and-you-miss-it affair. 'Well, what do you want to play?' he said to me.

'What do you mean?'

'In our film, who would you like to play?'

'Well, there's . . . there's Uncle Argyle. That's the part that's worth doing for me.'

'It's yours,' he said. 'You play Uncle Argyle.'

You can see why I liked him. If only more people did business that way.

So anyway, this was quite a turn-up. I had, through a combination of steely nerve and brilliant tactics (oh, all right then, dumb luck), landed myself a superb role in *Braveheart*.

To Caton-Jones I said, 'Mike, I've got a part in *Braveheart*.'

'Well, I don't want you to be in them both,' stated Caton-Jones.

'Why not?'

'It's the Scottish thing.'

Caton-Jones, I should make clear, is himself a Scot, but a Scot, as it turned out, with very little sense of his own country's history.

'Michael, there is 300 years between these two events. One is set in 1300 and the other one is set towards the end of the 1700s.' To my mind it was like the producers of *The West Wing* objecting to their actor also appearing in *Lincoln*, but of course Michael didn't see it like that. 'I don't want you to be in them both.'

'Well, in that case you'll have to give me more money. You have to pay for me not to be in *Braveheart*.' This was the thing. The shooting schedules worked perfectly, so there was no clash, no reason why I couldn't do both. Still he was humming and hawing, until I said, 'Look, I tell you what, I'll look entirely different. I'll play *Braveheart* with one eye,' I told him. 'How about that? I promise you I will not look the same.'

Reluctantly, he agreed.

I rang Mel.

'Mel,' I said. 'I've had a great idea!'

'What's the idea, Brian?' growled Mel.

'I was thinking I could play Argyle with one eye. I think it would *really* work.'

'Oh my God,' exclaimed Mel, 'that's a great idea. This is why we pay you the big bucks, Brian. It's for exactly that kind of inventive thinking.'

That's how I managed to keep both of those plates spinning and be in both *Rob Roy* and *Braveheart*, and in fact I had a ball making them. I enjoyed the Hollywood heroics of *Braveheart*, the whole massive epic-movie feel of it all, and I enjoyed *Rob Roy* because it was a great role and I loved working with Tim Roth, Liam Neeson and Jessica Lange. Not only that, but they filmed them at almost exactly the same time in the same place. No word of a lie, both productions were in the same hotel, which meant that I finished filming *Braveheart* on the Saturday and started *Rob Roy* the following Monday. I didn't even move rooms.

The only problem was my dislike of Caton-Jones. Now, I have in my time been a little bit of a diva. Just a tiny bit. There was in me – especially before I met Irina, who smoothed off a lot of the rough edges – a bit of an oikish element, and if I got a bee in my bonnet about something then I could be a bit of a pain in the arse. I remember once Michael Elliott taking me to one side and letting me know that I'd been too hard on somebody in the costume department, and I'm sure there are times over the years when I could have been more diplomatic. One thing I have learned to do, though, is let people get on with their jobs. My hunch that Caton-Jones was an arsehole was confirmed when, during the shoot, he fired the director of photography, Roger Deakins, which none of us could believe. Roger Deakins is one of the best DPs ever and is responsible for shooting *The Shawshank Redemption*, *Dead Man Walking*, almost every Coen brothers film, including *Fargo*, as well as *1917*. And Michael Caton-Jones made *Basic Instinct Two: Risk Addiction*.

Something else. Tim Roth and I were doing a scene and trying to talk things over with Caton-Jones. 'Michael, look, we could do it this way, or we could do it that way.' Different ways of doing it. Different levels of interpretation. At which point Caton-Jones came out with a classic. 'Listen,' he told us with the kind of patronizing tone that makes you want to kill, 'you guys do the acting and I'll do the directing.'

Liam at one stage pointed out that his character would not be sitting with his back to the door, making him more vulnerable to attack. But Michael wouldn't have it. 'That's my shot. I've got my shot.' His big influence was silent films, which says it all. He was not a man of text.

After I'd finished on *Rob Roy*, I went back to do a bit more on *Braveheart*. The film was still as bonkers and brilliant as it had been when I finished my first stint, running roughshod over historical accuracy, but still, a huge amount of fun.

What I found, also, was that Mel was exhausted. Absolutely cream-crackered. Matt Earl Beesley, the second unit director, tells the story of Mel's first day filming in Ireland. Prior to one particular scene that involved Mel having to run up a hill and jump on a horse, Matt took a look around and saw the entire assembled production – cast, crew, hundreds of extras – all banking on him being able to get up the hill, and thought, *This guy is not gonna make it two steps before he falls down from exhaustion. He's not even going to have the strength to call action, let alone the rest of it.*

But then, 'Action,' he croaks, and bugger me if he isn't scampering up the hill and jumping on the horse.

And so at last to the decision. Because the experience of making *Iron Will*, *Rob Roy* and *Braveheart* had convinced me of something, and it was this.

CHAPTER 39

In the 1990s I had reached a peak. I had been in the definitive inter-
pretation of *Titus Andronicus*. I had done *Rat in the Skull* in New
York, then *King Lear* and then *Frankie and Johnny*. I had won two
Olivier awards, one in 1984 for *Rat in the Skull* and one in 1988 for
Titus. I'd been nominated for two more, *Misalliance* in 1986 and
Fashion in 1988. In short, I felt that I had proved myself as a leading
man on the stage.

Film, then. My work in film had been a somewhat stop–start affair
but thus far unexplored and undeveloped, and if I remained in the
UK, likely to stay that way. After all, there's no real film industry in
the UK, while TV at that stage was run by suits. The 1960s and 1970s
were incredible in terms of television. As I write we're in another
golden age.

But the 1980s and 1990s? Not so much. Add to that the fact that
I had always had this thing about movies, believing that cinema is a
more egalitarian art form, whereas the theatre is essentially a feudal
construct, a structure in which you have to know your place – a
structure that says I as a Scot can play King Lear, but never, say, a
military officer, always just a sergeant.

So it was that having pursued my artistic muse in the theatre, now was the time to make that move to Hollywood where, although no longer quite the case of striking while the iron was hot, I still had a certain kudos in the wake of *Manhunter*. In other words, now was the time to go and break Hollywood.

As a leading man?

No.

Because, actually, when I sat down and took a long hard look in the metaphorical mirror, I didn't actually *want* to be a Hollywood leading man. What I wanted to be, I realized, was a character actor. I wanted to create those parts in the film where the character itself might be quite bland, but the actor makes it impactful. Of course the great lesson for that was Lecktor, because he's only on screen for a short time but makes a huge impact. In many ways, he overshadows everything that happens in the film. He's like that because that's the way Thomas Harris wrote him, as a malevolent, Machiavellian and manipulative presence. A mystery and a conundrum. It's where I feel that they went wrong with the character over time. Because the public grew so fond of him, he was given more time on the page and on the screen, and as a result lost so much of his mystique.

But although Lecktor is an almost unfairly glaring example of such a character, I do believe that it's possible to do it with any supporting turn. Indeed, I'd go as far as to say that you *should* do it with any supporting turn. It goes back to what I said right at the top regarding the quote in the Michael Powell book. And seeking solace in the old movies, which I do often, and with very little encouragement. Consider Bogart as an example. Bogart was around for a long time before he became the actor we now know. Before he was 'Bogart' he was a very good, serviceable actor. Fourth banana, then third, then second banana. Finally he got *Casablanca* and then *The Maltese*

Falcon and that was it; there was no looking back for Bogey, and for what was, tragically, just a short time – because he only lived until his late fifties – he was that iconic leading man we think of today.

I have a Bogart-related story, and here seems as good a place as any to tell it. I did a film with Lauren Bacall, who as I'm sure you know, was married to Bogart. She's dead now, of course, and in fact our film was one of the last things she ever did. *All at Sea*, it was called. Bacall was an interesting character. Bogart had been the love of her life, but when he died she found herself at the mercy of various other rapacious characters who had been hanging around Bogart but also fancied her. She wasn't treated well, and as a result had formed a hard outer shell that could make her seem aggressive and defensive, even though it clearly masked an incredible insecurity. I was giving quite a comedic performance in *All at Sea* and at one point she turned to the director and said, 'Why don't you laugh at me the way you laugh at him?'

She told me a story of the time she was married to Jason Robards. After Bogey had died, this was. Bogart was, of course, a great drinker. Robards was . . . a drinker. He would go off on regular three-day benders, and on one occasion was out in New York with Christopher Plummer at a bar called Frankie & Johnnie's on 46th Street in the theatre district. Who should walk in but Bacall, carrying a pair of co-respondent shoes, those brown and white shoes beloved of a certain era. She plonks them down on the bar, says to Robards, 'These are Bogey's, why don't you try and fill them?' and then leaves.

Ouch.

Anyway, so Bogart's a good example of one of those actors who just kind of creates their own value, working their way up from fourth banana. We call them character actors, but in a sense, everybody's a character actor. Just that you've got big characters and small characters.

Ah, you say, but what about somebody like, say, Arnold Schwarzenegger? Is Arnold Schwarzenegger a character actor? No, because he's not an actor. He's a star. He's a creature. That's the other thing in our profession, we have creatures. The Rock is a creature. Vin Diesel. Monroe went the other way. She started off as a creature but became an actor and found it hard to break her dizzy-blonde mould.

Therein lies one of the perils of first-banana status, I suppose. The dreaded pigeonhole. Another one? Responsibility. Fairly early on I decided, perhaps because of my experiences in the theatre, that I didn't want the responsibility of a picture on my back. The whole studio finances wrapped up in that one film, and that picture succeeding or, more to the point, *failing*, because of a single person, that person being me.

Never was there a better example of that effect in action than *Desperate Measures* from 1998. Michael Keaton and Andy Garcia led the cast, but as the film was being made you could tell that things weren't clicking. You could see the panic setting in. We shot the shit out of that film, and things got crazy. They had different scripts flying around. They had actors on standby in hotel rooms. It all cost an absolute fortune, none of which is the fault of either Michael Keaton or Andy Garcia. And yet when the picture fails? Which it did, with a *terrible* opening weekend, that's where the fingers point.

To be specific here, I'm talking about the leading man in a big studio picture, the kind of movie that lives or dies on its opening weekend. Ever since *Jaws* the opening weekend has been the big thing. The one saving grace of Covid is that it seems to have put paid to that, but historically, a bad opening weekend is a movie killer. File it with 'badly distributed' in the principle causes of a good movie's failure. In 2016, I made an excellent horror film called *The Autopsy of Jane Doe*. I would recommend you watch it at once, with the caveat that you'll need a stronger stomach than me, because it's very gory indeed. I'm not a particular lover of horror films, but I love being in them. Indeed, I was nominated for a Fright Meter Award for something I did in 2009, *Trick 'r Treat*, in which I played a scarred hermit who scares children. It was a job where I completely gave myself over to the director, Michael Dougherty. I decided that, as an experiment to myself, I would be a blank page. Whatever he told me, I didn't argue, I just did it. 'You want me to fall downstairs? Sure, I'll fall downstairs.' The only thing on which I allowed myself to have an opinion was the look of the guy, who I thought of as a cross between the horror director John Carpenter and Jerry Garcia.

I learned a lot from that experience. How we are sometimes our own worst enemy when we act. How we can get in the way of ourselves. And although it's not how I generally play roles, and it's not how I necessarily played roles from then on, it was certainly something that I took on board as an actor.

Anyway, the point I'm making isn't about *Trick 'r Treat*, it's about *The Autopsy of Jane Doe*, a *really great* horror film, actually. A small production, small crew, none of that bollocks you get on blockbusters, made with passion and enthusiasm by young filmmakers. Superb.

But then the problem is that it doesn't do very well, in the sense that it meets with approval from the horror community but not the world at large, and that's because it suffers a problem with distribution, the death of so many great films. *Wonder Woman* is never going to suffer a problem with distribution. Spider-Man's secret superpower is that he can appear on sometimes even more than one screen at every cinema in the country. This is the problem with these sorts of movies. They have squeezed out the small films. These days, for a small film to compete with blockbusters, you need a perfect storm of events: good distribution, good PR, good word of mouth, a good film in the first place. Once upon a time films like *Friday the 13th* and *Halloween* were able to break through on the strength of their word of mouth alone. Not any more.

So what I thought at the time, and still do, is that I just wanted to *act*. I wanted to be in a position where I could keep moving and not reach an impediment, one not of my own making that would prevent me doing that. I can't do anything about the failure of the studio to promote a movie. I can't do anything about test audiences. I can't do anything about interfering studio executives or disappointing opening weekends or poor distribution. These are the aggravating factors of the major studio movie. They're what you need to contend with if you want to be a big star. And fine if that's your heart's desire. The rewards are great. But if you want to be me? If you want to be a character actor? A perennial support? Then you turn up, do the job, take the money, which is slightly less than what the leads get but still worth having, thank you very much, and then you clock off. And you always, but always, live to fight another day.

Into the mix of all this cogitation was the fact that I knew my relationship with Siri could, and if I was honest *should*, draw to an end to free her to follow her bliss. I was about to celebrate my fiftieth birthday, always a moment when you find yourself swallowing hard, looking back with an appraising eye, looking forward with a sense of trepidation. I had this sense that a great shifting was in the offing. I was coming to a point of separation, not just in terms of my private relationship but also separation from the country. I felt that things needed to change.

And then a slightly odd thing happened. I had a phone call from Ian Talbot, artistic director of the open-air theatre at Regent's Park. 'We're going to do *Richard III*, and I know you've been in it. Do you fancy a crack at directing it?'

Did I want to direct *Richard III*? Well, not really, since I hadn't especially enjoyed playing Buckingham during the tour. Nor had I thought a great deal of the interpretation.

I'd think about it, I told Ian, and ended the call fully expecting that the next time we spoke I'd be telling him that I'd had a good old think and that my answer was thank you but no.

Then something happened in the interim. What happened was that I genuinely *did* think about it. Not only that, but during my ruminations, I changed my mind. I began to wonder if maybe this was the time to patch up my relationship with *Richard III*. Perhaps it was an opportunity to come to terms with the play and explore what I thought was missing from the NT production. Perhaps this was the time to do *my Richard III*.

Initially, I was keen to cast Eddie Izzard. I thought that he (nowadays, 'she', of course) would be excellent as an outsider like Richard, but sadly, Ian came up against opposition from the board. I chewed the end of my pen and thought again. My son had worked with the actor Jasper Britton, son of Tony. As a result of a childhood accident, Jasper walked with a pronounced limp. I thought he would make a superb Richard.

They bought it. Jasper was in, and I started to look at the play, which needed adapting and shortening for its Regent's Park run. One of the things I noticed was something Shakespeare does in his later plays. He gives his lead characters time off. Hamlet goes to England. Othello is out for the scenes of Roderigo and Iago. But the problem with Richard is that he's never off, so not only is it a bit exhausting for the actor, but it feels like overkill for the audience.

I looked at the script and I started to rearrange it with that in mind. I actually took Richard out of a couple of scenes. I boosted Buckingham's role. I also did something with the strawberries. At one point in the play the Archbishop brings strawberries on stage, but in the script nothing is made of them. Lord Hastings has been executed, so I had the head of Hastings brought in, wrapped in cheesecloth, with blood oozing through the cheesecloth, and then the characters eating the strawberries, with the red of the strawberry juice dripping down their hands like blood. Not only was it an impactful visual motif, but it had the effect of opening more doors for me, in that it influenced how I could shape the piece. I had lots of drums played, thanks to a composer, Jonathan Goldstein (who tragically died in a plane crash in 2019), who arranged an incredible drum-heavy score for me. With his help, I staged battle scenes using warring drummers and flashing imagery, the whole thing taking full advantage of the open-air setting so that the audience was subject to a sensory onslaught but not completely battered by it.

Jasper was brilliant in the role. He had a rather complicated relationship with his father, and Tony would hide in the bushes to see him at work. One time I spotted him in the foliage and went over. 'Tony, what you doing in there?'

'Shh, Brian,' he rustled, 'I don't want him to know I'm here. I'm just sneaking in. Mum's the word, eh?'

'Are you sure?'

'Oh yes. He'll get very upset. He does, you know. Really, Brian, it's very sweet of you to be concerned but I'm quite happy here in the bushes.'

He withdrew into the foliage, and I left him to it.

The play was a great success. I felt that I had delivered something of great worth and I'm happy to say that audiences and critics seemed to agree. As part of the long farewell that I was currently bidding to that era of my career, it was something of which I could be very proud.

One nasty taste left in the mouth comes from what happened between me and my female lead, Natascha McElhone. I readily admit that I had problems with Natascha during the production for reasons that aren't particularly serious but that slightly coloured our relationship, and as a result I'd be going home at night to Siri, moaning about her, as you do.

Sometime later, perhaps a year or so, I was in LA, lying in bed with Siri (yes, we were still together despite my niggling concerns) one early morning, when I got a phone call. It was Natascha, wanting to know if I would referee her for a green card. Fine, I said, no problem, and we left it there. I put down the phone.

'You hypocrite,' said Siri.

'You what?'

'I said you're a hypocrite.'

'Oh, really?' I said.

'Yes, really.'

'It's just that I was half asleep, and—'

'Half asleep or not, you're still being a hypocrite.'

I dare say that nobody enjoys being accused of hypocrisy, especially not by one's firebrand girlfriend. So I rang Natascha back. 'I'm sorry, but I can't recommend you for a green card. I can't be your reference.'

That was that. But the thing was that I felt absolutely terrible about it. I felt ashamed and, in fact, still do. And even though we've worked together since, and she was lovely, I never took the opportunity to say sorry about the way I had behaved, how I had been put on my mettle by my current girlfriend but was wrong, and how of course I should have been her referee.

Richard III was almost immediately followed by *The Music Man*, also at Regent's Park, a part I wanted as much for the sake of Margaret and Alan as myself. As a family, we used to love the film, and I was so keen to appear in this production that I offered to audition, which, at this stage in my career, I wouldn't normally have done. I was full of the joys of spring by then and thought that directing *Richard III* and then playing in *The Music Man* would be great fun.

I was right. It was. I'm hardly the world's most wonderful singer, but my songs were okay and, what's more, I got some excellent reviews for my movement and dancing. After Regent's Park we toured *The Music Man*, and while I'm not a great touring person, I saw it as part of my farewell to the UK. This is it. I'm going to finish this, get on the plane and start a new career in the US. I'm going to be a character actor.

And that's what happened. I got my nephew – this is Bette's eldest boy, David, who is actually only about eight years younger than me – to set up a place for me to live in LA, which I rented, and which subsequently became a halfway house for every Brit passing through the city. Siri came with me, although we were definitely coming to the end of our relationship, and I was happy there for a while, drawing my wages, doing as Fulton always said and following my mercenary calling. I was about to embark on my year of making action movies.

CHAPTER 40

Towards the end of 1995, I sat by a pool in LA for six weeks and saw a bunch of people, including Steven Seagal and the directors Renny Harlin and Andrew Davis. Andrew Davis had offered me the baddie in *Under Siege* in 1992, but I had turned it down and the part eventually went to Tommy Lee Jones. I'd regretted it and didn't intend to make that mistake again.

With the meetings over I jetted back home and waited for the phone to ring, deciding to record a few editions of the *Acting With . . .* series while I was twiddling my thumbs. I was flying up to Glasgow for one of those when I got a call. 'Dustin Hoffman is a no-show on this film, *The Long Kiss Goodnight*, and they want you to fly out at the weekend, take over and play the role.'

This was Thursday. They wanted me to shoot on Monday.

So I did. I recorded the *Acting With . . .*, flew to Toronto, was handed Shane Black's script – a very good script – went into the costume department on Saturday, got fitted on Sunday, and then filmed on Monday.

My very first scene was a driving bit in which I had to pick up Geena Davis and Samuel L. Jackson, who have just escaped the baddies' clutches. Samuel was droll and lovely. Geena was great.

You're always a bit nervous when you meet these people, who are so established. They look at you curiously. *Who is this guy? Where is he from, this Brit?* I may have been a big noise in the theatre but not in their world. At the age of fifty I felt like I was just beginning again.

I worked with an actress cast as my sister, Gladys O'Connor. Even though she was in her eighties, she was supposed to be my sister, which seemed a bit ridiculous, but there you go, that's Hollywood for you. I remember that Renny Harlin fell in love with her and asked her for a hug when we wrapped. She told me the story of how as a very young girl, maybe just six years old, she and her family had left Liverpool on the ship that departed in the wake of the *Titanic*, and how they had later come across the debris from the infamous passenger liner. She could remember seeing clothes in the water, and a wall of ice. She and fellow passengers stood on the deck, paying their respects and singing a hymn. An incredible story.

Ten days later, I was in the same airport in the same terminal, about to do another *Acting With* . . . when I got a call. 'Tommy Lee Jones is a no-show. Would you be interested?'

'What's the picture?'

As soon as the words were out of my mouth I realized it didn't really matter.

'*Chain Reaction.*'

Again it was Thursday and they wanted me to film on Monday. This time, however, I was let off the hook and didn't do the *Acting With* . . . Instead I found myself flying into Chicago and checking into the Four Seasons where my fellow guests included Keanu Reeves, Morgan Freeman and Rachel Weisz.

I had a meeting with the second assistant director.

'Is there a script? I'd like a script.'

'No, no, there's only the Tommy Lee Jones script, and we're not doing that now.'

I met Andrew Davis again, who was directing it. Andrew Davis, I found, was very excited to be working with me. He loved my work.

'So, script?' I said to him.

'Yeah, script.'

'Can't wait to see it.'

'Yup, that'll be Monday, Brian. We'll have a beats script for then.'

'A what script?' I had never heard of such a thing.

'It's just the beats of the scene. We know that this dramatic beat has got to happen, and then that dramatic beat has got to happen, and we work from that.' He stopped as though suddenly struck by a grand revelation. 'You've worked with Ken Loach, yes?'

'Yes.'

'He improvises?'

'Well, yes.'

'And you can improvise?'

'I can improvise, if you need me to improvise.'

'Great, that's great, Brian.'

It turned out that there were eight writers beavering away on the script, four pairs of two. But still nothing appeared. I joined Morgan Freeman in a set way underground at the bottom of the Chicago River. I've worked with Morgan many times – I would do so again that very year, in fact – but our first meeting was somewhat inauspicious given that he was, at the time, a very pissed-off bloke. Freeman is from Mississippi, and Chicago was way too cold for him. What's more, he'd been shooting the film for a while by this stage. He'd seen principals come and go, writers fired and hired, a sense of general chaos. Keanu Reeves was the lead on the film, of course; the lovely

Rachel Weisz the female lead. So it wasn't like Morgan had that Andy Garcia/Michael Keaton problem, this being more of a wages gig for him. But even so, he was feeling the strain.

I'm pleased to say, however, that although he was cold and pissed off and watching bedlam reign around him, Morgan Freeman remained an absolute gentleman. Being the very epitome of Morgan Freeman. The Morgan Freeman you would hope to meet. The Morgan Freeman you encounter in your dreams.

'Dare I ask if there's a script?' I asked him.

'No, Brian,' he purred, sounding exactly as you would want Morgan Freeman to sound, 'there is no script.' A weary pause. 'Not unless you count the beats script.'

The dreaded beats script. I can't remember exactly what the beats script said. I do know that nothing we shot made any sense, nor was the order in which we shot it reflected in the final production. What I do remember is that Morgan and I were required for a tracking shot along the tunnel. We're on the run. He's a sort of good guy/bad guy and I'm the bad guy/bad guy, and the idea was that we'd hurry up this tunnel together and then get into a lift.

That was it. Go up the tunnel, get in the lift. At which point Andrew Davis would call cut.

Fine. Until Andrew Davis said to us, 'Guys, I'm going to need you to improvise here.'

Eight writers working on this thing and we're asked to improvise. Oh, but I say 'we'. In actual fact, Morgan – cold, pissed-off Morgan – just drew his fingers across his lips, zipping them up. *Not me. I'm not improvising.*

Andrew looked at me. He was giving me his you-worked-with-Ken-Loach eyes. He said, 'Brian. Monologue?'

I nipped off to write some dialogue. We did the shot. Camera on the track. Getting to the lift, I'm doing my improvising and all is going well until . . . the Steadicam picks us up at the lift and, instead of calling cut, Andrew and the Steadicam comes into the lift with us and continues to shoot.

But I hadn't worked anything out for that that bit. I'd only worked on dialogue for the tunnel. So instead I started singing 'On Top of Old Smokey'.

'I don't think that's in the public domain, sing something else,' whispered Andrew, thinking on his feet. So I started singing 'Amazing Grace' instead.

And then, at last, he called cut.

And you know what? None of my improvising or singing made it into the film. We did it again with a bit of scripted dialogue that the many writers somehow managed to produce, which was good of them.

Keanu Reeves was an interesting case. This film was made during what I suppose you might say was his heartthrob period. Prior to that he had mixed huge films like *Point Break*, *Speed* and *Dracula* with more indie-ish stuff, *My Own Private Idaho* and *Even Cowgirls Get the Blues*. But despite choosing interesting work and being an interesting guy, he still had a reputation as a bit wooden. Maybe that was fair, at the time, but the thing about Keanu is that he's a seeker. He took himself off to a small theatre in Canada and played Hamlet. He stuck at it and he's actually become rather good over the years. He's become rather good because he's learned his job.

Brad Pitt the same. Like Keanu the initial appeal is all about the heartthrob looks, so he's had to learn on the job; he's had to dedicate himself to his craft. I love actors doing that. I love that ambition, that dedication, not to be better-looking and more famous or have a sexier partner, but to be a better actor, because the fact is that actors do not appear fully formed. I can think of just one off the top of my head: Marlon Brando playing Stanley Kowalski, when he's just there, this unknown doing something absolutely extraordinary and everything follows from there.

Working with Brad Pitt, I was impressed by his commitment to being an actor, his commitment to learning the job. Just to . . . learning. On *Troy* he was working with a lot of British actors from the classical tradition. Actors for whom dressing up in stupid costumes was mother's milk. But Brad puts on this leather stuff and of course he feels odd because he's never done it before. Actually, he looked magnificent. He had exactly the right classical beauty for it, but, firstly, he felt uncomfortable – he felt, actually, stupid – and secondly he didn't want to be known for his beauty; he didn't want to be this mere piece of eye candy. He wanted to be known as a worker, a guy doing his job and as a result he probably toiled harder than anyone on that show, which in itself is impressive.

Brad's not alone. Most big stars want to be actors. They want to perform. During a period when I was appearing in *Art* on Broadway – a moment in time to which I will return for one particular, very important reason – I was approached to appear in a Kevin Costner movie called *For the Love of the Game*. I played the owner of a base-ball team; Costner was the ageing but slightly over-the-hill star of the team. Incredibly, my first day's shooting on the film involved my character watching a tense baseball game in a packed stadium. Only, this being the magic of film, the stadium was empty. There was not another soul apart from me and the crew as I sat there acting my socks off, pulling faces, going *ooh* and *ah*, reacting away to God knows what, because I didn't understand baseball and still don't, and anyway there was nothing to react to.

Next I had scenes with Costner, and went along to the set, where they had rebuilt a suite of the Ritz-Carlton in exact detail.

As I arrived, the director, Sam Raimi, took me to one side. 'You must remember your status,' he told me. 'Your status is important because, you know, Kevin is a movie star, so he may be difficult.'

If this makes Sam Raimi sound clumsy and inexperienced and borderline rude, then it's not the impression I want to give. Sam is a great guy. Perhaps not necessarily an actor's director, but a great guy nonetheless. What's more, they were coming to the end of the shoot and everybody's nerves were a bit ragged.

'Well, Kevin did direct a film for which he won an Oscar,' I told him, thinking not of *The Postman* but of *Dances with Wolves*, 'so he must have some idea what he's doing.'

'Oh yes, ha ha, of course, but the point is don't let your status be affected.'

This was because my character in the scene was higher status than Kevin's character, but Sam was concerned that his real-life status – Kevin Costner being A Movie Star – might somehow bleed into and influence the scene, Sam not having heard of this thing we call *acting*.

'We've allowed you an hour's rehearsal,' finished Sam. 'I don't know if you need that, but that's what we've given you.'

And that was it. Briefing over.

So Kevin arrived, and he was clearly very tired because it hadn't been the easiest of shoots, but he was otherwise fine, and we started rehearsing. We found a place in the set, played there, then decided no, maybe not, we'd play it somewhere else, just working together running the lines of the scene. With that over I'd returned to my trailer when there came a hammering on the door.

It was Sam Raimi.

'What did you do?'

'Come again?'

'What did you do to Kevin?'

'What you mean? I haven't offended him, have I?'

'Oh no,' he shook his head, 'but he's never behaved like that.'

'Like what?'

'Well, the way he was with you. The way you were rehearsing together,' he said. 'He's never done that, not for the whole shoot.'

I looked at him. I said, 'Sam, did you ever consider treating Kevin as an actor rather than as a movie star, because I think that's what he wants, you know? He just wants to play the part.'

Possibly we both came away from that experience having learned something. Who knows? Maybe Sam merely left perplexed. But it does say something about the way that films are made, especially in Hollywood. It tells you that the people making them think that it's just about stars even when the stars in question want to apply themselves to the material and try to make the scene the best it can be. You see it time and time again. The stars, whether it's Brad Pitt or Kevin or Samuel L. Jackson, Keanu Reeves or Morgan Freeman, they just want the right conditions in order to do their work. Of course there are some who want to be a pain about it, but most actors, film stars or not, just want to act.

CHAPTER 41

The train rolled on. *The Glimmer Man* was in there. *Desperate Measures*. They came out at different times but were all made in 1996. Then there was *Kiss the Girls*. For *Kiss the Girls* I was reunited with Morgan Freeman, but it was another one where the director was a bit of a dickhead. I remember him having problems with the actress Roma Maffia, who had come in as a day player in the part of a forensic scientist.

Coming in as a day player is the toughest job. As the job title suggests, you've got one day to do your bit and make your point. One day in which all the attention is on you. A good director will do his or her best to empower that day player and bring the best out of them, so saying something like, 'You were much funnier at the audition,' isn't exactly the most helpful approach. Morgan Freeman stepped in on that occasion, I seem to recall.

Also in that show was Ashley Judd, who later became part of the #MeToo movement. Clearly what happened to her as a result of Harvey Weinstein affected her career, because her days as a leading actress were, unfortunately, numbered. Thankfully, I've only ever met that man once. He was a marginal producer in a play I did, but it did involve meeting him and I have to say he made my flesh creep.

There was something coming off him which was not very nice, and I'm not just saying this with the benefit of hindsight. There really was. I would have told you the same at the time.

What's so depressing about his – well, let's just call it what it is – 'reign of terror' in Hollywood, is that so many actresses suffered at his hands. So many careers destroyed, so many good actresses marginalized. I think it's terrible that an actress like Ashley Judd is now simply seen as a victim and that her victimhood comes second place to her acting.

Kiss the Girls was a decent enough picture. Of that batch, *The Long Kiss Goodnight* was my favourite. It did well with critics and although it wasn't initially profitable, it certainly seems to have stood the test of time, not that I keep much of an eye on that sort of thing. As I've said before, I don't revisit the work much, if at all, nor do I pay a great deal of attention to the film's fortunes. If this makes me sound detached and mercenary, then on the one hand, I apologize. But on the other hand, where have you been the last couple of chapters?

Why do films fail? Easy. The script. The truth is in the writing. You can dress it up, you can shoot the shit out of it, you can do it in Technicolor, Vistavision or Cinemascope, but if the writing isn't there, then nor is the film.

For years, and despite everybody and his father insisting that the script was paramount, the studio system looked down on writers and treated them badly. One of Alfred Hitchcock's most famous quotes is, 'To make a great film you need three things – the script, the script, and the script.' But there are a million others I could choose from. George Cukor: 'Give me a good script and I'll be a hundred times better as a director.' Steven Soderbergh: 'The key is – don't monkey around with the script. Then everything usually goes pretty well.'

Howard Hawks: 'You can't fix a bad script after you start shooting.' Richard Attenborough: 'There is nothing more important in making movies than the screenplay.'

You get the idea? Everybody can name great directors like Hitchcock and Spielberg. Who can name great screenwriters? That's why it was great to see, in the 1990s, writers come to the fore. Shane Black, Paul Schrader, Joe Eszterhas. These days, of course, all the good writing is on television. We see it from people like Peter Morgan, Aaron Sorkin, David Simon, David Benioff, Vince Gilligan, David Milch and, of course, my very own Jesse Armstrong, going all the way back to Stephen Bochco with *Hill Street Blues* being arguably the show that kick-started the TV revolution we're enjoying today.

Succession, as you can easily tell, is a writers' show. The writers understand and nourish each other, which is as it should be. If I wanted to change a word, just a single word of Logan's dialogue, I know that I'd have a fight on my hands. For example, I wanted to change the word 'nancy' to the word 'faggot', because to me, Logan is more likely to use the latter than the former. I won that one, and the dialogue was changed to 'faggot', but even the fact that we had the argument is symptomatic of the writer's ascendance in TV.

I sometimes feel that *Succession* focuses too much on the comedy at the expense of what is, essentially, a brilliant drama, but then again, when it comes to wrangling about lines, it helps that the writers mainly come from a comedy background. They have that tradition of flexibility, being quick on their feet. Of course, that does mean we get a lot of alternative lines. Kieran Culkin, for example, who had never improvised in his life, turns out to be the master of the alt lines and they'll give him loads. We'll do a scene and he's got five or six alt lines. We do takes of all five or six and eventually they'll pick one in the edit. That, again, is all to do with the ascendancy of the writer. It's the writers' medium for reasons I've already discussed, but also because you can tell a long-form story. It's got rid of the three-act drama. There's no longer a first, second and third act. In television it's all second act, which gives writers a better chance to explore themes and develop characters.

In cinema, that intimate, literate storytelling that you see in the older films has been lost. There are exceptions. I saw a picture recently, *Palmer*, directed by Fisher Stevens, who also stars in *Succession* as Hugo Baker, which was absolutely superb and featured an incredible performance from a young lad, Ryder Allen, proving everything I've said about child actors. That's an example of a smaller, intimate film, but it's a rarity these days in an age of Marvel and DC. The truth is losing out to spectacle.

Still, it's not really my problem. My responsibility as an actor is to follow my muse and put food on the table, which is why I did the slightly schlocky films like *The Glimmer Man* or *Desperate Measures* but also much smaller films such as *L.I.E.*, *The Escapist*, *Adaptation* and *Saltwater*. And yes, I've taken the superhero buck and would do again, but when it comes to throwing my support behind the smaller films, my record is good. In 2008, I made a film called *Red* with writer-director Lucky McKee, which I thought was great. They were constantly scraping around for money and there were all kinds of problems trying to get it made, but the intimacy and truth of the piece makes it one of my favourites. It includes a sixteen-minute take during which my character tells the story of the death of his wife and child. It's a scene that, firstly, I'm very proud of, and secondly something we were only able to do because it was digital.

Another one is *The Escapist* in 2006 which is a film that I helped over the finish line and, not uncoincidentally, is my favourite screen performance.

Enter Rupert Wyatt.

CHAPTER 42

In 2006, I was making a film called *Running with Scissors*. You wouldn't exactly call it a small, independent film. This, after all, was a picture starring Gwyneth Paltrow, Jill Clayburgh, Alec Baldwin, Evan Rachel Wood, Annette Bening and Joseph Fiennes. But neither, however, was it a huge production. It was the kind of mid-level studio-financed but literate film that we character actors love, and sure enough, I had a great time doing it.

I was worried I might have lost the part before it even began, actually. Reason being that between casting and the shoot beginning, I'd lost a lot of weight, about fifty pounds in all.

Now, if you're thinking, *Wow, Brian, how on earth did you lose fifty pounds? That's a diet I'd love to be on*, then firstly, it is not a diet you would love to be on, and secondly, I'll tell you.

It began in the late 1990s when I became friendly with the actress Patti LuPone. Just a friendship, nothing more. She was a drinking buddy. The kind of drinking buddy who introduces you to a whole new drink that you become rather fond of, and that drink was Cosmopolitans. I've never been much of a drinker and wasn't really then, but there was something about the taste of Cosmopolitans that got me on the hook.

Why? Because I fully admit to sugar addiction, that's why. In fact, I once made a TV programme about it. During the show, I was reunited with my sisters, Bette and May, and we talked about the amount of sugary sweets I would eat as a kid. Typically, they downplayed it, but it was in fact a huge amount that I would consume while sitting in the dark of the cinema as a wee bairn. Liquorice. Tons of liquorice. And midget gems. I loved the stuff and still would if not for the fact that I was diagnosed with type 2 diabetes.

So yeah, I've always had a sweet tooth. But I think that it was the Cosmopolitans that pushed me into the sphere of diabetes. And you know what? I can't even remember what it was that instigated the doctor's visits that saw me diagnosed with it. Just that one minute I was a guy who liked cocktails, the next minute I was a fucking diabetic.

I take medicine now. But one thing I have tried not to do is let it take over my life. It's something that has to be managed. I have to take pills every day and I exercise. But it's tiresome. I've tried to reverse it, and have done from time to time by losing a lot of weight, but I'm at the age now where I need my weight. They say you should have more weight when you're older; you should eat more protein and fewer carbs.

But still, it's something I've had to deal with. I just make sure not to give it too much stature in my life. I have diabetes. That's it.

Anyway, that occasion, just as *Running with Scissors* was about to kick off, was a time when I hadn't quite reconciled myself to it and was absolutely determined to lose weight and try to reverse it. I lost that fifty pounds but worried I might have lost the part into the bargain.

So when the director, Ryan Murphy, who you'll know from

creating *Nip/Tuck*, *Glee* and *American Horror Story*, came to my house, I greeted him dressed as Father Christmas in order to disguise the weight loss, which is random, but not *quite* as random as it sounds, since the script did in fact require me to dress up like Father Christmas, so at least I could excuse it as being in character.

In any event, the weight was never an issue; I went on to do the film and had a great time with all concerned. Gwyneth was a delight. Annette Bening was a joy to work with. Alec Baldwin, who I already knew, was great. And Evan Rachel Wood, also, was wonderful. At the time, she was just getting together with Marilyn Manson, who lived across the road from me in LA. Your next question: did I notice anything untoward about their relationship? Answer: no, but then again I wasn't really paying attention.

Anyway, the point of that very long introduction about *Running with Scissors*, which ended up being a good film, and one I'm very proud of, is that while I was making it I was also dealing with a young director called Rupert Wyatt. Rupert and I had made a short film together and Rupert was talking about developing it into a feature.

I wasn't especially keen, having magpie eyes for a different, perhaps bigger prize. By now I'd been a supporting actor for going on a decade and I was thinking that occasionally I'd like to play centre forward as opposed to left half. I talked to him about *Bad Day at Black Rock*, a film that means a lot to me, not only because it's a great film and it stars my favourite actor, Spencer Tracy, but because Tracy in it plays a man of a certain age but is still the lead.

To Rupert, I said, 'I think I've got it in me to do that kind of work.'

I left it with him. I'm not sure he was especially pleased with the outcome of that discussion. He had, after all, been keen to make his short film into a feature and was hoping that I would throw my weight – fifty pounds lighter, but still considerable – behind it. However, chastened, and probably grumbling about me under his breath like Muttley, he went away and produced a script called *The Escapist*, about a convict serving a life sentence who wants to break out in order to make peace with his daughter. The convict being me.

I thought it was brilliant.

'Rupert, I'm going to put this away safe somewhere, because I know that in the process of getting this made, the world and his wife are going to ask you to do rewrites, but I think we've got to keep this as a template. *This* is the film we've got to make, not some kind of rehash because of some producer's crappy taste.'

And, to cut a long story short, that's exactly what we did. We pushed that script through practically as it was originally written. Tim Roth dropped out, but because Joe Fiennes had been so astonishing in *Running with Scissors* I actually dragged Rupert Wyatt along to the opening. This in itself was rare for me. I hardly go to openings. Same with cast and crew screenings. If I'm forced to go to the premiere then I do my best to stand and wave for the cameras but then I'll leave before the film starts.

For Rupert, however, and for Joe Fiennes, I made an exception, and it worked out because Rupert agreed with me that Joe was perfect.

In the end we assembled a superb cast. We had Dominic Cooper, Liam Cunningham, Stephen Mackintosh – an excellent performance from Stephen Mackintosh – and Damian Lewis, and we made a film that I'm very, very proud of. A small, intimate film. A film where the performances are true to the word of the text and the word of the text is true to the characters.

A few years later I took a call from a producer wanting to know what I thought of Rupert Wyatt as a choice to direct *Rise of the Planet of the Apes.*

'Oh, aye, that would be fantastic,' I told him. 'He's a brilliant director. He's got a great imagination, superb visual sense. You could do a lot worse there.'

Rupert got the job, and indeed he cast me, so I had a ringside seat to watch as the project slithered almost out of his control because, as so often happens with these sorts of projects, where very promising directors are given a big film to do, that so-called golden opportunity comes with handcuffs. Rupert had been given a terrible script and the studio wouldn't let him touch it. He thought he was being hired as the young whizz-kid whose ideas would be greeted with delight, his creative vision nurtured; instead, he got treated like a journeyman. A hired hand.

The film did well, both critically and commercially, but I think Rupert came away from the experience somewhat bruised, and although he's continued working has certainly steered clear of block-busters. Whether that's by accident or design, I don't know.

Another smaller film that I'm very proud of was *L.I.E.* from 2001. This was set around the Long Island Expressway, and I played a guy called Big John Harrigan who was a chicken hawk, which meant that, while he wasn't exactly a paedophile, he would prey on the young, almost feral boys who hung around a pit stop on the expressway. Harrigan meets this kid, Howie, played by Paul Dano, a fantastic actor and actually a very good director as well, and rather than sexualize Howie, he realises that he needs parenting and so slips into that role instead. A beautifully written piece, despite three credited writers, including the director Michael Cuesta, it's got layers and ambiguity and all that chewy stuff we actors love, and the performances throughout are brilliant. Even mine isn't too shabby.

Plenty of folk warned me against the part. 'The guy's a paedophile,' they said.

I'd explain why he wasn't, strictly speaking, a paedophile, but they'd look at me like, *Who's counting? The guy's a paedophile*, and I began to wonder if I was being misled by an artistic imperative. Maybe I should listen to the doubters. After all, I wasn't keen on seeing my career sunk by a torpedo – with the emphasis on the 'pedo'. It wasn't like I *needed* the role.

It was my manager, Matthew Lesher, who put my mind at rest. I've been with Matthew about thirty years now, and he's an eccentric guy but quite extraordinary and also quite brilliant. He thought *L.I.E.* was a great script, insisted I took it, and I did. And it ended up being an acclaimed film, winning me various awards and attracting the attention of people whose attention was worth attracting. Bryan Singer, for instance, which is why you'll see me in *X2* and not Geoffrey Rush.

I'm sure that *L.I.E.* would have done better commercially were it not for the fact that it opened on the wrong weekend. It opened on the worst weekend it could possibly have opened, in fact. It opened the weekend of 9/11.

That morning I had been in Boston where I'd won a Boston Society of Film Critics Award for *L.I.E.*, which I shared with Denzel Washington for *Training Day*. The producers of *L.I.E.* were very keen for me to go, and of course I was happy to give the film whatever boost I could, the only fly in the ointment being the fact that I was supposed to get back to LA for a TV series called *The Bench*. At the eleventh hour, *The Bench* was cancelled (sets constructed and everything – total shitstorm) and because I knew that *L.I.E.* was opening in New York I decided to go there instead.

So I did that. Went to the opening and then on Tuesday morning was due to go back to LA so drove to Kennedy where my flight, United 24, was due to leave at 9 a.m. I boarded and took my seat, thinking how odd it was that there were a couple of empty seats on what was otherwise a packed plane. Sure enough, there was a wait because those passengers hadn't turned up. I assume the crew waited for as long as they feasibly could but then decided they'd have to take off regardless, empty seats or not.

We began taxiing down the runway, at which point the pilot came on and said, 'Ladies and gentlemen, my apologies, but we're going to have to pull over for a bit. There has been an incident at the World Trade Center. We think a light aircraft has hit it by accident.'

A collective gasp went up.

'Everything seems to be okay,' the pilot reassured us, 'but we're drawing up here anyway.'

The engines whined with deceleration as we pulled off to the side of the runway, a position from which I had a view across the bay to the Twin Towers. It took me a moment to work out what I was seeing. The brain takes a while to process the information. And then I realized that a funnel of grey smoke was pouring out of one of the towers. My first thought was that it reminded me of the fire effect you see on the Universal Studios tour, and then, still looking across, transfixed by this surreal sight, I saw the second plane hit. At the time, of course, I didn't know what I was witnessing because it was so far away. I just saw the orange of flame as the plane hit, followed by more smoke, thick and black, and I knew that something very, very terrible was taking place.

A couple of days later I was speaking to somebody who told me that the passengers who missed my flight were another group of terrorists. They had simply missed the flight, that was all. Otherwise . . .

Well, that was how it was sold to me. In actual fact, I just thought it was a little bit of hysteria. People trying to get into the drama, if you like.

But then, just this year, I discovered from a neighbour, an ex-CIA guy, that it was absolutely true; there *were* three people trying to get on that particular plane. These guys had turned up insisting they had to get on the plane but were turned away as latecomers. They had seats in first class with an accomplice in economy and the idea was that they were going to work together. That, at least, was what the intelligence services believed.

It's funny, because even now, I can't quite connect what I saw across the bay with the gravitas of the fact that almost 3,000 people would be dead before the end of the day as a result. It just seemed like a strange illusion.

All of which sombre reflection ushers us back to the subject of the script. And if the secret to a great film is a great script, what, then, is the secret to a great script?

The answer to that, I think, is a cohesive voice, which you get from the likes of Tony Gilroy, Shane Black and of course, most famously, Quentin Tarantino.

The trouble is, I really don't have much time for Quentin Tarantino. I find his work meretricious. It's all surface. Plot mechanics in place of depth. Style where there should be substance. I walked out of *Pulp Fiction*. I gritted my teeth and sat through *Once Upon a Time in Hollywood*, and although it wasn't as bad as I'd feared, it still wasn't good enough to convert me. Unlike seemingly the rest of the world – indeed, my sons – I am a Tarantino refusenik.

That said, if the phone rang, I'd do it. One of the guiding lights behind my decision to go to Hollywood, the two guiding lights, if you like, were Tim Roth and Gary Oldman, both of whom did at an early age what I should have done ten years before I actually did it, i.e. bugger off to Hollywood. They did all kinds of roles and broadened their range. Tim, of course, practically broke out with *Reservoir Dogs*; Gary, with an eye-catching cameo in *True Romance*. Got to admit: Tarantino didn't do them a lot of harm.

CHAPTER 43

As a young actor, I could see no further than the limits of my own theatrical ambition. My political sense was a rather grey, unformed haze, and although I suppose that in the recesses of that haze I thought that I was probably a socialist, that was about it. I stayed that way – a sort of semi-socialist, a socialist at heart if not in head – until there came a time when I was forced to confront and interrogate my own political feeling and form my thinking.

Of course, my family history had contributed to what was a growing political awareness. The injustice, the instability, the history of continuous displacement, my own and that of my forefathers. And while I had benefited from the great period of social mobility that was the 1960s, the 1970s was a very different feeling indeed. I had watched as, through that decade, England cemented a standing as 'the sick man of Europe', and the political stage was set for the arrival of a new voice, who duly arrived in the stentorian form of Margaret Hilda Thatcher. Sure enough, my political grey haze was approaching a state of dispersal.

So much has been said about the Iron Lady, both good and bad, but personally I'm grateful to her as the catalyst for my political coming of age. She and I have one thing in common: we are both the children of grocers. But there the similarity ends. Ultimately she was a force of devastation who destroyed British industry and laid waste to communities that to this day have never recovered; who sold the country's fortunes to a deregulated financial sector and encouraged a speculative culture with disastrous consequences; and whose premiership was defined by the pitched battles of the 1984 miners' strike, by inner-city riots and by the social unrest over the hated poll tax that eventually led to her political demise in 1990.

In foreign affairs, she dismissed the apartheid-fighting African National Congress in South Africa as 'a typical terrorist organization' and refused to back sanctions against the racist state. She drank tea with Augusto Pinochet while the former Chilean military ruler was being held under house arrest in London as part of an investigation into human rights abuses. She pursued policies that caused great suffering to millions of ordinary working-class men and women in this country, she decimated the manufacturing base, causing unprecedented mass unemployment. She used virtual police-state methods to suppress the miners' strike. The miners were effectively starved back to work. These were very cruel and heartless policies.

Thatcher's free-market economics in many ways paved the way for the current economic crisis. She was exceedingly light on regulating the financial and business sectors. Giving them free rein, stating that monetarism was the most important ideology and if push comes to shove, people had to be sacrificed for the greater good. She denigrated the idea of community, and as a far more divided society, we are still living with the legacy today.

These events subliminally entered my consciousness. The grey haze dispersed. I was now committed to socialism. I joined the Labour Party.

As I've became well-known in my field, I've become accustomed to people approaching me and asking for Lecktor quotes (I usually try and wriggle out of it on the basis that I'm not a performing monkey), while latterly I get fans requesting selfies or asking me to record answerphone messages as Logan Roy, more often than not telling the caller to fuck off.

If this is a minor downside of notoriety, the considerable upside is that I get comfortable seats on planes, good accommodation in excellent hotels and a trailer on set, the sort we call a two-banger, which is two apartments in one big trailer (on *Succession*, I share mine with the writers). The days of the big one-banger trailers are pretty much over, although I used to get a one-banger on the big Hollywood movies.

Otherwise, I have, like the superheroes in the comics I used to read, tried to use my powers for good, and so, as well as helping to get the odd film made – *The Escapist*, *Red* – I have also helped to support those causes close to my heart: diabetes charities being one of them, Age UK another. And socialism.

And that's what happened in the 1990s, when I came out for Labour.

I knew John Smith, the Labour leader prior to Tony Blair, and thought he was a good man. In fact, I read a poem at his memorial service at Westminster Abbey in 1994. As a result, I was well acquainted with his two protégés, Gordon Brown and Tony Blair. I was never entirely sure about Tony but liked Gordon. I've always thought that if they'd allowed Gordon just to be Gordon, the straight shooter that he was, then he would have been an ideal successor, but it was not to be.

Instead, after John's death, Tony became leader, and despite some minor reservations, I threw my support behind him because I believed in him and believed in his team. I thought they were a great, formidable bunch of politicians, and although there were a few elements of the campaign that I was uncomfortable with – I didn't like the fact that they were trying to put the boot into John Major, for example, who I considered to be a decent man, dealing with problems that were of Thatcher's making rather than his own – I lent my voice to the 'Enough Is Enough' party political broadcast. 'While the Conservatives look after the fat cats like gas and water company bosses, the rest of us have nowhere to hide. We have to work longer hours just to pay for the twenty-two Tory tax rises . . . enough is enough.'

And of course we won, Tony Blair became prime minister in 1997, and it was one of the most incredible times of my life to be there on that early May morning, 2 a.m. on the South Bank, tremendously excited about the possibility of a proper socialist Britain, where for the first time in living memory, the politics of my own country and those of England would be politically aligned.

I would, eventually, change my mind about Labour and come to think of that blissful May morning as something of a false dawn, because as things progressed I felt that the party lost its way. The straw that broke the camel's back for me was the Iraq crisis, but it was by no means the only problem I had by that stage, just, perhaps, the most fundamental and far-reaching. The one that tested me to breaking point. There were other things as well, of course, the fact that I felt very keenly an absence of the truth in the party, the fact that I saw Robin Cook and Clare Short, two very able and principled politicians, being sidelined.

Let down by a party that I had in some small way helped to power, a party that I had at one stage truly believed in, I felt politically homeless for a while. And I think that was painful for me, because as an orphan, you're always struggling with alienation; you always feel that you're only allowed to belong at other people's behest. It's like Blanche Dubois says in *A Streetcar Named Desire*, you're depending on 'the kindness of strangers'.

So I found myself looking back to my home country, and in doing so realized that the very notion of independence comes from a position of security. As a Scotsman living in Scotland, I never had that sense of security or national identity because my position as a Scot was not secure. My country had been subsumed into a United Kingdom and I had no say in the matter.

For that reason, and with no small measure of irony, it was only when I left my home country that I truly became a Scot. Being an émigré Scot gave me a sense of identity, and over the years what this émigré Scot came to realize and despise was that the parliament at Westminster could no longer see further than the end of its bridge. I decided that Scotland had earned the right to its nation status. It had come to it by means of a painstaking evolution. It had earned the right to control its own destiny. It would certainly make a better job of it than a Westminster parliament that has not the foggiest clue about Scotland's cultural, economic and social needs.

And that is why I came to embrace the idea of an independent Scotland and, ultimately, switched my allegiance entirely, endorsing the SNP, quitting Labour, actively campaigning for Yes Scotland. That's why you might see me in the papers every now and then, lending my voice to any initiative that helps advance the cause of Scottish independence.

I wasn't allowed to vote in the referendum in 2014 for citizenship issues, but that doesn't stop me working towards independence for the future, and it doesn't stop me believing that I will live to see the day when Scotland is autonomous. I believe that an independent Scotland will be outward looking, culturally confident, fiscally successful and an example to other small nations of how to hold their heads up high without taint. I believe that now, after all the signposts, more than at any time in our history we Scots have arrived at the moment to realize our potential.

And that, as Ben Elton used to say, was a little bit of politics for you there, ladies and gentlemen.

CHAPTER 44

Despite the fact that I had embarked on my new career as a character actor, living my mercenary life, that didn't mean I'd cut my ties with the theatre. Far from it. I continued with links to the stage both in LA and at home. For a start, I performed my one-man play, *St. Nicholas*, by the wonderful Conor McPherson, in 1997, while the following year found me back on Broadway appearing as Marc in *Art*. You may recall that I had something interesting to tell you about *Art*. So here it is.

The story actually begins seven years previously, when I was in Hamburg on tour with *King Lear*. After the performance, there was a party at which I met a young woman to whom I spoke for a long time. A long time. For most of the evening, in fact. After which I assumed I'd never see her again.

I was wrong about that. Later, when the tour reached Milan, we were in a restaurant and she walked in. I stood up, thinking (hoping) she'd come for me, but rather embarrassingly I'd got it wrong; she was not there for me at all. It turned out that she was having a relationship with somebody in the company.

So flash forward to when I'm doing *Art* on Broadway. I never like sitting backstage for hours before I go on stage. I'm slightly better now than I used to be, but in those days I had this thing about getting in and getting on rather than hanging around, and because *Art* was modern dress and performed without make-up I was able to cut things as fine as they slice the garlic in *Goodfellas*. Which is pretty fine.

So, anyway, I came in at my usual time, which was about 7.10 p.m. for a 7.30 p.m. start and there as usual was Jerry, the stage doorman, who said to me, in his broadest New York accent, 'Hey, there's a note for you,' pointing to my cubbyhole. 'Some woman left it. A really nice-looking broad.'

I plucked the envelope from the cubbyhole. Doing so, I had the strangest feeling. A thought that came to me, unbidden. *If you open this envelope, your life will change.* It was a thought that was as present and real as hunger or tiredness. A thought like a kind of shock that went through me.

I opened it. A note inside said something along the lines of, *Hi, I'm only in New York for a couple more days, and it would be nice to see you*, and it was signed 'Nicole Anson'.

Nicole Anson, I thought, digging in the memory vaults.

But I didn't know a Nicole Anson, did I?

And yet – and again you'd be forgiven for thinking this is all a bit woo-woo, but I swear to God it's true – I had a sudden image of the woman I had met in Hamburg and then in the restaurant in Milan. A memory that was tinged with embarrassment of that second encounter but also with genuine anticipation at the thought of seeing her again.

Generally speaking, in life, I'm not especially great at acknowledging things. It's a failing, I admit. It's all to do with this absence that I'm often talking about. And it's quite possible that in the normal run of things I might have let the note drift. Not out of discourtesy, just me being me.

But there was that feeling. That very strong feeling. A shifting. A sense of things that are meant to be.

I dialled the number she'd left and a woman answered. 'Hello?'

'Yes, hi, I was hoping to speak to Nicole?'

'Oh, I'm sorry, Nicole isn't here right now.'

'Ah, okay. Well, in that case, can you tell her that—'

'Oh, hang on a second . . .'

She came off the phone. Literally left me hanging. At that stage the company manager showed up and said to me, 'Hey, Brian, you've got a no-show tonight. Jean-Hugues Anglade isn't coming.'

What he meant was that of the four tickets I'd put by for guests only three were to be used. For whatever reason, Jean-Hugues Anglade wasn't able to make it.

At that moment the woman came back on the line. 'That was Nicole,' she was saying, 'She's on the other line.'

I asked if Nicole could ring me right away, left my number and put the phone down. Moments later, it jangled almost off the hook.

It was her.

'Where are you?' I asked.

'I'm on 59th and 7th.'

'Well, I'm on 45th and 7th,' I told her, 'and if you can get here . . .' I checked the time, 'in the next seven minutes, you've got a free ticket for the show.'

Nicole ran all the way down Broadway to the theatre and got her ticket. Having done the show, I was still slightly unsure as to exactly who she was, but when I went back to the reception room in which she was waiting for me, there she was – the woman from my vision.

That time in New York was a period during which I had taken up tango dancing, believe it or not, and so I took Nicole to tango that very night. Between you and me, I think it was my tango that did it. I think my skills on the dance floor impressed her enough to see me as partner material. Enough, anyway, that we spent most of the following day together. Afterwards she went to the airport and I said goodbye and then, with a heavy heart, went to the theatre for that evening's show.

Checking in at the airport, Nicole had discovered that her flight was overbooked. The airline was looking for volunteers to give up their seats, so she surrendered, then left the terminal where there happened to be a stretch limo waiting outside. 'I'll give you thirty bucks to take me back into the city,' she said to the driver, and he was going back anyway so he brought her in, took her to Broadway.

And stopped outside the theatre.

That's where she was when I next saw her. I was coming out of the theatre after the show and there at the kerb on Broadway was a stretch limo with Nicole inside.

'I don't have to leave for another four days,' she told me.

And that was it. We've been together ever since, and she is the great love of my life.

The mistake that I had made in previous relationships of always putting my career first, I've tried not to make with Nicole. Not always successfully, I will admit, but life is a work in progress. One thing I've realized is how important and enriching it can be to find areas in which you can work together, and we've done that a few times over the years. I've directed her in a couple of plays; we've appeared in films together. She's a formidable actress, and I'm not just saying that because she's likely to read this and thump me if

I don't – she genuinely has a rare talent that makes her a pleasure to work with.

Nicole, whose name is Nicole Ansari – not, as I had misread it, 'Nicole Anson' – is German – her parents live in Cologne – and yet despite that European heritage she's a born New Yorker. I'm not as infatuated with the city as she is – most of my friends these days are in LA or London, but Nicole absolutely loves the place and the place seems to love her back; everybody, in fact, seems to love Nicole.

Somehow I knew very early on that I was destined to have children with Nicole. And yet, funnily enough – and despite all I've said about her being my soulmate – she and I had reached a bit of a crossroads in our relationship during the early part of 2001. I was doing a film in Austin, Texas – *The Rookie*, with Dennis Quaid, which is a lovely film, directed by John Lee Hancock, who is a delightful guy and a great director – and she flew into Austin for what you might call 'crisis talks'.

'I think we should get married,' I said during the big talk.

'I think that's the best solution,' she replied.

(And yes, the story of us getting together is a lot more romantic than the proposal, but look, you can't have everything.)

We flew to Vegas to the Little White Chapel where a woman married us, as her mother played the theme from *Braveheart* on the piano, having made the discovery that I'd been in the film, and our first son, Orson, was conceived that night.

Torin came in 2004, two years later.

I have a little regret associated with Torin's birth, a little bit of karma, you might say. The thing was that during Nicole's pregnancy I had taken a job to be the voice of Aslan in the series of Narnia films, beginning with *The Lion, the Witch and the Wardrobe*, and so I flew to New Zealand at a point that was uncomfortably close to Torin's due date.

I was in Christchurch, which was beautiful, but feeling very guilty because of course there was absolutely no question of Nicole coming with me in her condition; moreover, there was every likelihood that I might still be away when Torin was born.

So anyway, I was trying to do the lion voice but there was nothing to go from, specifically no picture of the lion. Not only that, but I could sense something wrong, because the director kept telling me one thing, 'Pull it back,' while the sound guy was saying, 'You got to pick it up more,' which in many ways is the story of my acting career. But where in most cases the advice has proved a revelation, here it was just confusing and frustrating. I began to work myself up into a bit of a state, my mind constantly returning to the fact that my wife was heavily pregnant.

As it was, I got on a plane and arrived in time for the delivery. Nicole wanted to have a natural birth and Torin was at least in the right position, but he had to be induced because his blood pressure was decreasing and she had been in labour for too long. It pains me to admit it, but throughout that process, because I was dwelling on how badly the voice job had gone, I really wasn't as present as I should have been. I mean, I was *present*, as in I was there. Just not *present*. I wasn't there for my wife, who I think has forgiven me over time. I hope she's forgiven me.

The irony is that after all that, I was fired as the voice of Aslan. They were filming in Prague, and I'd flown there and they still didn't have an animated animal, but the director took me to one side, 'Brian, I'm going to have to let you go,' and that was it. The first time and only time I've ever been fired.

Liam Neeson did it in the end; he's got that great Northern Irish softness that really worked, whereas I was doing it more . . . me. Creatively, it was the right decision. Even so, there's a bit of me that believes I deserved to be fired because of Torin. At the time I thought to myself, *There's your just deserts, Brian. That's what you get for forgetting that it's not all about being an actor playing a role. You have to take life into account. Serves you fucking right.*

CHAPTER 45

One of the most interesting roles I have played, and in turn one of my favourite performances, is that of Hermann Goering in the mini-series *Nuremberg*. Goering was a fascinating character. A First World War fighter pilot, he was the second most decorated air ace after Manfred von Richthofen, absolutely passionate about his country.

At the end of the war, he flew his squadron into Switzerland, abandoned all of the planes there and walked back to Germany. He saw with horror the punitive conditions of the Versailles Treaty that followed in the wake of the war, had a breakdown and then went to live in Sweden, where he stayed for several years until he heard about this young man, Adolf Hitler, who was inspiring his countrymen back home.

From that moment on, Goering dedicated his life to Hitler. He became a believer of the whole Hitler myth – indeed, a perpetrator of that myth. But by the end of the Second World War, with the Nazis in disarray, Goering, who had tried to do a deal with the British, was regarded as a traitor and sentenced to death by Hitler.

It was that backstory that brought me into the character. If you play somebody like that, somebody that history regards as a terrible man, a war criminal, you're always looking for the humanity within them; you're in search of what makes them tick; you're trying to understand them as a human being. That's your way in as an actor.

This was something I felt about Lecktor and why my take was different to that of Anthony Hopkins. Though Lecktor was an intellectual, he was still an everyday kind of guy. And it was that element that gave him his essence. That was my entry point. Similarly, Logan Roy. In discussing the character with Jesse Armstrong before I'd even signed on, I had one question. 'Does he love his kids?'

'Yes,' Jesse told me.

And that was it. That's all you really need to know about Logan. Whatever terrible things he does, however awful he is, it comes from this bedrock of wanting the best for his children. It may be terribly twisted and wrong and immoral and all the other things you can say about Logan, but at least it comes from that place.

The flipside is the character where their humanity completely evades you. Playing Killearn in *Rob Roy* was interesting in the sense that it completely turned me around, and he remains the role that has been the most uncomfortable for me because I searched for that trace of humanity within him but came up short, because he's *so* vile, *so* awful. Playing him was like having to put on a set of dirty, wet clothes every day, and I didn't like it; I didn't want to be in this guy's skin.

I had no such problems with Goering. There was a tragic element to him. He was flamboyant and clearly a very funny man. He was a cross-dresser, and he remained fiercely loyal even after Hitler had sentenced him to death. He backed the wrong horse, but what he didn't do was to switch horses, and there's something in that loyalty that informs the Nuremberg process.

The worst thing the Allies did while he was in prison was to put

Goering on a diet and take away his meds. Not only did he lose a lot of weight, but his brain came sharply into focus and that's why he was able to run rings around prosecutors at the trial, at one stage giving a brilliant assessment of how and why Nazism came about.

Nuremberg, then, as in the TV programme, was a miniseries about the trial of Nazi war criminals following the end of the war, of whom Goering was the top-ranking. Christopher Plummer was in the cast, too, while the lead was Alec Baldwin, who in fact had recommended me for the role.

I like Alec a lot. He's not easy, but he's an extraordinarily bright guy. Playing Robert Jackson, who was the lead prosecutor in 'the Nuremberg Process', as they called it, was a difficult job, and it took its toll on him. Jackson was relatively badly prepared, which was not altogether his fault, but it did mean that he had trouble with the cross-examination. It didn't quite serve the movie to show Goering outwitting Jackson, but it is represented, albeit in a much more diluted form.

Another fascinating thing to happen was that during the trial, Goering went into denial about the extent of the Holocaust and his part in it. He was unable to accept that the Final Solution had been part of the Nazi plans.

There were some profoundly distressing Holocaust images shown at the real-life trial that we used in the series. There was one in particular, an image of a young woman being removed from a grave. Normally the hair was shaved, but this woman had long brown hair which cascaded as they brought her body out. Just that detail had a profound effect on me. I'd seen the images of dehumanized bodies before then. But I'd never seen a corpse like that, that had such a sense of humanity about it, and I used that as the moment that Goering lost touch with the reality of the situation. That's what happens. That's how people become inhuman. They don't necessarily lose who they are, they just go into denial about it; they convince themselves that two plus two equals five. That bad is good and vice versa.

So, yes, an endlessly fascinating role. Such a rewarding thing to create a feeling of . . . not sympathy, because you don't want that. But empathy, so that even though the guy is a terrible person, the audience still look forward to him being on screen, because they're asking themselves, *Where did this guy come from? What's going on?*

I think in that instance I presented a 360-degree human being, and that made it very rewarding. I must have done a decent enough job of it, too, because not only was I was nominated for a Screen Actors Guild award and Golden Globe, but I also won an Emmy for it.

I won't lie, I'm happy to get awards, even if I think the whole thing has got a bit out of hand. Once there was something very special about awards, but now it's a bit of a business, Oscars being a case in point. Once upon a time, something had to truly excel to get an Oscar, but now it's just because it goes out around Oscar time and contains the right sort of material in the right sort of performance. They do, after all, call it 'awards season', which I think is rather unfortunate.

Of course you have to be careful when being even mildly critical of awards. I've been up for many over the years. For *L.I.E.* I won that Boston Film Critics Award and a Satellite Award and was nominated for a few more. I was nominated for my cameo in *Frasier*, for *Adaptation*, for *X2* (a Teen Choice Award, that one – look at him, down with the kids), *Deadwood*, *Zodiac*, *Trick 'r Treat*. They can pile up, the nominations, so it's good to win one, and that's exactly what happened in 2020, when I won a Best Actor Golden Globe for *Succession*. Which of course was wonderful. It was tremendous for me and it was tremendous for my wife and it was a delightful evening, people like Leonardo DiCaprio coming up to me and saying, 'We've got to work together,' Brad Pitt making my re-acquaintance, bumping into Elton John who said to me, 'But Churchill. You were *the* Churchill.' Pacino doing the same, growling 'Churchill,' at me.

Well, yes. *Churchill*. I was robbed. It's the curse of Brian Cox. But we'll come to that.

CHAPTER 46

Without a shadow of a doubt, one of the best things about my job is the fact that I get to go all over the world and then, when I'm there, visit some of the best places. Which is why I am able to say things like, 'I was filming in the Palace of Versailles when I got the call about *The Bourne Identity*.' Which is true. I was.

The movie was *The Affair of the Necklace*. I remember that Christopher Walken was somewhat bemused by Jonathan Pryce, which is understandable, Jonathan being an interesting fish, kind of dark and gloomy at times. And if you can freak out Christopher Walken . . .

The call came from Doug Liman, director of *The Bourne Identity*, and it goes without saying that I signed up, and so, not long after having filmed at Louis XIV's abode, I was in Prague for the first *Bourne* movie.

I have to say, I had a great time doing it. Chris Cooper I loved. Matt Damon too. The director, Doug, well, he remained a somewhat, let's just say, 'eccentric' figure. I wouldn't say he was self-sabotaging, exactly, just that he would tend to get a bee in his bonnet about something and be unwilling to let it go. He was great with visuals, although not so great with narrative. There is a moment at the end in which Bourne jumps from the top of a stairwell and uses the corpse of a baddie to break his fall. That was Doug, all Doug. The trouble was that I don't think he really saw eye to eye with some of the high-ups and ended up taking an executive producer role for the sequel, with Paul Greengrass brought in to direct.

I met Paul prior to the shoot. He was great. A writer-director who had cut his teeth working on *World in Action* for Granada, he was unprepared for what Hollywood would throw at him, even after I warned him that they'd be hiring and firing writers left, right and centre.

As a result he came on board fully expecting to be sacked at any second, and so he did a rather clever thing. You remember the Moscow car chase in *The Bourne Supremacy*? Absolutely brilliant, one of the best in cinema history. Paul filmed that first, and it became his calling card. His way of saying, 'If you lose me, you lose this.'

Mind you, he still had problems with his writers. There were tussles between the credited writer, Tony Gilroy, and Brian Helgeland, who did an uncredited rewrite, as well as Paul himself who was also working on the script.

Perhaps I should have requested a credit myself. The final scene of *The Bourne Supremacy*, where my character, Ward Abbott, reveals all to Bourne, was shot no fewer than five times, and on one such occasion, Matt and I even wrote a version together, which we performed outside the building. A very fine job we did of it, too, even if I do say so myself.

We shot three of those endings, and having done that, I dusted myself off, thinking the job was done, and scarpered off to do *Uncle*

Varick at the Royal Lyceum in Edinburgh, marking a return there having directed and starred in *The Master Builder* by Ibsen in 1993 (the one starring Morag Hood, if you recall).

Uncle Varick was a Scottish adaptation of Chekhov's *Uncle Vanya* written by the extraordinarily brilliant and very eccentric Scottish playwright, John Byrne. I played Varick, stretching my legs in a performance that went from foundation-shaking anger to quiet despair. Right up my street, in other words.

We did the previews for that on Thursday and Friday. The opening was on Tuesday, giving us Monday off for some reason. Then I got a call from the *Bourne* people saying, 'There's going to be a plane waiting to fly you to Germany. We're doing some pickups.'

By this stage I was in full-on, moustachioed Uncle Varick mode, not clean-shaven Ward Abbott mode. Even so, off I went, back to *Bourne*, where I was fitted with a wig and had to shave, and if you watch the film it does indeed look glaringly obvious that Ward Abbott has changed his look quite considerably in the meantime. People say you can't tell, but I can guarantee that now you know, you won't be able to unsee it. Sorry.

Of course, I was killed at the end of that film. I remember seeing Doug Liman not long afterwards. 'I don't know why they killed you,' he told me. 'I would have kept you alive. You were such an important character. That was a big mistake.'

I didn't disagree, but even so, it hardly marred what was overall a great experience. What's more, *The Bourne Identity* changed my status as an actor. I guess you could say that it was the first of the big payday films. After that came *Troy, X-Men*, another *Bourne*. I was in a new league.

In fact, we were prepping *The Bourne Supremacy* while I was making *Troy*, but that wasn't the most memorable thing that happened during that time. It wasn't Brad Pitt looking like a Greek God. It wasn't even me having to stab Peter O'Toole.

No, this was a family matter.

It goes back to when Margaret was in her very early twenties and she went to Japan to teach English – on an island called Kozushima, ten hours by boat from Tokyo, off the Izu peninsula.

While she was there, the island was struck by a series of earthquakes followed by some equally destructive aftershocks. This was 2000, and I was making a movie called *The Reckoning*. I was worried sick about her, hearing how this remote place, which had once been a prison for political prisoners during the Edo era, was now the crumbling rock where she lived. As an employee of the Tokyo Prefecture Board of Education, however, Margaret was told she was fine to stay. So she accepted her earthquake kit and hard hat and began to fend for herself.

I have always regretted that I didn't get off my backside, go to Japan and 'rescue' my daughter, because I'm sure that the trauma of her isolation contributed to what happened next. Her need to take control. Control over everything to be safe, and this included her eating.

She became anorexic.

Margaret didn't come back to the UK. She went to Russia, and then to the States, getting a job with a management company in LA. It was only after both her mother and I went to visit her that we saw she was not in a good way, and this went on for some time. We were all sick with not knowing if she'd get better or just die. Watching as she seemed to waste away.

Seeing our despair, she announced she was going to go on a

twelve-step programme in Florida to address her addiction. By now, she was all of eighty pounds. The programme she intended to join could not accept her because of her frail condition, and after suffering what seemed to be heart problems she was admitted to hospital.

Margaret ended up in a drug rehab facility, and it was there that a saint of a nurse, Therese, clearly recognized that she was suffering from an eating disorder. She somehow got my number and called me. At the time, I was making *Troy* in Baja California in Mexico and I had to go to the director, Wolfgang Petersen, and throw myself on his mercy.

Wolfgang was completely wonderful, immediately rearranging the shooting schedule to give me two weeks off so that I could leave the set and travel to whatever facility could be found to accept Margaret. And continue the process of recovery.

Then, and with the help of the incredible Therese, we were able to find a centre that specialized in her disorder. Remuda Ranch in Arizona. The only problem with Remuda was that it was 2,000 miles from Florida. Though a predominantly Christian organization, Remuda's prime means of care for the patients was equine therapy.

There, at least, she would have the support she needed.

I visited her in families' week, sitting in on the group therapy sessions. In these I witnessed some incredibly memorable disclosures; Margaret was able to begin the long road back to health.

I am incredibly proud of her, of course, for many, many things. Her accomplishments are manifold. She has a gift for languages, speaks fluent Russian and these days is a highly sought-after teacher. Most of all, I'm proud of her for battling that terrible disease. For while I was hanging out on a film set with my pals, being star-struck by Peter O'Toole and messing about on chariots, Margaret was staring death in the face, and though it so nearly claimed her – because indeed she came very close – she now quite happily stares back.

CHAPTER 47

I've ended up playing a number of real-life figures in my time. Asked if I research them, the answer is usually no. I stick to the script, because the script is where you'll find that character. That's where the writer, who has no doubt done his or her research, has put the character, and the writer wants me to be a conduit for what's on the page, not some other idea that I discover during background reading, that he or she may have already considered and discarded, or is implied elsewhere. The story goes that Sir Ralph Richardson once quizzed Samuel Beckett for biographical details on Pozzo in *Waiting for Godot*, and Beckett told him that 'all I knew about Pozzo was in the text, that if I had known more I would have put it in the text.' Quite. Added to which, I've worked steadily, project after project, for six decades, and honestly, there just isn't the time to read extensively around every real-life character I've played.

In 2006, I found myself at the Royal Court playing Max in Tom Stoppard's *Rock 'n' Roll*, one of my perennial stints in the theatre, where the work is creatively fulfilling and rewarding but not necessarily financially rewarding. For *Rock 'n' Roll* I was playing a character based on the British historian Eric Hobsbawm, an extraordinary intellectual and lifelong Marxist. Nicole was in the play, too, which was the lovely icing on an already enticing cake.

The play is all about the importance of rock 'n' roll during the rise of socialism in Czechoslovakia between 1968 and 1990. As well as building to the climax of a Rolling Stones concert that was held in Prague in 1990, it also includes loads of references to Pink Floyd.

The first night of the play was great. Mick Jagger came, as did Václav Havel, who as well as being the former president of the Czech Republic and a leading light of his country's 'velvet revolution', was also a playwright in his own right and a friend of Stoppard's. All in all, an amazing first night at the Royal Court.

We ended up transferring from the Court to the Duke of York's Theatre, after which I had to leave on making-movie business, and David Calder took over from me with Dominic West taking the place of Rufus Sewell.

I rejoined the production when we played on Broadway from the end of November 2007 until March 2008. That was when we as a family moved from our house in Camden Mews to New York. Nicole breathed a happy sigh of relief that her spiritual homecoming had been achieved at last, and my young sons, knowing little else, embarked on lives as New Yorkers. We've been here ever since.

Anyway. To the play itself, and my main concern during that production was a section where my character has to sit and listen to Jan, played by Rufus Sewell, as he waxes lyrical about Syd Barrett of Pink Floyd. The problem was not Rufus, who is a fine actor. Nor was it Syd Barrett or Pink Floyd. The problem was that my character just had to sit motionless for about ten minutes, listening to Jan's monologue. Perhaps it's my natural restlessness, my need to be doing something even if that something is nothing, but it wasn't working for me.

I said to Tom Stoppard, 'Tom, Rufus is talking about Syd Barrett.'

Tom is the nicest, most gentlemanly guy, but he's got this thing about displacement of energy. He often talks about how he doesn't want to waste energy as he's getting older. The way this can manifest itself is in a somewhat listless disposition.

'Yes, he's talking about Syd Barrett,' he said, slowly, with the minimum use of energy. 'Is that okay, Brian?'

'That's fine. No problem with that at all. Just that . . .'

'Yes?'

'Give me a reason to be on stage. Why am I there? What am I *doing* there?'

He dodged the question. 'You're there to serve,' he said, by which he meant there to drive on the play, and I understood that, in a sense, although it didn't help with my problem which was that Eric Hobsbawm was a great socialist radical thinker, a philosopher at Oxford and I couldn't for the life of me think why he would be sitting listening to a lecture on Syd Barrett.

Tough shit for me. Some nights, when Rufus was doing it fast, it wasn't so bad. But when he really took his time and got into it, it made it hard for me to sustain and a very frustrating experience.

I was all right in the end; I did well out of it, people were kind about me. When we came to Broadway we lost a little bit of momentum because there was a strike that closed the show down for weeks, but it was still a major success.

Prior to that, Tom had been overjoyed to have a play on at the Royal Court. You wouldn't say he was fizzing with delight, because fizzing with delight involves more energy than he was willing to expend, but he was certainly delighted in his Tom Stoppardian way. Now, knowing my oft-repeated views on the occasionally feudal nature of theatre in the UK, and remembering John Osborne's experiences at the Court, you might well wonder how Tom Stoppard fared? Well, the answer is wrapped up in another question. How many Tom Stoppard plays after *Rock 'n' Roll* were performed at the Royal Court?

Answer: none.

In 2010, I played the speaker of the house, Michael Martin, in a TV thing called *On Expenses*, all about the whole expenses scandal and the disgraceful way that certain Tory MPs behaved. To my mind, Michael Martin seemed to be made the scapegoat. He was a good Catholic guy who played the bagpipes and I was very pleased to do the job because I'd always felt that he got the tap end of the bath.

I've played Stalin, too. And Nye Bevan. And Pablo Picasso. But my annus mirabilis for playing real-life figures came in 2013, when I played J. Edgar Hoover in a TV movie, *The Curse of Edgar*, Sir Matt Busby in *Believe*, and the BBC executive Sydney Newman in the story of Dr Who, called *An Adventure in Space and Time*, which also starred David Bradley as William Hartnell.

I suppose the most significant, though, is the big man. Churchill.

My Churchill film, just called *Churchill*, had the misfortune to come out in the same year as *Darkest Hour* starring Gary Oldman as Churchill and thus was afflicted by the Curse of Brian Cox, a phenomenon which was, I believe, coined by the film critics Simon Mayo and Mark Kermode to describe what happens when I play a character and then another actor picks up an Oscar for appearing in a different film as the same character.

It's not an especially virulent curse. There have only been two examples. Your prize for correctly naming the first one is something wet in the post, while *Churchill* was the second.

For that film, and in contradiction of something I said earlier, I did more than my usual amount of research. After all, this was a big starring role with a determinedly iconoclastic portrayal of Churchill. Dealing with the run-up to D-Day, the contention of Alex von Tunzelmann's script was that far from campaigning in favour of the operation, Churchill, profoundly affected by the slaughter he had witnessed first hand at Gallipoli, had in fact been against it.

Playing him, I saw Churchill as this little fat kid who went to Harrow (and having had my own experience of being a little fat kid, I had a sense of what that was like), but who then became this extraordinary guy, this journalist who embarked on the 'young Winston' years prior to becoming one of the great iconic figures of twentieth-century Britain. Our portrayal was of a man with a great and complicated history, not all of it perhaps as heroic as we might like to imagine, but a man who, like many others, returned from the First World War stricken by alcoholism. A man who in his prime-ministerial role showed the firm hand of leadership but in private was assailed by doubt. There's a bit of Lear in that portrayal. There's some Titus. There is blood and thunder, but also quiet contemplation.

And it was pretty good, all told. The trouble was that we went up against Gary's film, *Darkest Hour*. Ours was a small picture, Gary's was big. To add insult to injury, Gary then got an Oscar for it. The fact that he got the Oscar? I don't mind that at all. No, I know what you're thinking. I really don't. But what I do mind is that their film was cobblers. Ours might have been a little too heavy, and it certainly went against the popular belief that Churchill was not only in favour of D-Day but heavily involved in the planning, which I think made it unpalatable to many people, but at least it didn't have a scene in which Churchill catches a tube and begins talking to 'ordinary', cap-doffing people on the underground, asking them how they're enjoying the war and so on. Which is what they had in *Darkest Hour*.

In other words, ours was a more honest film, just that we didn't open in that wonderful window between Thanksgiving and New Year. The 'awards season'. We opened in the summer and so were eclipsed by a film that was more expensive but infinitely more shallow, a crowd-pleasing farrago. (And far be it from me to suggest that 'crowd-pleasing farrago' sums up the vast majority of awards ceremonies.)

While we're on the subject of playing real people, it would be remiss of me not to mention one of the weirdest. No – cut. Take two. *The* weirdest. In the same year as *Churchill* – 2017, to be precise – came a TV show called *Urban Myths*, a mix of comedy and real-life stories telling tales of legendary celebrity shenanigans. So, for example, the first one dealt with Bob Dylan flying to the UK to visit Dave Stewart, only to end up in the wrong flat. Was it true? Possibly not, but the show dramatizes it anyway. Did Cary Grant and Timothy Leary really take LSD together? Well, they do in an episode of *Urban Myths*.

Cast your eye down the episodes listed for season one and you'll see one called 'Elizabeth, Michael and Marlon', which concentrated on the story of Michael Jackson, Elizabeth Taylor and Marlon Brando jumping in a car together and fleeing New York after the 9/11 attacks. Whether this actually happened, it's difficult to say and the chances are we'll never know for certain since none of the participants are still with us. The official story, if 'official' is the right word, which it probably isn't, is that the night before, they'd all been at Madison Square Garden together, and then, when 9/11 happened, they decided to get out of the city so hopped on a bus. However, if you go on the internet, which in the interests of research, I just have, there are conflicting stories as to whether the journey took place at all and if it did, whether in fact it included all three participants. Besides which, for the purposes of our drama, we ditched the bus and put them in a car together.

At one point, Brando, Taylor and Jackson stop at a diner and the waitress is played by Carrie Fisher, who in real life, of course, was Elizabeth Taylor's stepdaughter, which makes your head spin. Meanwhile, I played Marlon Brando, which was great for me because I'd always wanted to play Marlon Brando. Doing his voice had long been one of my party pieces.

So I'm Brando, sitting in the back of the car with his suitcase. Elizabeth Taylor, played by Stockard Channing, was in the front driving, and next to her was Michael Jackson played by . . .

Who?

That was the question.

First they said, *What about Tilda Swinton?* That's a wacky thought. Tilda Swinton. For a while they tinkered with the revolutionary idea of getting an African American actress to play the African American man Michael Jackson, but their thinking was that Jackson was virtually white by 2001, so perhaps the part would be better played by a white man.

So in the end they went for . . . wait for it . . . Joseph Fiennes.

And, actually, Joe was rather good. There's no taking that away from him. The trouble was that Paris Jackson complained bitterly that a white actor had played Michael, and with some justification, it must be said, because as we all know, getting a white actor to play a black man – even a black man who was, for whatever reason, missing the requisite skin pigmentation – is, well, it's beyond the pale.

It was great, actually. It's very charming and funny and Joe looks convincing as Michael. But in light of the Jackson family protesting, which I think Paris had done in the time-honoured manner of tweeting about it, Sky bottled it, withdrew the episode and it remains unaired. Perhaps one day, in a less panic-stricken, cancel-culture-happy environment, we'll eventually get to see it, but I wouldn't hold your breath, because the fact is that we seem to be getting more cancel-happy, not less, a situation that not only do I find quite worrying, but also feel goes hand in hand with a general decline in courtesy throughout my industry. But then perhaps it is in a time of moral malaise that creatures like the 'Pink Pinocchio' and the 'Eton Clown' surface through a sea of lies. That the link between amoral deviance and irresponsible behaviour becomes, painfully, all too clear.

One of the watchwords associated with the current era is #BeKind, but it strikes me that cancel culture, in its adherence to a group sensibility, is anything but kind. There are certain figures who of course deserve all the punishment they get, but also abroad is a McCarthyist, vengeful element, which gives rise to an awful lot of collateral damage. People who don't deserve to lose their jobs find themselves unemployed. Those who might merely be adjacent to the genuine creeps find themselves ostracized.

Moreover, a combination of cancel culture and Covid seems to have changed codes of behaviour, giving people licence to hide behind healthcare protocols just as surely as they hide behind the language of 'woke'. What it has led to is a swiftness to judge, to dismiss quickly, to abdicate moral responsibility, and that to me is a nail in the coffin of creativity.

It's particularly apparent in the casting sphere, where young actors must now conduct auditions from home. They have to provide the camera and lighting and learn twelve pages of script, and very often will never get any feedback, not even a reply. I see this as being indicative of an overall erosion of standards, a lack of respect for the actor, and in a wider sense for the individual, who is forced to surrender individual thinking to the will of the crowd. Is that kind? This old, white dinosaur (currently making a crust from playing an old, white dinosaur) isn't so sure. We shall see.

CHAPTER 48

There has, unfortunately and unavoidably, been a great deal of death in this book, the product partly of my own longevity but also the fact that my profession tends to produce what you might call extreme and obsessive characters. Philip Seymour Hoffman, for example, with whom I worked on *25th Hour* for Spike Lee in 2002. He was the sweetest, funniest guy but he had a darkness to him. It's a matter of public knowledge that he had abused drugs and alcohol during his college years until, at twenty-two, he went into rehab and stayed sober for twenty-three years.

Clearly, he relapsed. Some years after the Spike Lee film, I did a couple of workshops with him. Whether he was back on the drugs then or not, I couldn't say, just that he was very edgy and argumentative, not at all the delightful man I had met before.

Sure enough, in February 2014, Philip was found dead in the bathroom of his Manhattan apartment of an overdose, at just forty-six. Sometimes it feels as though there are actors who get caught up in the lifestyle, who get swallowed up by it. River Phoenix would be one. Heath Ledger another.

And then you get those whose passing is nothing short of a freak and hideously tragic accident. In that case the name that immediately springs to mind is Natasha Richardson. I was making a TV mini-series, *The Day of the Triffids*, which starred Natasha's sister, Joely, when it happened. During a beginners' skiing lesson while on holiday in Canada, Natasha had hit her head. Complaining of headaches shortly afterwards, she was flown direct to New York.

Joely left the *Triffids* set to be with her in hospital, and although Natasha was still alive at that point, she died two days later of an epidural haematoma, and Joely returned for work with the weight of recent bereavement hanging heavy upon her. On the evening of Natasha's death, theatre lights on Broadway and in the West End were dimmed as a mark of respect. Meanwhile, on the *Triffids* set, Joely had to play a death scene. *My* death scene, in fact.

'Please don't let her film the death scene, that's just not nice,' I implored, but my pleas fell on deaf ears. In a world in which movies and TV trump everything in terms of importance, we had a schedule. And Joely had to film her scene (a fact that, when you think about it, throws Wolfgang's wonderful accommodation of my request to leave the set of *Troy* for an entire fortnight into even greater relief).

There is a somewhat tragic postscript to what is already a tragic story. Just one year later, I was making Ralph Fiennes's version of *Coriolanus*, which also starred Vanessa Redgrave, who was of course the mother of Natasha and Joely.

At the beginning of the shoot, Vanessa's brother, Corin, died of a heart attack at fifty. At the end of the shoot, two months later, her sister, Lynn, died of cancer at sixty-seven. This was the same Lynn Redgrave whose wig I had regularly rescued from the litter bin of her dressing room when I was but a child, and to have that connection, to see these terrible Redgrave tragedies up close, was heartbreaking. Absolutely heartbreaking.

During the writing of this book, we said goodbye to Christopher Plummer. I had first met Chris when I was playing opposite his wife, Elaine, in a BBC production of *She Stoops to Conquer.* As you may recall, I was overawed by Sir Ralph Richardson on that job, and when Christopher Plummer turned up the effect was the same. To me he was elegance personified, but the extraordinary corollary to that was that through Elaine I was introduced to the guy he worked out with, a character called Rusty Hood.

Rusty was a kind of minor stuntman in British movies. He had a basement flat in Earls Court, and on our workouts Chris and I would occasionally cross paths. I would always try to get away from Rusty's as quick as I could on the days that Chris would be working out because Rusty's really tiny apartment stank of the most appalling body odour and I was worried Chris might think I was responsible.

On the odd occasion that we did meet he would be so incredibly well dressed, just as if he were going on to lunch at one of London's fancy clubs, and he simply either ignored or perhaps didn't even notice the malodorous smell. In fact, thinking about it, in all my dealings with him he always had this air of undaunted grace. Never more so than when we worked together on *Nuremberg.*

To fellow Canadians he was more than just a celebrity. He was very much regarded as their royalty. He was also very much the product of that tradition of the great classical players of the past. From Garrick via Kean via Irving via John Barrymore via Larry Olivier via Paul Scofield. His career consumed him right to the very end. In fact, he was preparing to appear as Lear once again on celluloid. Apparently he could be heard by his wife Elaine quietly reciting his lines.

Chris died in Connecticut. Being no great fan of attending funerals, I didn't go. Memorial services in England are fine, but the funerals themselves are always acutely depressing. Especially if they're at Golders Green, which I find one of the most miserable places ever.

Another one, of course, was my brother Charlie. For while my three older sisters, Bette, May and Irene, soldiered on into their nineties, seemingly indestructible, Charlie was the first of us to go, of stomach cancer in 2007, aged sixty-nine.

I had always had a slightly complicated relationship with my brother. We had separate lives. He was much more working class than I am, with a lifestyle that encompassed his work – he ran a shop in Monifieth in Dundee – family and the pub. But he was a very funny man. He used to say that of the two of us, he was the actor in the family, and I think that in many ways he was right about that. In a sense his life was one long performance.

Years later, in 2014, I appeared in a sitcom, *Bob Servant*, about the owner of a burger van who runs for local office in the town of Broughty Ferry, very close to Dundee. During filming, there were so many locals who told the writer, Neil Forsyth, 'That turn he's doing, that turn of Brian's, that's Charlie Cox, that is.'

But, of course, Neil had never met Charlie and had no idea what they meant. As for me, well, I suppose I was channelling him a little. Charlie had that same sense of largesse and bonhomie you see in Bob Servant. If somebody came into the shop and he didn't have change, Charlie would say, 'Listen, I haven't got any shrapnel for you, so why not have a cabbage? In fact, have two cabbages.' That persona fed into a fantasy life into which he had retreated. When our father died, the world at large assumed that I as the youngest would have been hit the hardest, but as I've already discussed, I think that it was Charlie who really suffered; Charlie who disguised his tears at our father's funeral by frantically, obsessively, eating that orange;

Charlie who later joined the army and then came back somewhat brutalized, in my opinion. He still had that famous Charlie Cox sense of humour. One of his favourite jokes involving his army days was to say, 'I once saved our entire squad. I shot the cook.' And he was still retreating into that fantasy world, perhaps even more acutely. It was the westerns with him. He was always hitting what he called 'the mealy puddin' trail'. He'd say that the Apaches were after him. Except that he didn't mean the Apaches, as it turned out. He meant the VAT man.

Having been diagnosed with stomach cancer and told it was terminal, Charlie also had a touch of dementia at the end. At one point he said to me, 'Hey, Brian, have I left school yet?'

And I said, 'Aye, Charlie, you've left school. You left school some while ago.'

'I thought I had,' he said.

I hated to see him in that condition, made frail by his illness. He was remarkably accepting, but if challenged by his wife or daughters about his condition, he would bemusedly dismiss them. On one occasion, his wife Rosa remarked about the tightness of his dressing gown cord. Charlie's response was to untie and retie his cord several times, punctuating it when done, 'There, done, better now?' I could see that despite dementia, cancer and that he was dying, Charlie was in control, control even over small things, like a dressing gown cord.

But although I had felt a terrible sadness on hearing that he had been diagnosed with cancer, his actual death left me somewhat hollow. I don't think that I really came to terms with it, not until years later, when I began to pine for him, when it hit me unexpectedly hard, that in a family always dominated by women, he was my brother. And not only had our relationship never quite developed or evolved in the way that I would like it to have done, but there was no longer the opportunity for it to do so.

In short, I had lost him. And I had lost any possibility of what there might have been between us. Which left me with regret. It left me wondering, as these things so often do, what constitutes a good death?

Putting the question to one side for a moment, the human experiment can be labelled as . . . disappointing. But as a species, we are, at times, exceedingly vulnerable. Our vulnerability lies in the inability to understand life and its purpose. We hunt for the tools to make sense of it all: religion, science, politics, sport, the theatre. We explore and search for meaning by discovering new worlds and climbing mountains, and a great many of us find tremendous solace and comfort in these activities, but the one thing that is absolutely certain is that we are born and that we will die. The rest is propaganda.

Throughout my adult life I've had moments of crisis, when I needed help and perspective. When my first marriage fell apart, for example. When my relationship with Irina came to an end. When Margaret was so very ill.

In the early 2000s a combination of the domestic and career issues I described brought me to another crisis point, when I visited a Jungian therapist, who brought me to understand how my family, especially my sisters, Bette, May and Irene, held me in their hearts.

The second time was in the middle of the *King Lear* tour. By now I had split from Irina and was effectively homeless. I knew I was in deep shit.

At this point, I was introduced to the work of Peter Ouspensky and his book *In Search of the Miraculous*, which in turn led me to the work of George Ivanovich Gurdjieff, a Russian philosopher.

Gurdjieff taught that most humans live their lives in a state of hypnotic 'waking sleep', but that it is possible to awaken a higher state of consciousness and achieve full human potential.

He taught that a person must expend considerable effort to effect that transformation that leads to an awakening, attaining that higher level of consciousness. He believed that inner growth and development are real possibilities that nonetheless require conscious work to achieve. Gurdjieff called his discipline 'The Work'.

I was introduced to the formidable Betty Gloster, a disciple of Gurdjieff, who was grace personified. Extremely caring and patient. Whenever possible while on tour, I would fly into London for a private work session with her.

One of the precepts of the Gurdjieff work is 'self-remembering'. That is, if a man spends his life in a constant state of sleep, he needs prompts to awaken him. She gave the simplest of exercises, one being that every time I touched a door handle I would awake and remember. And it worked.

The third major crisis I had was a period during which I found myself questioning my marriage and career, and this time of reflection led me via the work of Victor Frankl to logotherapy. I had read his seminal work *Man's Search for Meaning*, a book inspired by Frankl's time as a Jewish physician in Nazi concentration camps. Frankl's basic tenet is that the primary motivational force of an individual is to find a meaning to his or her life and that everything can be taken from a man but one thing: the last of the human freedoms – to choose one's attitude in any given set of circumstances.

We actors live in a constant state of insecurity and rejection. Either by possible employers or critics of our work on stage or screen. It could drive you mad, and sadly it has been the case for some who are unable to cope with the rejection. Me, I've had sixty years of these conditions. And I've had to learn the hard way not to attach myself to these insanities.

And that's logotherapy in essence: don't attach. Our main motivation for living is our will to find meaning in life, and life has meaning even in the most miserable of circumstances. I take some comfort from that, believe it or not, while at the same time feeling a great sense of existential horror at the idea of the world without me. I do believe that we simply flick off, like an appliance. You don't get a choice how. You can only choose your attitude at the time. That's how you make it a good death.

CHAPTER 49

As for Charlie, I think that he would have recognized a little of himself in Bob Servant. He'd certainly have seen the funny side. For me, Bob was partly Charlie – perhaps less so than the good people of Broughty Ferry believed – as well as that Scottish vaudeville tradition of which I'm so fond, and a little bit of Rab C. Nesbitt, which I love.

It also represented a case of me reconnecting with my roots. After all, Bob Servant came in the wake of that period during which I had thrown my support behind Scottish independence, after the referendum, and also when I was rector at the University of Dundee.

Because, yes, I was, for a time, exactly that. Some bright spark in the students' union decided that, as I was a Dundee boy, I should be put up for the post. I was and I won unanimously, remaining rector for six years. They wanted me to go on for a third term, but I decided that I had gone on long enough, plus the travel to and from Dundee was proving arduous.

The rector is an elected position, and the job is to ensure that the interests of staff and especially students are paramount when it comes to any decisions made by the university's governing body. At the time I had plenty of criticisms of the system, one of those being the gap that exists between a school student, who comes from a structured, organized system of education, and a student at university, faced with the notion of independent learning. I felt that a lot of kids weren't prepared for independent learning, even at eighteen, and that the transition could and should be better handled. I tried my best as rector to address that.

I tried to be a present, proactive rector. One of my main jobs, and an aspect of the post that I found particularly rewarding, was my student surgeries. For example, through my experiences with Margaret, I was able to identify that one of my students suffered from anorexia, and help them allay their disquiet. Another was suffering anxiety about their exams, and so I suggested they write an essay all about a student taking an examination and how they got through that process. It was something that went back to my logotherapy, and I'm happy to report that that particular student went on to do well in their exams and flourished.

I would go in about once a month for a couple of days, and I have to say, I really enjoyed the work, finding it fulfilling and gratifying. When it came time for me to leave, a sour note was struck when they wanted me out at short notice to allow a new rector to take over, and though they were very apologetic about it, I must admit to being slightly pissed off because I did a lot of work for that university. I put in a lot of time and effort and I felt that in many ways I had been summarily dismissed.

Still, it remains an interesting era, especially as it formed part of that period during which I felt a sense of myself rediscovering my Scottishness, reconnecting with that part of my past. That, *Bob Servant*, and then to cap it all off a production of *Waiting for Godot* at the Lyceum in Edinburgh. I had worked at the Lyceum over a number of years through my friend, Kenny Ireland, the Lyceum director who back in the day had helped give Billy Connolly his start by putting him on *The Welly Boot Show*. Kenny died of cancer in 2014 and taking over as artistic director at the Lyceum was Mark Thompson, who got in touch. 'We want to do something for the fiftieth anniversary of the company,' he said. 'What do you suggest?'

'I've never done a Beckett,' I told him.

Incredible, when you think about it, but true.

'What about *Godot*?'

'*Godot*. Yes. You and . . . who else?'

'What about Bill Paterson?'

Bill and I had worked together on screen a few times. The time I played Pablo Picasso? He was in that too (directed by Sharon Maguire, who later went on to the *Bridget Jones* films). We had also done a film, *Complicity*, starring Jonny Lee Miller and Keeley Hawes, in 2000, so I knew him as a friend and I knew him to be a wonderful, wonderful actor.

Waiting for Godot is basically a two-hander in which the characters, Didi (me), and Gogo (Bill) sit waiting for the arrival of someone called Godot, having various profound conversations. It's a difficult play, especially when you are, well, I was sixty-nine and Bill was seventy when we did it.

'Bill,' I said, when I called him, 'the Lyceum's fiftieth anniversary is coming up and I've suggested that you and I can do *Godot*.'

'Oh, that's interesting,' he said, and then paused. 'It's a lot of lines.'

'Yeah, I know. I think we can manage that though, can't we?'

'I suppose so,' he said, and then paused. 'But I'm worried about my legs.'

That one threw me.

'What?'

'My legs, Brian. You know, the long things between my hips and my feet. They're not what they once were. Tell you the truth, I'm a wee bit worried about them.'

'Oh, I'm sure your legs will be all right. Gogo sits down a lot, Bill, you know that. He's mainly looking at his boots.'

'Aye,' he said. 'Aye, I suppose you're right.'

Sure enough, that's the way the play works. As Didi, I'm the big boisterous one, running around all the time, whereas Gogo, with the exception of one sequence when we're both running around, pretty much just sits there. So that thing about the legs? That was just Bill being Bill. The main thing was that we were a huge hit. Packed houses every night. Great reviews, some of the best of my career.

Early last year, just before Covid hit, there was talk of reviving it. Three years ago, and despite the fact that it had been packed out in Edinburgh, the English management wouldn't look at it, thus there wasn't the opportunity to transfer it to the West End. Since then, however, *Fleabag* has happened for Bill, and *Succession* for me. Suddenly these two old duffers are big names with commercial potential and people are interested in doing *Godot* again.

I rang him. 'Bill, you know there's a possibility that with the success of Logan and *Fleabag* we could do *Godot* again.'

'Oh yes,' he said, 'I think I can still remember the lines. But, you know, Brian, I've got one little concern.'

'What's that, Bill?'

'My legs, Brian, I'm worried about my legs.'

CHAPTER 50

One of the pleasures of being a partner in a relationship is the double joy of working together. I believe I've been extraordinary lucky in earning that double joy.

In my past relationships I endeavoured to establish working relationships on stage as well as off. First in 1989 with Irina as Vivie in *Mrs Warren's Profession*, then with Siri who played Hilde Wangel in *The Master Builder* in 1994.

As for Nicole, she had long established herself as a pretty formidable actress before we met up again, with her work in Zurich and at the Volkstheatre in Vienna. She seemed to me to be ripe for something extraordinary.

Now, the very nature of working on stage provides a deepening understanding of shared goals through the dramatic form. The play being the thing, as the Bard so rightly put it, requires a profound commitment to its meaning and delivery.

Some years ago, Nicole was sent a play, *Sinners*, by the Israeli writer Joshua Sobol. It deals with the sensitive subject of a Middle-Eastern English professor, Layla, who has had an affair with one of her young married students, Nur, and has been sentenced to death by stoning for her adulterous affair. Layla sits in a hole in the centre of the stage, completely covered from view, while her young lover has to collect and prepare the stones for her stoning.

I read only one page of the script and knew instantly that not only was this was a play I wanted to direct, but I very much wanted to do it with Nicole. The resonance of the play in the present climate was and is so profound, that I found it completely irresistible.

In 2016, through the auspices of Greensboro Arts Alliance in Vermont, under the direction of the visionary Sabra Jones, Nicole and I were invited to stage *Sinners*. I would direct and Nicole would star as Layla.

This was Nicole's second summer season in Greensboro, which Sabra had run for over ten years, employing a complementary blend of local amateur actors and professionals. She had created a unique and committed theatrical community, performing at the highest professional level. The perfect setting for a work as controversial as *Sinners*, away from the glare of New York.

We performed in the nearby town of Hardwick at the Hardwick Town House, which had started life as a primary school, later to be converted to a miniature Italian opera house, complete with incredible acoustics.

The work was intense – the simple density of the text, the physical choreography of the young man's stone collection – but Nicole was amazing in her grasp of the professor's fervent defence of female sensuality, channelling the frustration of a Middle-Eastern woman living at the mercy of a time-worn patriarchy. The character of Layla is so clearly defined that her articulate humanity requires a blunting and blending of the edges, but one of Nicole's gifts and strengths as an actress is her ability to completely inhabit the paradox of character.

The location of the play is simply 'any country where this could happen', but in Iran, in the wake of the Islamist revolution, the barbaric practice of stoning women to death had become widespread, particularly in remote communities, and Nicole's Iranian roots awakened a strain of her DNA history – a history which lies, in different forms and influences, in all of us.

The part of the young man was doubly hard. At first his role was clearly underwritten, but this, of course, is the advantage of developing a work over two or three years. The luxury of work in progress, the refining and redefining of a piece of theatre. And our actor, Arash Mokhtar, would go on to do a stellar job.

Our opening in Hardwick was greeted enthusiastically and proved that the play had legs. The play challenged that Vermont audience to acknowledge how easy it is to dismiss oppressive regimes, tyrannical theocracies, as somehow 'other', but when the differences in style and scripture are peeled away, you see how systemic patriarchy is.

But our heroine is not the only victim, and the play is a dialogue between Layla and her lover, Nur.

Initially, Arash Mokhtar did a wonderful job as Nur, despite the slightly underwritten part. Our work over the next year or so was to redefine Nur as the catalyst of Layla's woes. This was the task I set our writer Joshua. With the most economic stroke of his pen, Joshua elicited a deeper and more profound understanding of Nur's own dilemma. How Nur too is also a victim. A victim of the cultural traditions laid down by his father, and how these traditions demand adherence, at any cost to his manhood, to his own sexuality and self-respect.

So when the play was reproduced in London at the Playground Theatre in 2020, with a new Nur, Adam Sina, we very much achieved the balance that had been just out of reach first time around.

Sinners is not simply an admonition against the violence inflicted on Layla and Nur, but also the swansong of two individuals whose love is unacceptable in their society.

In the final moments of the play Sobol creates an almost magic-realist event when Layla rises out of her prison hole and greets Nur in the form of a dance.

For me as the director this was also a moment to review and address the contradictions of the romance, beauty and passion of Islamic culture. I enlisted the choreography of Shah Ghalam (wonderfully reinterpreted by Laya Torkaman in London) and the music of Fareed Shafinury.

The music and dance allow the essence of the story to transcend the play's specific circumstances. And become a celebration of these two people – without their constraints, or without the elements that brutalize them – a celebration of their true passion, their true love. The essence of who they are and what is possible for them. And . . . for all of us.

CHAPTER 51

Succession is a satire about families. About dynasties. It's about entitlement. It's a critique of the fact that non-elected individuals can have an effect on policy. It's about Logan Roy trying to teach his spoiled, entitled children the value of hard work. Teaching them the hard way. Teaching them in a way that is not always – hardly ever – moral or ethical, but teaching them nonetheless, because he wants the best for them, and because they are, at the end of the day, however spoiled and entitled they might be and whatever individual flaws they possess, his children, just as Waystar Royco is his child, just as certain privileged employees also enjoy that status.

I was in London in 2016 when my manager, Matthew, rang and said, 'There's an interest in you for this show about a media family, written by some guy, er, Jesse Armstrong.'

At this stage, it was just an idea, something in the ether. Unlike Matthew, I had heard of Jesse Armstrong. He was one of the co-creators of *Peep Show* and had also written for *The Thick of It* so I assumed the show would likely feature some kind of satirical element. Other than that it was anyone's guess. I had conversations with Jesse and the producer, Adam McKay, an ex-*Saturday Night*

Live writer and regular collaborator of Will Ferrell, who was also to produce. I liked what they had to say.

So I said yes, returned to the States and embarked on the pre-prep. Then we did the first read-through and something happened – something just clicked into place. I've talked before about jobs I've done such as *The Game* or *The Straits*. Ensemble pieces. I was in a season of *Deadwood* having been approached by David Milch, the showrunner. Milch began his career writing for Stephen Bochco on *Hill Street Blues*. He's an incredibly literate, philosophical man, a bit of a genius and an all-round good egg. I had already seen *Deadwood* at the time and thought it was the most extraordinary thing I'd seen in years so to be approached about doing the third season was great. It was an interesting character as well: Jack Langrishe, a Chicago theatre owner who had ended up in Deadwood where he tried to start again.

Now, David had his problems. Alcohol, heroin, gambling. I won't rake over them here because he's a good person and sometimes bad things befall good people and he is indeed one of the good guys. It was thanks to David, in fact, that we were able to get Nicole a much-needed green card, but that's another story.

The other great thing about doing that season was, of course, Ian McShane, who for a certain generation of TV viewers will always be *Lovejoy* but, and without wanting to do *Lovejoy* down, is a much, much finer actor than that particular legacy might suggest. Happily he's proved it over and over since, with things like *Sexy Beast*, while Al Swearengen in *Deadwood* was a quite extraordinary creation.

So, it was a very happy show. I was looking forward to coming back for season four when my character was going to open his theatre and we would do *The Mikado* – which is exactly what happened in the real-life *Deadwood* – but then things fell apart, some kind of pissing contest, which meant that the fourth series never happened and instead HBO and David agreed to make a film in place of another series.

I had approaches about doing the film, but by then I was tied up with *Succession*. Although I was sad about not being able to rejoin *Deadwood* and regretting the fact that my character had no real conclusion in the story, I was excited for *Succession* by then and anyway, that's just the way it goes sometimes. It wasn't like I was ever going to turn down *Succession*, because that read-through? Wow. The whole cast was there. The cast as we know them today, and I'd been blown away by them, every single one.

Next, we did the pilot, after which we had to wait for the pickup, which came pretty soon, after which things seem to have gone from strength to strength. We've had excellent press, consistently good word of mouth, the cast have grown into their roles, the storylines have stayed true to Jesse's original vision.

The funny thing was that before I had my initial talks with Jesse and Adam, it was sold to me as a one-shot deal, that Logan would die at the end of the first season. *Sure*, I had thought. *That's the story of my career. One-season parts.* As I've said before, every actor likes to get that long-standing, recurring gig, and not just for the money and the security, but also because it's a wonderful thing to follow that particular narrative from its very beginning to its very end. But still, I was okay with that. Later on, we were having yet another conversation, just going through ideas, with me talking stuff off the top of my head, as you do, when I said to them, 'So it's just a one-season part, right?'

From the other end of the line came an almighty pause, so long that I thought we'd lost the connection.

'Maybe not, Brian.'

Turned out they were as keen on Logan as I was. They enjoyed the dynamic that arose from a situation where, instead of Logan departing the story and the kids fighting it out for themselves, he remained very much on the scene, pulling the strings in ways that are sometimes as confusing to the viewer as they are to the kids themselves. Which kids does he prefer? Is it Shiv, Sarah Snook's character, who might be his equal? Is it Jeremy Strong's Kendall, a monster of Logan's making? Is it Roman, played by Kieran Culkin, the dark horse? It's probably not Connor (Alan Ruck), if I'm honest.

As for Logan, I just love playing him. I love the fact that I can play him as reined in and bottled up. One of the writers, Tony Roche, said to me the other day, 'You do stillness like nobody I know, it's just incredible. One doesn't have to write for you. One just has to give you stage directions and then film,' and that's one of the things that I really like about it, too. The economy of Logan's dialogue. I negotiated a driver with HBO, and on the way to and from the set, I'll sit in the back with my assistant, the wonderful Mickey, and we'll run lines together. Mickey enjoys the fact that Logan doesn't have too many lines. We both love the fact that the dialogue suits me, the actor. Sometimes it can be almost distressingly easy to put on my Logan Roy skin, but I understand why, because as well as being what it's about – wealth, entitlement, et cetera – *Succession* is also about displacement. It's about how Logan is classically displaced, taken from his childhood home when he was very young. And you know what? I know somebody else who feels displaced, who left Scotland at a young age. Somebody else who feels a certain disgust with the rest of the human race, who feels that humanity is a failed experiment. My view is that at some point very early on in his career he returned to Scotland to work at DC Thomson where he learned his trade as a local journalist but then he became this avaricious empire builder and was eventually corrupted by it. So he's got all these layers, he's got all these nuances. He is not necessarily one thing nor is he entirely another.

And yet, and yet. There is still that element to him that I find constantly intriguing. You're constantly asking, *Who is he, this guy?*

A great character, then, and I sincerely hope that after the third season there will be another one, and if that turns out to be the last, then . . .

Then what . . .?

EPILOGUE

I began with a story about myself and Nigel Hawthorne on an aeroplane. Well, dear old Nigel passed in 2001 of pancreatic cancer. His last film was a made-for-TV Christmas comedy, *Call Me Claus*, in which he starred opposite Whoopi Goldberg. Nigel had the title role in that one. He was Santa. It was made the year he died.

And that's the way it goes. Sometimes people retire. Sean Connery. Gene Hackman did it. But mostly you go on until you drop dead of one thing or another, because at the end of the day, it's not the kind of job where you can't wait to collect your pension and your carriage clock and leave. There's a part of you that remains the kid on top of the coal bunker, singing Al Jolson songs. You never stop wanting to show off, working out that insecurity, expiating yourself of your guilt. You never stop.

In my case, I continue to make movies around the filming of *Succession*, but mainly as a way of funding stints at the theatre, because even though films were always my first love as a wee boy, it's theatre that has had the most profound effect on me.

The last thing I did in the theatre prior to Covid was a Broadway play called *The Great Society*, in which I played the lead, President Lyndon B. Johnson.

Initially I'd been told that it was just a reading of the play, but then I got in the door and they assumed crash positions and said, 'Actually, Brian, we were hoping you'd agree to do the whole play.'

'You what?'

'The whole play. Is that a problem?'

'Yes, it's a fucking problem; of course it's a problem. I've got to learn this text in three weeks.' Did I mention it was 160 pages and very dialogue heavy? For me, a seventy-three-year-old, to learn 160 pages in three weeks, even with the help of the redoubtable Mickey, was a tall order. Perhaps too tall.

But what happened was that I began to really, really enjoy the piece. I was too short to play Lyndon Johnson, but it didn't matter because what I came to realize was that Johnson reminded me of my dad, and for that reason I found myself channelling my dad into the performance. That was my 'in'. After that, I knew the script would follow.

By the end of rehearsals, I knew 80 per cent of the script. I knew it chronologically, so it was only the end of the play that eluded me. Even so, the opening night loomed.

'Would you wear an earpiece?'

'I've never worn an earpiece before,' I said, and then had an image of myself up on stage, blank mind grappling to find the words that would not come, 'but I'll give it a go.'

Enter Mickey, who is the dearest man imaginable, and who via my earpiece talked me through that final twenty per cent of the script so that we got through the previews. By opening night, I knew it all, but even so, I kept Mickey there. I'd got used to him by then, and besides which, that mind-blank image was still playing in my head.

Point being, I got through it. I got through it, and the director, Bill

Rauch, called me a 'stage beast'. Age of seventy-three, 160 pages of script and a pretty good performance in just three weeks. Exhausting, yes, but the theatre feeds you. It's that astonishing relationship you can achieve with the audience; it's the fact that you never get bored, you're always feeling an immediacy, a sense of a new experience unfolding. It's exhausting, especially the rehearsal process, but it's also a great source of energy. It's why we actors are always drawn back, because no matter how well paid and seemingly comfortable it might be on the dark side in TV and film, relaxing in our two-bangers between scenes, having HBO drivers ferry us to and from home, it's all beaten into a cocked hat by being crammed into a dressing room at the Birmingham Rep. Which is why I'm more likely to go the Nigel Hawthorne route. Why I only ever really see this stopping when I die. And when that happens, I can only hope I make a good death, with dignity and grace, with my loved ones nearby.

All I ask is that when that moment comes, the funeral isn't at Golders Green.

And, dear God, don't let Michael Gambon do the eulogy.

AFTERWORD

The fear of committing words to the page is manifold.

A life comprises so many fractured elements. The nervousness that accompanies putting pen to paper, trying to illustrate and make sense of one's life, ultimately induces an inner state of . . . well . . . sheer panic. A rabbit-in-the-headlights feeling.

What did I leave out?

Who did I leave out?

Have I misremembered events?

Have I been unfair, unkind?

Am I a hostage to some elaborate, self-induced, hermetic fantasy?

Sticking with the rabbit metaphor - let's not forget, also, that my book is called *Putting the Rabbit in the Hat* – and to paraphrase that other well-known performer, Bugs Bunny:

'Well, that's me, folks . . . warts and all.'

ADDENDUM

In my assessment of my fellow performers, I confess I can be a bit harsh and sometimes too hasty for my own good, appearing somewhat glib at times.

Acting is a tough job sometimes. We all suffer the strain and deal with the potential rejection every time we put ourselves on the line by walking on a stage or standing in front of a camera. Players live such a roller-coaster existence, it is sometimes very hard not to fall out of the carriage. I have been accused of disrespecting certain actors. This is far from the case; I have the utmost respect for anyone who tackles the craziness and insecurity of our profession, whatever reservations I may have about their approach to the craft.

Johnny Depp has, without question, a loyal and powerful fan base (which I have often borne the brunt of) and is clearly loved by many. At his best, he has the gifts of a great silent screen player, with performances of rare sensitivity in movies such as *Gilbert Grape* and *Donnie Brasco*.

Michael Caine certainly is an institution. An institution that created *Alfie* and Peachy Carnehan in *The Man Who Would Be King* with the great Sean Connery. But also an institution who has always honoured his working-class roots and the Micklewhite family he was born into.

Edward Norton, who wanted to try writing and directing, has, again with time and tide, showed his worth with his excellent creation *Motherless Brooklyn*.

And the individual I accused of being an arsehole, well . . . that was almost thirty years ago and I'm sure he's changed. Because people in the movie world shift and change throughout their lives, even directors.

We all do. In the last months, my teenage boys have, both at different rates, emerged from their hormonal tunnels. They recently attended funeral of their grandfather, the elegant Nossy Ansari, an absolute prince among men. They loved their Opa. His passing and the depth of their mourning provoked a delicate shift in their growth as young men. His loss was the first they had suffered. Both recognized, as their elder half-brother Alan had done at his uncle's funeral thirty years before, the profound nature of such a passing.

It's like how I felt about the wonderful women who have shared part of my life. That regretful sadness I have felt at the end of these relationships – saying goodbye to that joy, that tenderness, the privileged intimacy we were allowed to share. The loss of what you achieved with a partner always leaves a deep and lasting sorrow. For me it seems unavoidable.

In the Catholic Church, they talk about 'temporal punishment' that attaches itself to the soul after forgiveness for sins and errors has been received. I feel I've experienced my own form of 'temporal punishment' when every relationship I've had came to its natural and sometimes painful conclusion.

I hope to know no such sorrow with my present partner and confidante: my wife, the beautiful, steadfast Nicole. She has been my rock, and I wanted to end this addendum honouring her and the joy she has brought me.

INDEX

Abbate, Mickey, 264

Acting With . . . (TV series), 286, 287

Adaptation (2002 film), 297, 324

Addy, Mark, 134

Adler, Stella, 166

adobe-style dwellings, 263

Adventure in Space and Time, An (2013 film), 335

Affair of the Necklace, The (2001 film), 326

Age of Kings (1960 TV series), 93–4

Age UK, 310

Aida (Verdi), 62

Albee, Edward, 69

alcohol, 80–87, 92, 106–7, 139, 189, 249, 265, 266, 270, 277, 336

All at Sea (2010 film), 277

Allen, Ryder, 297

Allen, Woody, 117, 137–9

Alma (play), 211

Alpha Beta (Whitehead), 35

American Dream, 184

American Horror Story (TV series), 301

And Then There Were None (1945 film), 47

Anderson, Lindsay, 36, 60–61, 124–31, 144, 150–52, 154, 181–2

acting guidance, 126–8, 152, 154, 196, 197, 214, 255

Britannia Hospital (1982 film), 112, 125, 130

homosexuality, 129

In Celebration (1969 play), 124, 127, 150, 151, 166, 181

In Celebration (1975 film), 125

Is That All There Is? (1992 documentary), 154

This Sporting Life (1963 film), 52, 60, 124, 130, 137, 154

Whales of August, The (1987 film), 130

Anglade, Jean-Hugues, 316

Aniston, Jennifer, 78

anorexia, 329, 350

Ansari, Nicole, *see* Cox, Nicole

Archer family, 39

Aris, Jonathan, 134–5

Armstrong, Alun, 50–51, 140, 150

Armstrong, Jesse, 296, 322, 357

Art (Reza), 291, 314

Arts Theatre, London, 60

As You Like It (Shakespeare), 95, 104

Ashcroft, Edith Margaret 'Peggy', 245

Assembly Hall, Edinburgh, 120

Astor Place Riot (1849), 119

Atkins, Eileen, 221

Attenborough, Richard, 296

attitudinizing, 127

Autopsy of Jane Doe, The (2016 film), 279

Avatar (2009 film), 136

Avengers, The (TV series), 76

Avon river, 187

Ayrton, Norman, 254

Bacall, Lauren, 277

Bad Day at Black Rock (1955 film), 301

Badel, Sarah, 233

Baker, Thomas, 143

Baldwin, Alexander 'Alec', 299, 301, 323

Balliol College, Oxford, 242

Barbican, London, 231, 232, 237

Barker, Ronald, 177

Barrett, Roger 'Syd', 333–4

Barrymore, John, 214, 343

Basic Instinct II (2006 film), 273

Bates, Alan, 36, 52, 124, 129, 130, 137, 181, 245

Batman (comic book), 42

Baxter, Stanley, 110, 233

Bean, Sean, 265, 267, 268

Beano (comic book), 42, 68

Beatles, The, 69

beats scripts, 288–90

Beazley, Sam, 252

Becket (1964 film), 84

Beckett, Samuel, 58, 91, 170, 332, 350–52

Being Human (TV series), 134

#BeKind, 339

Believe (2013 film), 335

Bench, The (TV series), 304

Benedict, Paul, 251–2

Bening, Annette, 299, 301

Benioff, David, 133, 296

Bennett, Alan, 26–7, 155

Bennett, Jill, 151, 152, 154

Bergman, Ingmar, 133

Berkoff, Steven, 142–3

Bernard, Jeffrey, 5

Berry, Halle, 210

Béthune, Pas-de-Calais, 11–12

Bevan, Aneurin 'Nye', 335

Biden, Joseph, 14

Big Romance, The (Holman), 150

Billy Liar (1963 film), 161

Birdies, The (play), 109

Birmingham Repertory Theatre, 94, 95–9, 100, 101–2, 104, 364

Birth Without Violence (Leboyer), 32

Black Watch, 12

Black, Conrad, 146

Black, Shane, 296, 306

Blackpool, Lancashire, 18

Blair Atholl, Perthshire, 20

Blair, Anthony 'Tony', 310

Bloom, Orlando, 83

Blue Film, The (1975 TV film), 262

Bob Servant (TV series), 344, 349, 350

Bochco, Steven, 296, 358

Bogarde, Dirk, 50

Bogart, Humphrey, 276–7

Bolam, James, 124–5, 183

Bombay, India, 194–7, 198

Boorman, John, 60

Borderers, The (TV series), 98–9

Boston Film Critics Award, 304, 324

Boston, Massachusetts, 304

Bourne Identity, The (2002 film), 326–7, 328

Bourne Supremacy, The (2004 film), 327, 328

Bowie, David, 116

Boxer, The (1997 film), 43–4, 165

Bradford, Barbara Taylor, 10

Bradley, David, 252, 257, 335

Bram Stoker's Dracula (1992 film), 290

Branch, Tony, 242

Brand (Ibsen), 156

Brando, Marlon, 49, 54, 58, 59, 150, 166, 291, 337–8

Braveheart (1995 film), 80, 269–74

Brecht, Bertolt, 74, 94, 183

Brian Cox's Russia (2017 TV series), 248

Bridge on the River Kwai, The (1957 film), 50, 52, 141

Bridget Jones films, 117, 134, 351

Britannia Hospital (1982 film), 112, 125, 130

British Academy of Film and Television Arts (BAFTA), 261

British American Drama Academy (BADA), 242

British Broadcasting Corporation (BBC), 25, 91, 115–16

Age of Kings (1960), 93–4

Being Human (2008–13), 134

Bob Servant (2013–15), 344

Borderers, The (1968–70), 98–9

Brian Cox's Russia (2017), 248
Changeling, The (1974), 187, 203
Churchill's People (1974–5), 269
Combing Down His Yellow Hair (1971), 155
Dad's Army (1968–77), 233
Day of the Triffids, The (2009), 342
Death of a Salesman (1966), 115
Doctor Who (1963–), 48, 92–3, 335
Doomwatch (1970–72), 140
Fall and Rise of Reginald Perrin, The
     (1976–9), 119
Fawlty Towers (1975–9), 119
Fleabag (2016–19), 352
Game, The (2014), 134–5, 136, 358
Grushko (1994), 268
Hamlet at Elsinore (1964), 262
Hedda Gabler (1972), 115
Knight in Tarnished Armour, A (1965), 114
Life and Loves of a She-Devil, The (1986), 262
Likely Lads, The (1964–6), 125
Lost Language of Cranes, The (1991), 261
Lovejoy (1986–94), 358
Nationwide (1969–83), 199
On Expenses (2010), 335
Porridge (1974–7), 112
Quatermass Experiment, The (1953), 118
Rab C. Nesbitt (1988–2014), 349
Requiem for a Heavyweight (1957), 115
She Stoops to Conquer (1971), 116, 120, 145,
     155, 343
Spooks (2002–11), 117
Taming of the Shrew, The (1980), 233
Television Centre, 115–16
Thérèse Raquin (1980), 186–91
These Men Are Dangerous: Stalin (1969), 155
Thick of It, The (2005–12), 357
Top of the Pops (1964–2006), 115
War and Peace (1972), 200
Year of the Sex Olympics, The (1968), 118,
     119, 120, 144
Yes Minister (1980–88), 194
Z-Cars (1962–78), 140
British Linen Bank, 62
Britton, Jasper, 281–2
Broadmoor Hospital, Berkshire, 258–60

Broadway cinema, Dundee, 47
Broadway, New York, 206, 207, 291, 314–17,
     333, 362
Brook, Irina, 250, 252, 253, 257–8, 272, 346,
     353
Brook, Peter, 75, 78, 79
Broughty Ferry, Angus, 344, 349
Brown, James Gordon 310
Bryant, Michael, 142
Büchner, Georg, 201, 203
Buckingham Palace, London, 184
Buckstone Club, London, 87
Bundy, Theodore 'Ted', 225–6
Burton, Richard, 84, 85
Busby, Alexander Matthew, 335
Bush Theatre, London, 219
Byrne, John, 328

Caine, Michael, 85, 262
Caird, John, 231
Calder-Marshall, Anna, 75
Calder, David, 333
Call Me Claus (2001 film), 362
Cambridge Theatre Company, 194
Camden, London, 263
Cameron, James, 136
Camus, Albert, 45
Canada, 13–14, 24, 30, 158
cancel culture, 339
cannabis, 80, 263–4
Capaldi, Peter, 140
Captains Courageous (1937 film), 54
Caravaggio (1986 film), 81
Carpenter, John, 279
Carroll, Lizzie, 115
Casablanca (1942 film), 276
Cash, Paul, 235
Casino Royale (1967 film), 110
Catholicism, 7, 19, 29, 54, 159, 205
Caton-Jones, Michael, 270–73
CBE, 183–5
Cellier, Peter, 97–8
Central School of Speech and Drama, 65,
     80–82
Chain Reaction (1996 film), 287–90

Changeling, The (1974 TV play), 187, 203

Channing, Stockard, 338

Chaplin, Kiera, 10

Chapman, Paul, 92

character actors, 277–8, 284

Chariots of Fire (1981 film), 254

Charleson, Ian, 254

Chekhov, Anton, 60, 79, 95, 244, 245

Chekhov, Michael, 76

Cheltenham Ladies' College, 229–30

Chernobyl disaster (1986), 265

Chester, Cheshire, 18

Chicago, Illinois, 287–90

Chidlow, Bill, 28

Chile, 309

Chinatown (1974 film), 164

Chipperfield's Circus, 192

Christchurch, New Zealand, 319

Christian Scientists, 253

Christie, Agatha, 47, 58, 170

Churchill (2017 film), 162, 325, 335–7

Churchill, Winston, 5, 335–7

Churchill's People (TV series), 269

Cider House Rules, The (1999 film), 187

cinemas, 47–50

Citizens Theatre, Glasgow, 110–11

Clair, René, 47

Clark, Jim, 168

Classics Illustrated, 42–3, 44, 46

Clayburgh, Jill, 299

Cleese, John, 177, 233

Clift, Edward Montgomery, 52, 165

Cloning of Joanna May, The (1992 TV film), 261, 262, 264, 268

Clooney, George, 78

Clue (1985 film), 194

Clurman, Harold, 166

Cocktail Party, The (Eliot), 120, 221

Coen, Ethan and Joel, 273

Colbert, Claudette, 137

Combing Down His Yellow Hair (1971 TV play), 155

Comedy of Errors, The (Shakespeare), 91–2

Comedy Theatre, London, 251

Complicity (2000 film), 351

Connery, Sean, 93, 115, 184, 362

Connolly, William 'Billy', 351

Conroy, Jarlath, 150

Convey, Colum, 151

Conway, Jeremy, 264

Cook, Robin, 311

Cooper, Christopher, 326

Cooper, Dominic, 302

Cooper, Gary, 90

Corbett, Ronald, 177

Coriolanus (Shakespeare), 153, 214, 232, 342

Cornwell, Bernard, 265

Coronation (1936), 17

Costner, Kevin, 291–3

Cotton, Oliver, 172, 177, 213

Court Jester, The (1955 film), 56

Courtenay, Thomas, 52, 116, 150, 213

Covent Garden Hotel, London, 43

Covid-19 pandemic (2019–21), 52, 220, 278, 352, 362

Coward, Noël, 79

Cox, Alan, 23, 31–2, 33, 122, 201, 229, 231

Cox, Bette, 7–8, 17, 20, 24, 30, 68, 160, 184, 284, 300, 344, 346

Cox, Caroline, 25–8, 31–2, 104–8, 112, 122, 155, 201, 203

birth of children, 31–2

divorce, 229–31, 235

New Year's Eve parties, 35–6, 153

Three Musketeers performance, 156, 157

stillbirth of twins, 26–8, 155

wedding, 104

Cox, Charles 'Chic', 5–7, 13–20, 21–3, 28–9, 36

Cox, Charlie, 5, 7–8, 18, 23–4, 344–6, 349

Cox, Hugh, 12–13

Cox, Irene, 7–8, 17, 30, 49, 54, 158, 344, 346

Cox, Margaret, 32, 122, 201, 229–30, 248, 329–31, 333, 346, 350

Cox, Mary Ann 'Molly', 4–7, 11, 13, 16–20, 24–30, 54, 158–60, 234

Cox, May, 7–8, 17, 18, 20, 24, 30, 160, 300, 344, 346

Cox, Murray, 259

Cox, Nicole, 33–4, 185, 211, 219–20, 315–20, 353–6

Cox, Orson, 33, 318

Cox, Torin, 33–4, 318–20

Cranham, Kenneth, 186

Crawford, Cheryl, 166

Crawford, Joan, 35, 189

Criterion Channel, 52

Cromwell (Storey), 50–51, 150, 170

Crosby, Harry 'Bing', 56

Crown, The (TV series), 53–4

Crucible, The (Miller), 243–9

Cuesta, Michael, 303

Cukor, George, 295

Culkin, Kieran, 126, 128, 296, 360

Cunningham, Liam, 302

Curious Incident of the Dog in the Night-Time, The (2016 film), 118

Curse of Edgar, The (2013 film), 335

Cushing, Peter, 191–2

Czechoslovakia, 333

Dad's Army (TV series), 233

Dalida, 12

Dalziel, Larry, 99, 114, 115, 226, 229

Damon, Matthew, 326

Dances with Wolves (1990 film), 292

Dandy (comic book), 42, 68

Danger Man (TV series), 204

Dano, Paul, 303

Danton Affair, The (Gems), 231, 232

Danton's Death (Büchner), 201, 203

Dark of the Moon (play), 90

Darkest Hour (2017 film), 335, 336, 337

Darling (1965 film), 161, 167

David Copperfield (Dickens), 42–3

David, Eleanor, 131

Davies, Howard, 231

Davies, Ray, 77

Davis, Andrew, 286, 288–90

Davis, Bette, 35

Davis, Bette, 130

Davis, Geena, 286

Davis, William 'Bill', 72

Day of the Locust, The (1975 film), 161

Day of the Triffids, The (2009 TV series), 342

Day-Lewis, Daniel, 43–4, 165, 255

DC Thomson, 42, 68–9, 361

De Laurentiis, Agostino 'Dino', 225

De Niro, Robert, 98, 166

Dead Man Walking (1995 film), 273

Deadwood (TV series), 324, 358

Deakins, Roger, 273

Dean, James, 47, 49, 54, 150, 165, 243

Death of a Salesman (Miller), 115

Defence of the Realm (1985 film), 112

Demme, Jonathan, 226, 227

Demolition Man (1993 film), 3

Dench, Judith, 117, 209, 213

Dennehy, Brian, 222, 263

Departed, The (2006 film), 80

Depp, John, 137

Desperate Measures (1998 film), 278, 289, 294, 297

Desperately Seeking Susan (1985 film), 53

Devine, George, 149

Dewar, Bill, 41, 57

Dews, Peter, 93–4, 95, 96, 100, 104, 199

diabetes, 111, 300, 310

Diamond, Gillian, 169

DiCaprio, Leonardo, 325

Dickens, Charles, 43, 44

Diesel, Vin (Mark Sinclair), 278

Dirty Harry (1971 film), 75

Do the Right Thing (1989 film), 133

Doctor in the House (1954 film), 50

Doctor Who (TV series), 48, 92–3, 335

Doctor Zhivago (1965 film), 143

Don't Start Without Me (Rayburn), 155

Donner, Lauren Shuler, 212

Donner, Richard, 212

Doomwatch (TV series), 140

Dorfman Theatre, London, 175

Douglas, Michael, 198

Dover Road (Milne), 68

Downton Abbey (TV series), 24

Dr Jekyll and Mr Hyde (Stevenson), 44

Dracula (1992 film), 290

Drymen, Stirling, 39

Dublin Carol (McPherson), 151, 218

Duellists, The (1977 film), 75

Duke of York's Theatre, London, 77, 205–6, 333

Dumas, Alexandre, 42, 156

Duncan, Lindsay, 186

Dundee, Scotland, 4–9, 11, 13, 30, 36, 39–42, 47–52, 160

cinemas in, 47–50

Repertory Theatre, 57–63, 64–71, 72, 73, 76, 124, 150, 214

St. Nicholas production in, 219

University of Dundee, 349

Dunkirk evacuation (1940), 12

Duvall, Robert, 200

Dylan, Robert 'Bob', 337

Ealing comedies, 50

Earls Court, London, 118, 343

East of Eden (1955 film), 49

eBay, 43

Edinburgh, Scotland, 74, 91–4, 95, 100–101, 109, 120, 183, 328, 350–52

Edward Scissorhands (1990 film), 137

Efremov, Oleg, 242

Elizabeth II, Queen, 183, 184

Elliott, Denholm, 151

Elliott, Marianne, 118

Elliott, Michael, 84, 102–3, 116, 118, 120–23, 125, 144, 197, 204, 225, 272

Elphick, Michael, 81

Elton, Benjamin, 313

Emmy Awards, 324

emotional memory technique, 166

English Stage Company, 149

Entertainer, The (Osborne), 149

Equity, 106, 114

Escapist, The (2008 film), 297, 298, 302, 310

Eszterhás, József, 296

Evans, Edith, 79, 253

Evans, Robert 'Bob', 164, 167

Even Cowgirls Get the Blues (1993 film), 290

Evening Standard, 118, 246

Excalibur (1981 film), 60, 81, 82

existentialism, 45

expiation, 209, 215, 250, 259

Eyre, Richard, 251, 252, 255, 256

Fall and Rise of Reginald Perrin, The (TV series), 119

Far from the Madding Crowd (1967 film), 161, 167

Fargo (1996 film), 269

Fargo, Sarah, 264

Farrow, María 'Mia', 139

Fashion (Lucie), 232, 235–6, 243, 275

Fawlty Towers (TV series), 119

Feast, Michael, 80

Ferrell, John William 'Will', 358

feudal society, 13, 153, 184, 275, 335

Fiennes, Joseph, 299, 302, 338–9

Fiennes, Ralph, 214, 342

Fife's, Dundee, 64

Finlay Street, Bishops Park, 153

Finney, Albert, 36, 50–52, 54, 104, 120, 150, 154, 170, 171, 184–5, 203, 213

Fisher, Carrie, 338

Five Finger Exercise (Shaffer), 60

Fleabag (TV series), 352

Fleming, Tom, 91, 94, 183

Fonda, Jane, 166

Fools Rush In' (Sinatra), 42

For the Love of the Game (1999 film), 291–3

Forbes-Robertson, John, 214

Ford, John, 54

Forrest, Edwin, 119

Forsyth, Neil, 344

Forth and Clyde Canal, 10, 45

France, 11

France, 326

Frankie and Johnny (1991 film), 187

Frankie and Johnny in the Clair de Lune (McNally), 251, 252, 275

Frankl, Victor, 347

Franz Kafka's It's a Wonderful Life (1993 film), 140

Fraser, Ronald, 86

Frasier (TV series), 324

Freeman, Morgan, 287, 288, 293, 294

Friday the 13th (1980 film), 280

Fright Meter Award, 279
front-foot acting, 209
Fulham, London, 119, 153, 203

Galileo (Brecht), 74, 94, 183
Gambon, Michael, 87, 97–9, 104–6, 227, 252, 364
Game, The (2014 TV series), 134–5, 136, 358
Game of Thrones (TV series), 80, 133–4, 217
Garcia, Andrés 'Andy', 278, 289
Garcia, Jerry, 279
Garrick Club, London, 90, 155
Garrick, David, 343
Gartcosh asylum, North Lanarkshire, 11
Gaskill, William 'Bill', 150
Geoffrey, Peter, 252
Georgy Girl (1966 film), 66
Gere, Richard, 78
Gerry's Club, London, 87
Getting On (Bennett), 26–7, 155
Giant (1956 film), 47–8
giardia, 265–6
Gibson, Alan, 192
Gibson, Mel, 269, 270–74
Gielgud, Arthur John, 95, 117, 137, 175–7, 180, 214, 253
Gill, John, 172
Gill, Peter, 186, 201, 203
Gilligan, Vince, 296
Gilroy, Anthony 'Tony', 306, 327
Gish, Lillian, 130
Glasgow Citizens Theatre, 64
Glasgow, Scotland, 10, 110–11
Glass Menagerie, The (Williams), 73
Glee (TV series), 301
Gleeson, Brendan, 83, 136
Glimmer Man, The (1996 film), 1–2, 294, 297
Gloster, Betty, 347
Goddard, Jimmy
Godfather films, 164
Godley, Campbell, 64
Goering, Hermann, 321–4
Goldberg, Whoopi, 362
Goldblum, Jeffrey, 78
Golden Globes, 324, 325

Golders Green, London, 344, 364
Goldsmith, Oliver, 116
Goldstein, Jonathan, 282
Goodfellas (1990 film), 134, 315
Gordon, Hannah, 64
Gorrie, John, 114
Grainger, Gawn, 61
Grant, Cary, 53, 57, 337
Gray, John, 2
Great Depression (1929–39), 16
Great Society, The (Schenkkan), 264, 362–4
Green, Vanessa, 264
Green's Playhouse, Dundee, 47, 48
Greene, Graham, 262
Greengrass, Paul, 327
Greensboro Arts Alliance, 354
Grimes, Frank, 129, 130
Group Theatre, 166
Grushko (1994 TV series), 268
Guess Who's Coming to Dinner (1967 film), 54
Guinness, Alec, 74–5, 220–21
Guinness, Matthew, 74–5, 221
Gumshoe (1971 film), 112
Gurdjieff, George, 346–7
Guthrie, Tyrone, 110

Hackett, George, 41
Hackman, Gene, 227, 362
Hall, Peter, 169, 170–74, 178, 231
Halloween (1978 film), 280
Hamill, Mark, 130
Hamilton, Victoria, 135
Hamlet (Shakespeare), 64, 75–6, 94, 95, 189, 214–16, 233, 237, 282
Brook's production, 75–6
Classics Illustrated version, 42
Day-Lewis' performance, 255
Grimes' performance, 129, 130
Hamlet at Elsinore (1964), 262
McKellen's performance, 208
O'Toole's performance, 79, 83
Olivier's performances, 95, 98, 101
'rogue and peasant slave' speech, 214
'to be, or not to be' soliloquy, 39

Hammer House of Horror (1980 TV series), 191–3
Hammersmith, London, 73
Hampstead, London, 119
Hancock, John Lee, 318
Hannibal (2001 film), 224
Hardwick, Vermont, 354
Hardy, Oliver, 145, 192
Hardy, Thomas, 44
Hare, David, 187, 227–8
Harlin, Renny, 286, 287
Harris, Julie, 49, 166
Harris, Richard, 52, 61, 85, 129, 137, 150
Harris, Rosemary, 79
Harris, Thomas, 222, 226, 276
Harrison, Reginald 'Rex', 137, 154
Harrogate, North Yorkshire, 141
Harry Potter films, 80, 117, 136
Hart, Ian, 140
Hartnell, William, 335
Havel, Václav, 333
Hawaii, 51
Hawes, Keeley, 351
Hawks, Howard, 53
Hawthorne, Nigel, 1–3, 90, 362, 364
Hay Fever (Coward), 79
Hazeldine, James, 142
HBO, 359, 360, 364
Heartbeat (TV series), 200
Hedda Gabler (Ibsen), 115, 150, 151
Helgeland, Brian, 327
Hell on Frisco Bay (1956 film), 47
Hemmings, Nolan, 267
Henderson, John, 57, 61, 95, 214
Henry IV (Shakespeare), 93
Henry V (Shakespeare), 93, 95
Henry VI (Shakespeare), 93
Hepburn, Katharine, 54
Her (2013 film), 139
Hidden Agenda (1990 film), 252, 255–6
Higgins, Clare, 252
Hill Street Blues (TV series), 296, 358
Hilltown, Dundee, 50
Hird, Thora, 116
His Girl Friday (1940 film), 53

Hitchcock, Alfred, 133, 295, 296
Hitler, Adolf, 321
Hobsbawm, Eric, 332, 334
Hodge, Patricia, 262
Hoffman, Dustin, 164, 165, 167
Hoffman, Philip Seymour, 341
Hogmanay, 17–19
Holly, Buddy, 42
Hollywood, California, 161–9
Holman, Robert, 150
Holmes Place, London, 198, 204
Holocaust (1941–5), 323, 348
Honky Tonk Freeway (1981 film), 161
Hood, Morag, 200, 328
Hoover, John Edgar, 335
Hope, Leslie 'Bob', 56, 57
Hopkins, Anthony, 200, 224, 225, 226, 227, 322
Hordern, Michael, 102–3
Howard Hawks, 296
Howard, Trevor, 86
Hudson, Rock, 48, 52
Hughes, Tom, 134
Hurt, John, 86, 103
Hutchinson, Ron, 76, 151, 206, 207, 213, 217, 222, 223, 224, 275

I and Albert (1972 musical), 176
I Love My Love (Weldon), 199–200
Ibsen, Henrik, 95, 118, 120
Brand, 156
Hedda Gabler, 115, 150, 151
Master Builder, The, 200–201, 260, 268, 328
Peer Gynt, 84, 94, 95
When We Dead Awaken, 120
If.... (1968 film), 125
In Celebration (Storey), 124, 125, 127, 150, 151, 166, 181, 254
In Search of the Miraculous (Ouspensky), 346
In the Ghetto' (Presley), 140
Inadmissible Evidence (Osborne), 60, 152
India, 194–7, 198
Inspector Morse (TV series), 92, 261
Iran, 33, 34, 355

Iraq, 311

Ireland, Kenny, 350–51

Irish famine (1845–52), 14

Irish Republican Army (IRA), 206, 256

Iron Will (1994 film), 268–9, 274

Irving, Henry, 95, 343

Is That All There Is? (1992 documentary), 154

ITV, 115

Cloning of Joanna May, The (1992), 261, 262, 264, 268

Downton Abbey (2010–15), 24

Hammer House of Horror (1980), 191–3

Heartbeat (1992–2010), 200

Inspector Morse (1987–2000), 92, 261

Prisoner, The (1967), 110

Red Fox (1991), 86

Redcap (1964–6), 116

Rising Damp (1974–8), 119

Shades of Greene (1975–6), 262

Sharpe (1993–2008), 265–8

World in Action (1963–98), 327

Izzard, Eddie, 281

'J'attendrai' (Dalida), 12

Jackman, Hugh, 210

Jackson, Glenda, 75–9, 205

Jackson, Michael, 337–9

Jackson, Paris, 338–9

Jackson, Philip, 223

Jackson, Samuel Leroy, 286, 293

Jagger, Michael 'Mick', 117, 333

James, Henry, 69–70

Japan, 329

Jarman, Derek, 81

Jaws (1975 film), 256, 278

Jericho Mile, The (1979 film), 223

Johansson, Scarlett, 139

John, Elton, 325

Johnson, Dwayne, 278

Johnson, Lyndon, 362–4

Jolson Story, The (1946 film), 18

Jolson, Al, 362

Jones, Gemma, 117

Jones, Sabra, 354

Jones, Tommy Lee, 286, 287, 288

Judd, Ashley, 294–5

Julius Caesar (Shakespeare), 169, 174, 175–80

Jung, Carl, 346

jute industry, 8, 14

Kanner, Alexis, 75

Kaye, Danny, 56, 57, 233

Kazan, Elia, 49

Keach, Stacy, 75

Kean, Edmund, 343

Keaton, Michael, 200, 278, 289

Keeler, Christine, 78

Kendal, Felicity, 10

Kennedy, Jacqueline, 78

Kennedy, John Fitzgerald, 118

Kennedy, Robert 'Bobby', 118

Kerensky, Alexander, 141, 142

Kermode, Mark, 335

Kick Theatre Company, 232

Kidnapped (Stevenson), 44

Killiekrankie, Perthshire, 20

Kind of Loving, A (1962 film), 52, 161

King Lear (Shakespeare), 73, 102, 120, 156, 208–10, 227, 237, 250–60, 275, 314, 346

Kinks, The, 77

Kismet, London, 87

Kiss the Girls (1997 film), 294, 295

Knack, The (Jellicoe), 125

Kneale, Nigel, 118

Knerr, Catherina Ren, 264

Knight in Tarnished Armour, A (1965 TV play), 114

Koch, Edward, 261

Kozushima, Japan, 329

L.I.E (2001 film), 210, 297, 303–4, 324

Labour Party, 309–12

Ladd, Alan, 47

Lambert, Gavin, 128

Lange, Jessica, 272

Langton, Simon, 187–9

Larg's, Dundee, 40

Last Hurrah, The (1958 film), 54
Last of the Mohicans, The (Cooper), 42
Laurel, Stan, 145, 192
Laurie, John, 233
Lawrence of Arabia (1962 film), 52, 82, 84, 141, 143
Lawson, Wilfred, 84
Laya Torkaman, 356
Lean, David, 52, 143, 212
Leary, Timothy, 337
Leboyer, Frédérick, 32
Ledger, Heath, 341
Lee, Spike, 132–3, 341
Leigh, Mike, 75
Lenin, Vladimir, 142
Leningrad, Russia, 268
Lesher, Matthew, 264, 304
Levin, Bernard, 179–80
Lewis, Damian, 302
Lewis, Jerry, 47, 233
Life and Loves of a She-Devil, The (1986 TV series), 262
Life in Movies, A (Powell), 2, 276
Life of Galileo (Brecht), 74, 94, 183
Likely Lads, The (TV series), 125
Liman, Doug, 326–7, 328
Lincoln (2012 film), 43, 271
Linklater, Kristin, 72–3
Lion, the Witch and the Wardrobe, The (2005 film), 318–20
Lipman, Maureen, 75
Lithgow, John, 223
Loach, Kenneth, 252, 255–6, 288, 289
logotherapy, 347–8, 350
Loitering with Intent (O'Toole), 83
London Academy of Music and Dramatic Art (LAMDA), 33, 72–9, 89, 118, 254, 255
lone wolf (game), 8, 41–2
Loneliness of the Long Distance Runner, The (1962 film), 52
Long Kiss Goodnight, The (1996 film), 286–7, 295
Look Back in Anger (Osborne), 149, 152
Loot (Orton), 119–20

Los Angeles Times, 224–5
Los Angeles, California, 158, 161–9, 283, 284, 286
Lost Language of Cranes, The (1991 TV film), 261
Lourdes, France, 20
Love from a Stranger (Christie), 58
Love's Labour's Lost (Shakespeare), 156
Lovejoy (TV series), 358
Lucie, Doug, 232, 235–6, 243
Lucille Lortel Awards, 221
LuPone, Patti, 299
Lyceum, Edinburgh, 74, 91–4, 95, 100, 183, 328, 350–52
Lynn, Jonathan, 194, 196–7
Lyon Street, Dundee, 30, 36, 41–2
Lyttleton Theatre, London, 175

Macbeth (Shakespeare), 42, 194–7, 198, 220–21
Mackay, Fulton, 24, 109–13, 118, 197, 233, 236, 285
MacKerrell, Vivian, 80, 81
Mackintosh, Stephen, 302
Macrae, Duncan, 109–10, 197, 233
Macready, William Charles, 119
Madness of King George, The (1994 film), 3
Maffia, Roma, 294
Maguire, Sharon, 351
Mahler, Alma, 211
Mainly About Lindsay Anderson (Lambert), 128
Major Barbara (Shaw), 203
Major, John, 311
Maltese Falcon, The (1941 film), 276–7
Man with a Flower in His Mouth, The (Pirandello), 199
Man's Search for Meaning (Frankl), 347
Manahan, Sheila, 112–13
Manchester Royal Exchange Theatre, 120, 199
Manhunter (1986 film), 145, 210, 222–8, 229, 269, 276, 310
Mann, Michael, 223, 224, 225, 226

Manuel, Peter, 225
Marathon Man (1976 film), 164, 167
Marchant, Stephen, 252
Margaret, Countess of Snowdon, 181–3, 200
Marigold (play), 60
marijuana, 80, 263–4
Marilyn Manson (Brian Warner), 301
Marlowe, Christopher, 170
Martin, Dean, 47
Martin, Michael, 335
Massey, Anna, 186
Master Builder, The (Ibsen), 200–201, 260, 268, 328
Master of Ballantrae, The (Stevenson), 44
Matalon, Vivian, 89–90
Match Point (2005 film), 137–9
Matheson, Eve, 252
Mathias, Sean, 261
Mayo, Simon, 335
Mayor of Casterbridge, The (Hardy), 44
McArdle, Jimmy, 270
McCann, James, 12
McCann, Patrick, 10–11, 45
McCarthy, Joseph, 243
McDowell, Malcolm, 129
McElhone, Natascha, 283, 284
McGann, Paul, 267
McGoohan, Patrick, 121, 204
McGregor, Ewan, 46
McIlvanney, Hugh, 242
McKay, Adam, 357–8
McKee, Edward Lucky, 297
McKellen, Ian, 208–10, 213, 245, 251, 252, 256, 261
McKern, Reginald 'Leo', 103, 120
McNally, Terence, 251
McNeice, Ian, 139
McOwen, Michael, 73
McPherson, Conor, 151, 218–21, 225, 314
McShane, Ian, 358
McWha, Geordie, 5
Melville, Herman, 41, 42, 44, 121–3, 204–5, 206
Menzies, Tobias, 53

Merchant of Venice, The (Shakespeare), 64, 66
method acting, 43, 164–5
#MeToo movement, 294
Meyer, Michael, 118
Meyers, Jonathan Rhys, 139
Michael Chekhov Acting Studio, 76
Michelangelo, Antonioni, 133
Mick-Macks', 7, 17
Midnight Cowboy (1969 film), 161
Midsummer Night's Dream, A (Shakespeare), 31
Mikado, The (Gilbert and Sullivan), 358
Mikkelsen, Mads, 225
Milch, David, 296, 358
Mildenhall, Richard, 242
Miller, Arthur, 115, 243–9
Miller, Jonathan, 102, 233, 239, 240, 244
Miller, Jonny Lee, 351
Milne, Alan Alexander, 68
Milne, Carl, 110
Milton, Ernest, 214
miners' strike (1984–5), 309
Mirren, Helen, 117
Misalliance (Shaw), 231, 275
Moby-Dick (Melville), 41, 42, 44, 121–3, 204–5, 206
Mokhtar, Arash, 355
Monifieth, Dundee, 344
monologues, 217–21
Monolulu, Prince, 4–5
Monroe, Marilyn, 101, 166, 278
Monroe, Vaughn, 42
Montrose, Angus, 13
More, Kenneth, 50
Morgan, Peter, 296
Morocco, 33
Morton, Samantha, 139
Moscow, Russia, 242–9, 250, 256, 327
Mourning Becomes Electra (O'Neill), 73
Mrs Warren's Profession (Shaw), 251, 353
Murder on the Orient Express (Christie), 170
Murdoch, Rupert, 146
Murphy, Ryan, 300–301
Murphy's War (1971 film), 83

Murray, William 'Bill', 167
Music Man, The (play), 284
My Cousin Vinny (1992 film), 194
My Own Private Idaho (1991 film), 290

National Theatre, London, 79, 100–103, 116, 156, 168–9, 181, 186, 201, 231
Hamlet, 255
Julius Caesar, 169, 174, 175–80
King Lear, 250–56, 257, 259–60
Princess Margaret's visit, 181–3, 200
Richard III, 250, 251, 256–8, 281
Tamburlaine the Great, 170–74
National Theatre of Scotland, 220
Nationwide (TV programme), 199
Neal, Siri, 219, 262, 268, 269, 280, 283, 285, 353
Neeson, Liam, 272, 320
Nelligan, Kate, 186, 187
Nettleton, John, 172
new realism, 149
New York, United States, 76–7, 119, 206, 207, 291, 314–17, 333, 362
New Zealand, 319
Newman, Paul, 166
Newman, Sydney, 335
Nicholas and Alexandra (1971 film), 140–43, 161, 164
Nip/Tuck (TV series), 301
Nissen huts, 101
Nixon, Richard, 60
Nolan, Christopher, 42
North by Northwest (1959 film), 199
Northern Ireland, 43, 206, 252, 256
Norton, Edward, 132
Nottingham Playhouse, 155
Nunn, Trevor, 34
Nuns on the Run (1990 film), 194
Nuremberg (2000 miniseries), 321–4, 343
Nuts in May (1976 film), 75

O Lucky Man! (1973 film), 125, 130
O'Connor, Gladys, 287
O'Hara, David, 80
O'Herlihy, Gavan, 267

O'Neill, Eugene, 73, 76, 77, 205, 222
O'Toole, Peter, 52, 79, 82–4, 137, 143, 150, 329, 331
Oberon, Merle, 47
Observer, 242
Old Vic, London, 80, 151, 170, 218
Oldman, Gary, 151, 222, 307, 335, 336
Olivier, Laurence, 95, 100–103, 137, 343
Entertainer, The (1960 film), 149
Gambon, relationship with, 97–8
Hamlet, 97–8
King Lear, 102–3, 120
Marathon Man (1976 film), 164, 167
Nicholas and Alexandra (1971 film), 142
Othello, 79, 97–8
Romeo and Juliet, 253
Wuthering Heights (1939 film), 47
Olivier Awards, 222, 231, 275
Olivier Theatre, London, 175
Omen, The (1976 film), 212
On Expenses (2010 TV film), 335
On the Waterfront (1954 film), 49, 141, 199
Once Upon a Time in Hollywood (2019 film), 306–7
Orange Tree Theatre, Richmond, 199, 251
Orton, John 'Joe', 119–20, 156, 222
Osborne, John, 36, 58, 149, 151–4, 335
Oscars, 54, 133, 140–41, 161–2, 227, 292, 324
Othello (Shakespeare), 64, 79, 94, 95, 97, 104–7, 199, 282
Our Lady of Victories, Dundee, 38–41
Ouspensky, Peter, 346
Owen, Clive, 131
Owen, William 'Bill', 124, 127

Pacino, Alfredo 'Al', 166, 325
Page, Anthony 'Tony', 59, 150
Palace Variety Theatre, Dundee, 233
Palmer (2021 film), 297
Paltrow, Gwyneth, 299, 301
Paramount Studios, Hollywood, 161
Parry, Natasha, 251
Paterson, William 'Bill', 91, 206
Patinkin, Mandy, 223

Patton (1970 film), 141

Paul Schrader, 296

Peacock, Trevor, 116, 145

Peckinpah, David Samuel, 92

Peep Show (TV series), 357

Peer Gynt (Ibsen), 84, 94, 95

Penny for a Song, A (Whiting), 231

People's Friend, 69

People's Journal, 69

Petersen, William 'Bill', 223

Petersen, Wolfgang, 330, 342

Philanderer, The (Shaw), 130–31

Picasso, Pablo, 335, 351

Picnic (Inge), 68

Pink Floyd, 333

Pinochet, Augusto, 309

Pinter, Harold, 170

Pirandello, Luigi, 199

Pirates of the Caribbean films, 136–7

Pitlochry, Perthshire, 20

Pitt, Brad, 290–91, 293, 325, 329

Place in the Sun, A (1951 film), 50

Planet of the Apes (1968 film), 141

Playground Theatre, London, 355

Plaza Cinema, Dundee, 50

Plowright, Joan, 79

Plummer, Christopher, 262, 277, 323, 343

Point Break (1991 film), 290

Poker Players, The (play), 245

poorhouses, 10–11

Pope John Paul II (1984 film), 203

Porridge (TV series), 112

Portman, Eric, 86

Portmerion Antiques, 253

Postlethwaite, Peter, 50–51, 150

Postman, The (1997 film), 292

Powell, Greg, 267

Powell, Michael, 2, 276

Prague, Czech Republic, 319, 326, 333

Presley, Elvis, 140

Pressburger, Emeric, 2

Prestatyn, Denbighshire, 19

Previn, André, 139

Prick Up Your Ears (1987 film), 222

Prince of Tides, The (1991 film), 187

Prisoner, The (TV series), 110

Pryce, Jonathan, 136, 245, 326

Pulp Fiction (1994 film), 306

Putney, London, 73, 201

Quaid, Dennis, 318

Quatermass Experiment, The (1953 TV series), 118

Queen's Theatre, London, 155

Rab C. Nesbitt (TV series), 349

Raimi, Samuel, 292–3

Raising the Curtain (gala), 245, 250, 256

Rankin, Ian, 220

Rat In The Skull (Hutchinson), 76, 151, 206, 207, 213, 217, 222, 223, 224, 275

Rauch, Bill, 363–4

Ray, Nicholas, 128

Rayburn, Joyce, 155

Red (2008 film), 297, 310

Red Dragon (2002 film), 224

Red Fox (1991 TV film), 86

Redcap (TV series), 116

Redgrave, Corin, 342

Redgrave, Lynn, 65–7, 342

Redgrave, Vanessa, 214, 342

Reeves, Keanu, 287, 288, 290, 293

Regent's Park Open Air Theatre, London, 281–4

Requiem for a Heavyweight (1957 TV film), 115

Reservoir Dogs (1992 film), 307

Richard II (Shakespeare), 93, 94, 95, 239

Richard III (Shakespeare), 93, 95, 208–10, 237, 250, 251, 256, 281–4

Richardson, Cecil Antonio 'Tony', 149, 150

Richardson, Joely, 342

Richardson, Natasha, 342

Richardson, Ralph, 95, 116–17, 137, 175, 332, 343

Rickman, Alan, 191

Rigby, Terence, 98

Ring, The (2002 film), 136

Rise of the Planet of the Apes (2011 film), 303

Rising Damp (TV series), 119
River Phoenix, 341
Riverside Studios, 186
Road to Morocco (1942 film), 56
Rob Roy (1995 film), 86, 269, 270–74, 322
Robards, Jason, 277
Roberts, Rachel, 154
Robinson, Andrew, 75
Robinson, Bruce, 80
Robinson, Edward, 47
Rock 'n' Roll (Stoppard), 34, 151, 332–5
Rock, The (Dwayne Johnson), 278
Rolling Stones, The, 333
Romeo (comic book), 68
Romeo and Juliet (Shakespeare), 94, 95, 96,
      105, 245, 253
Rookie, The (2002 film), 318
Rosie, George, 69
Rossiter, Leonard, 119–20, 130
Roth, Timothy, 272, 273, 307
Royal Academy of Dramatic Art (RADA),
      111
Royal cinema, Dundee, 47
Royal Command Performance, 183
Royal Court Theatre, London, 124–5, 145,
      146, 149–55, 170, 181, 206–7, 214,
      218, 332–5
Royal Exchange Theatre, Manchester, 120,
      199
Royal Opera House, London, 139
Royal Shakespeare Company, 170, 176,
      231–4, 235–41, 242, 243, 259
Ruck, Alan, 360
Rumpelstiltskin, 92, 105
Running with Scissors (2006 film), 299–302
Rush, Geoffrey, 210, 304
Russell, Rosalind, 53
Russia, 242–9, 250, 256, 268, 327
Ryan's Daughter (1965 film), 143
Rylance, Mark, 259

Saint George's Hospital, London, 32
Saint Michael's School, Dundee, 41
Saint Nicholas (McPherson), 218–21, 314
Saint, Eva Marie, 49, 199

Saltwater (2000 film), 218, 297
Santa Fe, New Mexico, 263
Sartre, Jean-Paul, 45
Satellite Awards, 324
Saturday Night and Sunday Morning (1960
      film), 50, 154
Saturday Night Live (TV series), 167, 357–8
Saville, Philip, 262
Scales, Prunella, 145, 245
Schaffner, Franklin, 141–3
Schlesinger, John, 161–9, 175–80
Schneider, Romy, 219
schtick, 207, 208, 212–13
Schwarzenegger, Arnold, 278
Scofield, Paul, 144–5, 185, 253, 343
Scotland's Story (TV series), 255
Scott, Peter Graham, 98–9
Scott, Ridley, 75
Scottish Education Authority, 73
Scottish National Party (SNP), 312–13
Screen Actors Guild, 324
Seagal, Steven, 1–2, 3, 103, 286
Seagull, The (Chekhov), 60
Secrets from the Workhouse (2013
      documentary), 10
Seidelman, Susan, 53
September 11 attacks (2001), 304–6, 337–8
Sewell, Rufus, 333–4
Sexy Beast (2000 film), 358
Shades of Greene (TV series), 262
Shaffer, Peter, 60
Shafinury, Fareed, 356
Shah Ghalam, 356
Shakespeare, William, 3, 39, 95–6
    As You Like It, 95, 104
    Coriolanus, 153, 214, 232, 342
    Hamlet, see *Hamlet*
    Henry IV, 93
    Henry V, 93, 95
    Henry VI, 93
    Julius Caesar, 169, 174, 175–80
    King Lear, 73, 102, 120, 156, 208–10, 227,
          237, 250–60, 275, 314, 346
    Love's Labour's Lost, 156
    Macbeth, 42, 194–7, 198, 220–21

Merchant of Venice, The, 64, 66

Midsummer Night's Dream, A, 31

Othello, 64, 79, 94, 95, 97, 104–7, 282

Richard II, 93, 94, 95, 239

Richard III, 93, 95, 208–10, 237, 250, 251, 256–8, 281–4

Romeo and Juliet, 94, 95, 96, 105, 245, 253

Taming of the Shrew, The, 232, 233–4, 235, 238–40

Timon of Athens, 176

Titus Andronicus, 197, 232–3, 235, 236, 237–40, 246, 253, 275

Shakespeare pub, Edinburgh, 101

Sharp, Alan, 270

Sharpe (TV film series), 265–8

Shaw, Fiona, 233

Shaw, George Bernard, 95, 117, 130, 203, 231, 251, 353

Shaw, Martin, 75, 191

Shaw, Robert, 111, 262

Shawshank Redemption, The (1994 film), 273

She Stoops to Conquer (1971 TV play), 116, 120, 145, 155

Sher, Antony, 186

Sheridan, Jim, 43

Short, Clare, 311

Shot at Glory, A (2002 film), 200

Shrapnel, John, 88

Sid and Nancy (1986 film), 222

Sight & Sound, 128

Signoret, Simone, 220

Silence of the Lambs, The (1991 film), 224, 226–8

Sim, Alastair, 233

Simon, David, 296

Simple Spymen (Chapman), 68

Sina, Adam, 355

Sinatra, Frank, 42

Singer, Bryan, 210–12, 304

Sinners (Sobol), 353–6

Smith, John, 310

Smith, Margaret, 79, 117

Smithereens (1982 film), 53

Snelling, Mr (dentist), 201

Snook, Sarah, 360

Snowdon, Antony Armstrong-Jones, 1st Earl, 181

Sobol, Joshua, 353

socialism, 308–12, 333, 334

Society of West End Theatres, 151

Soderbergh, Steven, 295

Sorkin, Aaron, 296

South Africa, 309

South Bank, London, 170–71

Soviet Union, 242–9, 250, 256, 265

Spacey, Kevin, 269

Sparks, David, 73

Spean Bridge Hotel, Highlands, 86

Speed (1994 film), 290

Spider Man films, 279

Spiegel, Samuel, 141–3

Spielberg, Steven, 256, 296

Spooks (TV series), 117

Square, The (play), 91

St Petersburg, Russia, 268

Stafford-Clark, Max, 151, 206–7, 213

Stalin, Joseph, 142, 155, 243, 335

Stallone, Sylvester, 1, 3

Stanislavski, Konstantin, 166, 243

Star Wars films, 130

Stark, Kathleen Norris 'Koo', 262

Staunton, Imelda, 245

Steiger, Rodney, 115

Stevens, Fisher, 297

Stevenson, Robert Louis, 44

Stewart, David, 337

Stewart, Patrick, 210

Stockbridge, Edinburgh, 93

Stoppard, Tom, 34, 151, 332–5

Storey, David, 50, 150, 225

Strachan, David, 42

Straits, The (2012 series), 135–6, 358

Strange Interlude (O'Neill), 76, 77, 205–7, 222

Strasberg, Lee, 165–7

Stratford-upon-Avon, Warwickshire, 80, 130, 171, 231, 232, 240

Streetcar Named Desire, A (1951 film), 50, 312

Streets of San Francisco (TV series), 198

Strictly Sinatra (2001 film), 140

Strong, Jeremy, 165, 360

Strong, Mark, 252

Succession (TV series), 10, 77, 83, 126, 145–8, 254, 296, 310, 322, 325, 352, 357–61

Sunday Bloody Sunday (1971 film), 161

Sunday Post, 101

Superman (1978 film), 212

Superman (comic book), 42

Sutcliffe, Peter, 225

Sutherland, Donald, 262

Sutherland, Muir, 266

Swander, Homer, 198

Swift, Jonathan, 125

Swinton, Tilda, 338

Talbot, Ian, 281

Tale of Two Cities, A (Dickens), 43, 44

Tamburlaine the Great (Marlowe), 170–74

Taming of the Shrew, The (Shakespeare), 232, 233, 235, 238–40

Tams, John, 266

Tarantino, Quentin, 306–7

Tay river, 8, 61, 124

Taylor, Elizabeth, 47, 337–8

Tchaikovsky, Pyotr Ilyich, 245

Terry, Nigel, 81–2, 87–8, 122, 230, 233

Thames TV, 116

Thatcher, Margaret, 258, 308–9, 311

Thaw, John, 91, 92, 116, 261

Theatre in Education, 181

Theatre Royal, Windsor, 208

There Will Be Blood (2007 film), 43

Thérèse Raquin (1980 TV series), 186–91

These Men Are Dangerous: Stalin (1969 TV play), 155

Thick of It, The (TV series), 357

Thirty-Minute Theatre (TV series), 154

This Is Spinal Tap (1984 film), 251

This Lime Tree Bower (McPherson), 218

This Sporting Life (1963 film), 52, 60, 124, 130, 137, 154

Thomas, Dylan, 69

Thomas, Jeremy, 225

Thompson, Mark, 351

Thorson, Linda, 76

Three Musketeers, The (Dumas), 42, 156

Three Sisters (Chekhov), 244, 247

Timmerman, Bonnie, 223, 224

Timon of Athens (Shakespeare), 176

Titanic, RMS, 287

Titus Andronicus (Shakespeare), 197, 232–3, 235, 236, 237–40, 246, 253, 275

Tom Jones (Fielding), 66

Tomelty, Frances, 150

Top of the Pops (TV series), 115

Tracy, Spencer, 54–5, 57, 85, 91, 150, 301

Training Day (2001 film), 304

Traverse Theatre, Edinburgh, 91

Treasure Island (Stevenson), 44

Trick 'r Treat (2007 film), 279, 324

Trocchi, Alexander, 44–6

Trotsky, Leon, 142, 161

Troy (2004 film), 52, 82–4, 87–8, 291, 328, 329, 330, 342

True Romance (1993 film), 307

Trump, Donald, 1, 146–7

von Tunzelmann, Alex, 336

Turner Classic Movies, 52

Turner, Lana, 56

25th Hour (2002 film), 132, 341

Ukraine, 265, 268

Ulliel, Gaspard, 225

Uncle Vanya (Chekhov), 79, 145, 245, 328

Uncle Varick (Byrne), 327–8

Under Milk Wood (Thomas), 69

Under Siege (1992 film), 286

United Kingdom, 184, 312

United States, 184

University of California, Los Angeles, 199

University of Dundee, 349

Urban Myths (TV series), 337–9

Valembois, Zelie, 11, 12

Van Gelder, Nicki, 264

Venice, Italy, 211

Verbinski, Gore, 136

Verdi, Giuseppe, 62
Vermont, United States, 354
Versailles, France, 326
Vikings, 34
Villiers, Jimmy, 86
Vincent Square, Westminster, 25
Visconti, Luchino, 219
Volkstheatre, Vienna, 353

Waiting for Godot (Beckett), 91, 332, 350–52
Waiting for Guffman (1996 film), 251
Walken, Christopher, 326
Walker, Alexander, 256
Walter, Harriet, 254
Walters, Julie, 251
Wanamaker, Zoë, 31, 61
War and Peace (1972 TV series), 200
War Horse (2011 film), 118
Warner, Deborah, 232, 233, 236, 238–9, 246, 251, 253–4, 257
Warrington, Cheshire, 30
Washington, Denzel, 304
Watson, Emily, 43, 165
Wayne, John, 90
Wednesday Play, The (TV series), 114
Weinstein, Harvey, 294–5
Weir, The (McPherson), 218
Weisz, Rachel, 287, 289
Weldon, Fay, 199, 262
Welly Boot Show, The (1972 musical), 351
West Wing, The (TV series), 271
West, Dominic, 333
West, Timothy, 245
Whales of August, The (1987 film), 130
What the Butler Saw (Orton), 156
When We Dead Awaken (Ibsen), 120
Where the Wild Things Go' (Monroe), 42
Whitehead, Ted, 35

Whithouse, Toby, 134
Williams, Roger, 45, 150
Williams, Tennessee, 73
Williamson, Nicol, 58–61, 81, 92, 124, 196
Williamson, Susan, 73
Wilson's, Dundee, 70
Wilton, Penelope, 186
Withnail and I (1987 film), 80
Wodehouse, Pelham Grenville, 12
Wolf (1994 film), 187
Wonder Woman (2017 film), 279
Wood, Evan Rachel, 299, 301
Wood, Natalie, 128
World in Action (TV programme), 327
World War I (1914–18), 11, 12, 13
World War II (1939–45), 11–12, 15, 117, 321
Wuthering Heights (1939 film), 47
Wyatt, Rupert, 298, 301–3
Wyndham's Theatre, London, 218

X-Files, The (TV series), 72
X2 (2003 film), 208, 210–12, 324, 328

Year of the Sex Olympics, The (1968 TV play), 118, 119, 120, 144
Yes Minister (TV series), 194
You Will Meet a Tall Dark Stranger (2010 film), 117
Young Adam (Trocchi), 45–6
Young Sherlock Holmes (1985 film), 135, 229
Young, Frederick, 143

Z-Cars (TV series), 140
Zodiac (2007 film), 324
Zola, Emile, 186
Zoo Story, The (Albee), 69